LOTUS ELISE AND EXIGE 1995–2020

THE COMPLETE STORY

Johnny Tipler

Foreword by Clive Chapman

THE CROWOOD PRESS

First published in 2021 by
The Crowood Press Ltd
Ramsbury, Marlborough
Wiltshire SN8 2HR

enquiries@crowood.com

www.crowood.com

This impression 2026

British Library Cataloguing-in-Publication Data
A catalogue record for this book is available from the British Library.

For product safety-related questions contact:
productsafety@crowood.com

ISBN 978 1 78500 842 9

Lotus Elise S2 painted specially for this book by French watercolour artist, Laurence B. Henry (www.laurencehenry.hautefort.com)

Typeset and designed by D & N Publishing, Baydon, Wiltshire

Printed and bound in India by Thomson Press India Pvt. Ltd.

Acknowledgements

After completing a quartet of books about Porsches, discussions with The Crowood Press determined that a book about the Lotus Elise would be welcomed.

This is my second book on the Elise, Crowood having published the first one in 1999, and it's been a real pleasure composing this one. It's a very different story. When I wrote the first one, the vast majority of Elise variants did not exist, and that book focuses very much on the hands-on construction methodology of what became known retrospectively as the Series 1 model. Twenty years on, the timeline contains many more variations on the Elise theme. During this time I also wrote extensively for the in-house *Lotus Club International* magazine, edited by Caroline Parker, with images provided by the official works photographer, Jason Parnell.

Elise book one was facilitated by press officers Alastair Florance and Prunelia Stuart; as fortuitously Alastair is still helming the media department at Lotus Cars, Elise book two has also been compiled largely thanks to him. Some of the leading figures from the original Elise days are still in evidence, and it was a real pleasure to natter with Richard Rackham again, as well as Russell Carr, whom I got to know when composing my Evora book, and Barney Hatt from the factory's Design Studio. Major influencers in the Elise story include Gavan Kershaw, Andy Pleavin and Neil Thomas, all of whom feature large in the text as they describe their respective roles and their particular roles in the cars' evolution and construction. We also hear from Italian Lotus racing driver Stefano D'Aste, and independent Lotus salesman and commentator Guy Munday provides an objective take on the cars and the company. TV presenter Vicki Butler-Henderson describes teaching her sister how to drive a circuit in an Elise. And, crucially, I have also been fortunate enough to meet the woman that the car is named after: none other than Elisa Artioli, who drives everywhere in the very Elise that her grandfather Romani Artioli gave her. The cover image is of her in this car near her Trieste home, taken on a shoot by Rémi Dargegen.

I also want to thank Ron Simons, ebullient owner-operator of RSRSpa and RSRNürburg, with whom I've had the pleasure of driving one of his Exiges around Spa-Francorchamps, plus Kostas Sidiras for photos.

Images are everything, and I've been blessed with a welter of great shots provided by various sources. So, many thanks indeed to everyone who has contributed photos of Elises and their ilk, including William Taylor from his Coterie Press Images archive, Stephanie Ewen of Red Fin Photography and Design, Simon Clay, Jason Parnell, Antony Fraser, Laura Hampton and Raven Cozens-Hardy. Steve Bennett trawled though his archives from his days as editor of *Cars and Car Conversions* and *Circuit Driver* publications to provide some outstanding images. Individual snappers whose work also appears in the book include Rémi Dargegen, Paul Harmer, Kostas Sidiras and Tom Wood. Tim Price very kindly provided archived Elise catalogues. I'm also delighted to include fabulous Elise and Exige artworks by Laurence B. Henry, Stephanie Arnwine and Taralee Guild.

CONTENTS

Clive Chapman and the Elise 260 Cup. Son of Lotus founder Colin Chapman, Clive runs Classic Team Lotus, restoring, fettling and racing a broad spectrum of famous Lotus racing cars.

JASON PARNELL

FOREWORD

The Lotus Elise embodies the spirit of Lotus.

The Elise concept was founded on a fundamental innovation: a chassis made of bonded aluminium extrusion. Bonded aluminium harked back to the F1 World Championship-winning Lotus type 25, while extruded aluminium avoided the significant investment costs of pressed aluminium. Designer Richard Rackham had come up with a lightweight, stiff, 'simple' chassis design that was well suited to low-volume production. Just the kind of win-win-win-win scenario that led to the success of so many of the illustrious predecessors to the Elise.

Undoubtedly my father would have approved of the chassis. Immediately he would have gone on to demand, 'How else can we exploit the benefits of aluminium extrusion?', which is exactly what Richard and his colleagues did, realizing elegant extruded door hinges, pedals and uprights.

This 700kg (1,540lb) car, with stiff chassis, low centre of gravity and low polar moment of inertia, was styled by Julian Thomson in a body that appealed to everybody. Immediately it became another iconic 'see it and smile' Lotus. Crucially, this low-volume, high performance British sports car was pitched at a price that made it relatively affordable, especially for the existing Lotus enthusiasts. The Elise fitted the bill in so many important ways, at a critical time, to secure a future for the marque. To his credit, Romano Artioli had led the company to a vital success, implemented by project manager Tony Shute and his team.

Lotus enjoys a healthy relationship with media, public and customers. They are keen for the marque to succeed. When the Elise arrived, and its many attributes became apparent, it gave them something to affirm their enthusiasm. The steering feel, responsiveness, speed through the corners and practical drivability are its greatest assets in practice. The driver feels a real connection from the steering, through the tyres onto the road. Just as a Lotus should be.

The wonderful 1950s Lotus Elite turned out to be more of a track car than a Grand Tourer. The Lotus Elise truly is both. And the chassis platform lent itself to being adaptable in so many ways, as numerous iterations were developed for road and track. In keeping with many previous associations with major manufacturers, Lotus pulled off a brilliant deal with GM for the VX220. As the fantastic success of the S1 Elise started to level out, this enabled Lotus – with the generous 'indulgence' of GM – to develop the Series 2 Elise. This was a classic triumph of Lotus ingenuity; a fundamentally different car that would broaden the appeal to more customers had been realized and brought to fruition with maximum efficiency. Importantly the development programme included Federalising the car, whilst managing to keep the weight below 750kg (1,650lb). The Series 2 has been even more successful.

I have always liked the minimal specification of the interior. There is everything a driver needs, and not much more. Function is everything. My father loved designing racing cars because of the relative lack of legislation and compromise. Of course, he was proud of the Lotus road cars, and recognized their importance; but he could get frustrated by the compromises, especially arising from what the marketing department insisted should be taken into consideration. I am sure he would have recognized the Elise as being a true Lotus. However, I should say he also had ambitions to drive the marque upmarket, so he would have been delighted with the Evora and ecstatic with the Evija.

The Evija is Lotus's latest flagship model, launched in July 2019. It is a world-beating hypercar reckoned to produce 2,000 horsepower from its electric propulsion system, clad in supercar bodywork incorporating cooling ducts and aerodynamic surfaces honed to perfection in typically superlative Lotus fashion.

I hope Lotus Cars will manage to keep the Lotus spectrum broad, with an Elise at one end and an Evija at the other. The Evija will come top in many aspects spectacularly. The Elise will continue to come top in others, and at a price that will be relatively affordable to many drivers, who will continue to appreciate the engineering elegance and efficiency that it represents. Long live the Elise!

Clive Chapman

TIMELINE

1994 Elise 'step-in car' concept begins to gel.

1995 Testing of the prototype Elise M1-11.
Elise debuts at Frankfurt Show.

1996 Malaysian DRB-HICOM Group's Proton subsidiary acquires major stake in Group Lotus.

1997 Lotus Elise Trophy introduced in Italy, staged by Peroni Promotions.
Sport Elise Sprint 190 announced in March.
Elise-based GT1 race cars in action in FIA GT Championship.
Lotus Cars matches international quality control standard ISO QS 9000.
Water-based paint first trialled.
May sees 1,000th Elise built.

1998 Proton ups its holding to control 80 per cent of Group Lotus.
From initial output of 750 vehicles, annual Elise production is now running at 3,300 units.
September sees Lotus's fiftieth anniversary celebrations; half the 1,500 Lotuses in attendance are Elises.
Sport 135 model introduced.

1999 143bhp Elise 111S with developed VVC K-series engine announced at Geneva.
Minimalist 340R concept car launched (340 units made).
Motorsport Elise unveiled at Earls Court.

2000 Lotus builds GM's VX220 Speedster in normally aspirated format.
Sport 160 and Sport 190 are introduced in May.
177bhp (192bhp in track-spec) Exige S1 launched.
Series 2 Elise is announced in October, still using Rover K-series powertrain.

2001 Series 2 Elise on sale.
Upgraded 135R version becomes available.

2002 In production from May, the Elise Type 111S features Rover K-series VVC engine, revised transmission ratios, round tailpipes with flap valve, three-tier rear diffuser, larger radiator, and polished nickel-finish eight-spoke wheels.

2003 Sport Elise 135R becomes available, developed in consort with the Lotus Ride & Handling Department with enhanced driveline and running gear.

2004 Series 2 Exige goes on sale.
Federal Elise goes on sale in the USA.
189bhp 111R becomes available in Europe and rest of world.
Toyota ZZ 1.8-litre twin-cam engine and six-speed gearbox replace K-series driveline.

2005 243bhp supercharged Sport Exige R released at Geneva in March (fifty units built).
Elise 111R and Sport Racer models shown.
Limited run (fifty cars) of Lotus Elise Sport goes on sale.

2006 Exige S and Europa 2.0 launched at Geneva.
Tesla Roadster electric prototype is unveiled, built on Elise chassis.
ProBax seats, LED tail lights and ECUs introduced. Lotus decals on rear changed to embossed lettering.
North American Exige goes on sale in the USA.
220bhp supercharged Exige S unleashed.

2007 Federally correct lights and bumpers are fitted, having been exempt for three years.

In production from May 2002, the Elise 111S was powered by the K-series VVC 4-cylinder unit, with different gearing, new exhaust with flap valve and round tailpipes, plus three-piece rear diffuser and eight-spoke powder-coated wheels.

WILLIAM TAYLOR

Elise S released and 111R renamed Elise R. Spec includes airbags, ABS brakes, electric windows, and carpet.

2008 Elise 270E ethanol-fuelled model is up and running. Main models are the 134bhp, five-speed Elise S, 189bhp six-speed Elise R and 218bhp six-speed, supercharged Elise SC. Exige S 240 is available with 240bhp.

2009 Exige S 260 is released.
Stealth black Exige Scura is launched.
Highly tuned Exige GT3 becomes available for competition.

2010 Base model Elise S and Exige offer 9 per cent reduction in CO_2 and better fuel economy.

2011 Fresh styling cues include new front clam featuring almond-eye headlights, Evora-like mouth and air intakes; revised rear bumper and engine cover; all-in-one integrated headlights including LED daylight running lights and LED direction indicators; and better aerodynamics with 4 per cent reduction in drag coefficient. Entry-level 134bhp 1600cc Toyota 1ZR-FAE engine is introduced.

2012–20 Exige S Roadster is in production.

2013 Exige V6 Cup, Exige V6 Cup R, Elise S Club Racer and Elise S Cup R are introduced.

2014 Elise S Cup is introduced.

2015 Exige 360 Cup is introduced.

2016 Elise 250 Special Edition, Elise Race 250, Exige 350 Special Edition and Elise 3-Eleven are introduced.

2017 Elise Sprint, Elise Cup 260, Exige Race 380, Exige Cup 380, Exige Cup 430 are introduced.

2018 Exige Cup 430 Type 25, Exige Sport 410, Exige Type 49 and Type 79 are introduced.

2020 Elise Classic Heritage Editions based on Sport 220 reflect Lotus F1 racing car colour schemes: Types 18, 49, 72 and 81.
Exige Sport 410 Twentieth Anniversary model comes out.

Full frontal: the 2020 Elise Cup 250 weighs 931kg (2,053lb), having no power steering or air-conditioning, using a lighter lithium-ion battery, carbon-fibre seats and lighter forged-alloy wheels.

LAURA HAMPTON

INTRODUCTION

In production for twenty-five years, the Elise is a model that has steadily evolved. The original car, conceptually a true Lotus complying exactly with the mantra 'performance through light weight,' employed traditional construction practices, based on a radically innovative chassis. The Series I Elise opened the gates for the Series 2 (S2) model and its principal derivative sibling the Exige, while the concept matured steadily, with powertrain revisions, styling facelifts and chassis modifications through the next twenty years.

Representing the bedrock of Lotus production, the Elise and Exige capably epitomize the concept of a lightweight sports car with highly proficient handling and power delivery. Their production was sustained through four corporate upheavals, as the company enjoyed periods of stability punctuated by sudden changes of management and ownership.

Named after Elisa, the granddaughter of Lotus's owner at the time, Romano Artioli of Bugatti fame, the Lotus Elise was launched at the Frankfurt Show in 1995. During the next twenty-five years it not only established itself as the embodiment of what Lotus stands for, it retained a unique place in the international sports car market. To put it bluntly, for most of the last quarter of a century, no other manufacturer has come up with a car to rival seriously the Elise or the Exige.

Look around: the most obvious – and numerous – sports cars on the road are, by some way, evolutions of the Mazda MX5 (Miata in the USA), a shameless copy of the 1960s Lotus Elan – though tediously reliable in a way the Elan never quite managed to be. Going up a notch, the Porsche Boxster was made in far fewer numbers than the MX5, though many more than the Lotus Elise and its derivatives. Lotus Seven successors such as the Caterham Seven and Westfield have an aesthete following of their own. Then there are the soft, 'hairdresser' cabriolets like the Audi TT and the Mercedes-Benz SL R231, while the harder-edged Alpine A110 and

Smiling faces, both: separated by fifteen years' evolution, the Series I and Series 2 Elises here point up the fundamental difference in stylistic character, the purer, rotund contours of the original car contrasting with the mature sophistication of the 2011 model year car.
WILLIAM TAYLOR

Elisa Artioli was feted during a visit to the Lotus Cars factory in July 2018, and we caught up at the nearby Bird in Hand pub.

Porsche Cayman are construed as Exige rivals. The point is, there's nothing out there that does the sports car job as well and in as focused a fashion as the Elise.

The original Elise, known retrospectively as the Series 1 or S1, is a classic beauty, with a purity of form carried over into the Series 1 Exige, born out of the early one-make Autobytel race series. The S1 Elise was in production for five years, the S1 Exige for four years. Late in 2000, the new millennium ushered in the Series 2 Elise, built on the same radically innovative extruded aluminium chassis, but clad in very differently styled bodywork. The key players in the initiation, productionizing and development of the Elise were designers Richard Rackham, who is credited with the car's radically innovative chassis; Julian Thomson, who styled the Series 1 model; senior development engineer Tony Shute; and director of vehicle engineering Roger Becker, who was also the prime mover in productionizing the Exige and the Evora. Becker had worked at Lotus for forty-four years – since the Cheshunt days – and had a hand in developing every car the company had built since 1966, including the original Elan, the Esprit and the Elise. His son Matt worked with him from 1988 to fine-tune all aspects of ride and handling – alongside former Team Lotus F1 star John Miles, who acted as a consultant.

Launched at the NEC Motor Show, revisions on the Series 2 Elise included lowered chassis rails along the cockpit sides, revised suspension with new hubs and hub carriers, larger-diameter wheels – shod with Bridgestone Potenza tyres – a new soft-top and window guides. The stage was set, as far as the general style and makeup of the car was concerned, for the next two decades.

The Series 2 Elise 111R came out in 2004, with – arguably the most important aspect of Elise production, certainly from a marketing point of view – the Federal version with North American specification. Coincidentally, the S2 Exige also appeared in 2004. The third major innovation for 2004, and a move that further consolidated the model's place in the sports car pantheon, was the adoption of the Toyota ZZ 1.8-litre twin-cam engine and six-speed gearbox, replacing the K-series driveline.

Viewed in profile, the front and rear clamshells of the Series 1 Elise display minimal overhang ahead of and to the rear of the wheels.
WILLIAM TAYLOR

A feature of the Lotus sixtieth anniversary commemoration at Snetterton in September 2011 was an attempt to field a record number of Lotus cars on track; at some corners it was gridlock!

An Elise 111S finished in Storm Titanium on Ipswich quay. Available in 2002, the S2 Elise retained the 1798cc Rover K-series engine, and now allied to a close-ratio G6 gearbox. WILLIAM TAYLOR

The following year, the 243bhp supercharged Toyota-powered Sport Exige R was released at the Geneva Show, alongside the Elise 111R and Sport Racer models. A limited run of fifty Lotus Elise Sport went on sale. In 2006, the Exige S and Europa 2.0 were launched at Geneva. In a significant step, perhaps with less fanfare than it deserved, the Tesla Roadster electric prototype was unveiled, a model built on the Elise chassis. Also in 2006, ProBax seats, LED tail lights and ECUs were introduced, while Lotus decals on the rear were changed to embossed lettering. The North American Federal-spec Exige went on sale in the USA, and the 220bhp supercharged Exige S was released.

Federally correct lights and bumpers were fitted for 2007, having been exempt for three years. The Elise S was released and the 111R was renamed the Elise R. The general spec now included airbags, ABS brakes, electric windows and carpet.

At the Geneva Show in February 2005, Lotus Cars' Lotus Sport division introduced the Sport Exige 240R, a limited edition – fifty cars built – powered by the 243bhp supercharged version of its 4-cylinder Toyota VVTL engine.

PAUL HARMER

New models to appear in 2007 were the Type 121 Europa, a restyled model with a plusher cabin, and the 2-Eleven, the bare-bones track-day antithesis.

For 2008, the left-field bio-ethanol-fuelled Elise 270E was released, plus the one-off green technology Eco Elise, whose bodywork clamshell was composed of 'sustainable' materials including hemp, eco-wool and sisal, with water-based paint. It also had solar panels inset into the hardtop to assist powering the electrical circuit. Mainstream models were the 134bhp five-speed Elise S, the 189bhp six-speed Elise R and the 218bhp six-speed supercharged Elise SC. The Exige S 240 was also available with 240bhp. The Exige S 260 was released the following year, along with the stealth-black Exige Scura, while the highly tuned Exige GT3 was available for competition usage. In 2010, the base model Elise S and Exige offered a 9 per cent reduction in CO_2 emissions and better fuel economy, with combined figures of 37.2mpg, or 31mpg for the USA (7.6ltr/9.1ltr/100km). The Elise R and Elise SC returned 29mpg and 28mpg respectively (9.8 and 10ltr/100km).

As for those corporate upheavals, they serve as milestones in the Elise and Exige saga: Romano Artioli's Bugatti concern bought Lotus Cars from General Motors in 1993, and relinquished control in 1996, with ownership passing to Malaysian car maker Proton, though Artioli remained at Lotus as special projects director till 1998. Having spent the best part of forty years at Lotus, Mike Kimberley was appointed CEO in 2005, but was forced to retire early in 2009 due to having a bad back – though not before he had overseen the launch of the Evora. In his wake, in 2010 Proton allowed former Ferrari merchandizing director Dany Bahar and his insidious cohort to take Lotus into what proved an overly ambitious programme, aimed at rivalling Italian supercar makers such as

Launched at Geneva in 2007, the Type 123 2-Eleven was conceived as the Elise line-up's 'circuit car', fitted with the supercharged 4-cylinder Toyota VVTL engine. This is Ian Fenwick's 2-Eleven race car entering the pits garage at Snetterton in 2019.

STEPHANIE EWEN

The Eco Elise was on show in the Greener Driving Pavilion at the British Motor Show at London's ExCel in July 2008; bodywork clamshells were composed of 'sustainable' materials including hemp, eco-wool and sisal, with water-based paint. It also had solar panels inset into the hard-top to assist powering the electrical circuit.
WILLIAM TAYLOR

Ferrari and Lamborghini. There was, briefly, a ruthless drive to go upmarket, with 'lifestyle' the overarching and superficial watchword, and when that proved an impossible dream, the Malaysian government shifted control from Proton to DRB-HICOM, a state-owned car distribution conglomerate. In the process, key Lotus engineering and executive staff resigned or were stood down.

Sadly, the Malaysians did not fully comprehend or appreciate what they had at Hethel, and no major investment was made in creating new product or doing more than evolving the existing product lines. In fairness, this is partly because they caught a cold over the Bahar programme. Nevertheless, it felt like stagnation had set in. Then, in 2017, salvation arrived in the shape of the Chinese global automotive company Geely. This bullish conglomerate, which also bought a 49 per cent share of Proton, had already taken over Volvo in 2010 and made beneficial changes there, and similar promises were made for Lotus. In 2020, *The Economist* magazine declared that Geely 'might well succeed where others had failed'.

Returning to the evolution of the Elise platform line-up, fresh styling cues unveiled in 2011 included a new front clam, featuring almond-eye headlights, an Evora-like mouth and air intakes, revised rear bumper and engine cover. All-in-one integrated headlights included LED daylight running lights and LED direction indicators. Aerodynamics were better, with a 4 per cent reduction in the drag coefficient. The entry-level 134bhp 1600cc Toyota 1ZR-FAE engine was introduced, broadening the field still further.

Announced at Frankfurt, the Exige S is a quantum leap in the model's specification, endowed with the 3.5-litre Toyota V6 annexed from the Evora, installed in an enlarged chassis. The Exige S Roadster came out in 2012, featuring the Toyota 3.5-litre V6 engine and extended chassis like its coupé sibling, making it the fastest soft-top ever to roll off the Hethel production lines. Apart from having no roof, the Roadster differed from its coupé sibling in lacking front splitter and rear spoiler. The Exige V6 Cup, Exige V6 Cup R, Elise S Club Racer and Elise S Cup R were hot on its heels. Available from February 2013, the track-focused, road-going, Exige V6 Cup's 3.5-litre Harrop-supercharged Toyota 2GR-FE V6 engine develops 345bhp. The no-frills Exige V6 Cup is 60kg lighter than the standard V6 Exige, and the double-wishbone suspension incorporates slightly stiffer springs and two-way adjustable dampers for crisper response and tauter handling. The engine lid and complex cantilevered rear wing is supported by a pair of hydraulic struts, rather than a single manually hoisted prop.

The Elise Club Racer was 24kg lighter than the 'standard' model by virtue of having normal amenities deleted, including carpets, radio, speakers, passenger footrest, central locking, mudflaps and sound deadening, together with installation of lightweight motorsport battery and body-coloured seats. Unveiled in June at Canary Wharf and Le Mans, the Exige LF1 paid homage to Team Lotus's 81 Formula 1 World Championship victories. The references to the F1 squad's commercial liveries are slightly ambiguous, with black bodywork, gold wheels and red highlights. Just eighty-one were built.

The Elise S came out in 2006, designated an entry-level car producing 134bhp from its normally aspirated Toyota 1ZZ-FE 4-cylinder engine. It could still do 128mph (206km/h), with a 0–60mph time of 5.8 seconds.
ANTONY FRASER

Changes and upgrades were subtle yet frequent variations on the theme. At first glance, the Exige 360 Cup looks similar to the standard Exige V6 Cup, though the 2015 incarnation features a revised matt-black front lid and roof, with Motorsport Red highlights on the front splitter, tow-eye and the front of the lid, plus, most obviously, Motorsport Red wheels.

The Elise S Cup was next up, and for 2016 another rash of limited editions hit the road in the shape of the Elise 250 Special Edition, the Elise Race 250 and the Exige 350 Special Edition. The Exige 360 Sport was effectively an evolution of the 2012 Exige S, though lighter and with suspension revisions, including front camber doubled from 0.40° to 0.80°, front toe from 0.06° to 0.12°, and rear camber from −1.9° to −2.1° – the maximum possible. The Elise 260 also featured remodelled bodywork, increasing downforce by an amazing 44 per cent over the Cup 250. The louvred front arches and splitter conspired with the motorsport-derived rear wing and diffuser to generate 180kg of downforce at 151mph (243 km/h). Introduced in autumn 2016, the Special Edition Exige 350 Sport celebrates the company's 50th anniversary. Tipping the scales at 1,099kg (77kg less than the previous generation Exige S), weight saving comes from lightweight forged wheels, lithium battery, carbon seats and vented two-piece brake discs. Aerodynamic enhancements include the revised front access panel, improving air flow exiting the horizontally mounted radiator, and louvred tailgate panel. Its controls feature Lotus Dynamic

Lotus Cars' motorsport development manager Johnny Lamb puts the facelifted 2011 Elise through its paces. Power for the standard base model came from the normally aspirated 1598cc 4-cylinder Toyota unit, enabling 0–60mph in 6.0 seconds and 0–100mph in 18.6 seconds.
ANTONY FRASER

Unveiled at the 2010 Geneva Show, the facelifted 2011 model year Elise retained the basic tried-and-tested suspension componentry involving unequal-length wishbones, Eibach coil-over Bilstein dampers and front anti-roll bar.
ANTONY FRASER

The Exige V6 Cup of 2014 was equipped with Lotus Dynamic Performance Management, enabling engine and traction settings to be switched between Touring, Sport and Race.
WILLIAM TAYLOR

Rough with the smooth: photographed on Norwich's medieval cobbled Elm Hill, 2016's Elise 250 Cup produced 243bhp at 7,200rpm and 184lb ft of torque from 3,500 to 5,500rpm, enabling 0–60mph in 3.9 seconds and a top speed of 154mph (248km/h). Aerodynamically, its new front splitter, side sills, rear diffuser and wing generated 66kg (146lb) of downforce at 100mph and 155kg (342lb) at full speed.
JASON PARNELL

The Elise 260 of August 2016 featured mildly remodelled bodywork, increasing downforce by an amazing 44 per cent over the Cup 250. The louvred front arches and splitter conspired with the motorsport-derived rear wing and diffuser to generate 180kg of downforce at 151mph.
WILLIAM TAYLOR

Generating interest at the 2012 Goodwood Festival of Speed, the Exige S Roadster ushered in the 3.5-litre Toyota V6 annexed from the Evora, installed in a longer chassis like its coupé sibling. As the convertible roof negated the need for a rear wing, the front splitter was also absent. It was the fastest soft-top ever to roll off the Hethel production lines.

Performance Management (DPM), selected by dashboard switch to provide Sport and Race settings. This increases throttle response while lowering traction slip thresholds and removing understeer recognition, thereby allowing greater driver input before the system intervenes. The range also includes the Elise 250 Special Edition, Elise Race 250, and Elise 3-Eleven.

The Exige S Roadster came out in 2012, with the Exige V6 Cup, Exige V6 Cup R, Elise S Club Racer and Elise S Cup R hot on its heels. The Elise S Cup was next up, and for 2016 another rash of limited editions hit the road in the shape of the Elise 250 Special Edition, the Elise Race 250, the Exige 350 Special Edition and in 2017, the Elise 3-Eleven, the Elise Sprint, the Elise Cup 260, the Exige Race 380, the Exige Cup

380 and the Exige Cup 430. The final swathe of commemorative special editions and Heritage models arrived in the guise of the Exige Cup 430 Type 25, Exige Sport 410, Exige Type 49 and Type 79. All were fine-looking cars, serving to highlight and showcase the marque's hugely successful racing lineage.

The limited-edition Type 79 Exige 430 mimicked the hallowed black-and-gold colour scheme of the JPS-Lotus Type 79 from 1978, with which Mario Andretti and Ronnie Peterson contested the 1978 F1 World Championship, the American star emerging with the Driver's title and Team Lotus the Constructors' trophy. Also available were the Exige Cup 430 Type 25, Exige Sport 410 and Gold Leaf-hued Exige Type 49. The mainstream line-up for 2019 and 2020 now featured the Exige Cup 430, its 430bhp 3.5-litre V6 engine from the Evora GT430 shoehorned in to make it the fastest Lotus road car ever, posting a 3.2sec 0–60mph time and a 180mph (290 km/h) top speed. The Elise Cup 250 differed from the regular Elise Sport and Sprint models by its aero addenda, incorporating front splitter, bargeboards, rear diffuser, and rear wing that generated 125kg of downforce at 140mph (225 km/h). It also had two round rear light clusters instead of four, and a polycarbonate rear screen.

We'll find out some of the design and production methodology in subsequent interviews with the likes of Gavan Kershaw, Russell Carr and Andy Pleavin, who bring the Elise story right up to date by explaining the strategies, fine-tuning and construction processes.

There's no substitute for getting out and about with these cars, and I was fortunate enough to have contributed extensively to the in-house publication, the *Lotus Club International* magazine, available in dealerships and dispatched to registered Lotus owners. Editor Caroline Parker – who worked in the PR and marketing department – and in-house photographer Jason Parnell and I would regularly undertake road trips in Elise and Evora press cars for drive stories to publish in the magazine, forging a close working rapport between the three of us, and visiting some amazing locations in the process. I draw on some of these expeditions for the Elise and Exige driving experiences recounted further on in the book.

Hot off the production line, an array of Elises and Exiges on display during a factory open day, July 2006.

RICHARD RACKHAM INTERVIEW

The time-served and thoroughly proven Elise chassis was designed by Richard Rackham. Before Lotus, Richard worked for Aldridge Engineering, consultants in Long Stratton, Norfolk, on the design of a Formula First racing car. Geoff Aldridge started off designing FI cars for Lotus, and the consultancy was a major supplier of expertise to Lotus. Richard worked in the handling department under Roger Becker, and carried out much of the design work for the racing Esprits, including Le Mans 1993, after which he was involved in the Elise project.

JT: What does the Elise mean to you now, three decades on?

RR: The Elise is basically a download of everything that I have learned about making normal road cars handle properly, and how to design racing cars. Basically, I have made a racing platform with sufficient adjustments in it to make the most of its limitations as a road car. That's why its handling is so good: everything that needs to be tuneable can be tuned, but without upsetting other areas. It's not just car handling but all the other associated factors as well. We wanted it to be a car that you immediately feel at home with when you sit in it. That means creating the right environment.

There are half a dozen fundamental things on a car that need to be independently adjustable, and if you have those, you can make the most of it, instead of having to make major compromises. Certain elements of the Esprit racing programme filtered down to the Elise, like stiffness, and the ability to adjust the cambers, which is how the tyres lean, and also the sort of feeling you get in a race car – the directness of the gearshift and the steering ratios. Good racing cars have everything in just the right place – the relationship of the gearshift to the wheel, where the pedals are in relation to each other and the body and the seating position. It goes back to Chapman's principles in its concept, construction and light weight, which is why we don't need to have a great deal of power to make it a performance car. It is a very frugal car in terms of fuel and

Mastermind of the bonded and riveted extruded aluminium chassis, Lotus chief engineer Richard Rackham also masterminded the Evora chassis design. Posed here with three evolutions of the Elise, he collected the prize at the 2019 Autocar Awards when the Elise received the Readers' Champion title.
LOTUS CARS

consumable items like tyres and brakes; the brakes last virtually indefinitely. You can run constantly over three days on a circuit and you won't need to replace any brake pads or discs.

JT: To what extent are seats and cabin dimensions relevant to gaining type approval?

RR: The inside of the car is designed around the seating position, and the seat relates to where your hips are and where your legs go. We also refer to where the knee is in relation to the dash, so that if you have an accident you go forward and your knee hits the dash and stops you submarining under the dash. When cars are crashed for the type approval test they have the seats installed and we nominate the point where the occupants' hips are in the car, and that's where the crash dummies are put in. The crash test dummies are a certain size, so the inside of the car is designed around these dimensions. Your car passes the test with what is deemed to be the average-sized person on board. In fact, we only had to pass the 'Reg 12' trolley test, which is where you drive the car straight into a brick wall at 30mph (48km/h). The requirement for that is that the steering column doesn't move more than about 5in (125mm) in the horizontal or up or down. That test was very good for the Elise. I think it moved about an inch (20mm or 25mm) in either direction, so we were well inside the limit and the car was virtually drivable after that. Most cars are completely destroyed.

There are about twenty fundamental tests involved in obtaining European type approval, and the Elise really only stumbled on one of them. This was all to do with the rake of the windscreen – Lotus couldn't square that with the required vision lines and wiped areas – so there had to be a significant rethink on the slope of the screen. They had to change the angle of rake and make it more upright to comply.

JT: Could you explain a bit more about the construction of the chassis?

RR: There is no industry standard for bonding aluminium. It doesn't exist. You can't go and buy it off the shelf, and when you start looking around, many companies will sell you an adhesive but they won't sell you the process. Neither will they sell you any guarantee, so that had to be driven completely from the ground up by Lotus. The Lotus system, which is the only system in production in the world, is based around available technology with a certain amount of innovation. It's very complex, involving the selection and grade of pre-treated aluminium, the handling of it, and the special technique used to prepare the surfaces for anodizing. After bonding, the sections are joined together with these simple Ejot rivets. Then samples are tested for corrosion, and there's also durability testing. It's a very big chunk of the chassis story.

JT: What's the legacy of the extruded chassis?

RR: The legacy of the extruded aluminium chassis is that it facilitated production of cars produced by other companies, including the Tesla Roadster, the Vauxhall VX220 and Aston Martin's VH platform cars, and we have been suppliers to McLaren as well. We hardly have any quality issues or reliability issues because a) the

Smart yet purposeful, the cockpit of the 2016 Elise 260 displays exquisite trim details, driver-oriented instrumentation and gauges, plus a pair of figure-hugging seats.
WILLIAM TAYLOR

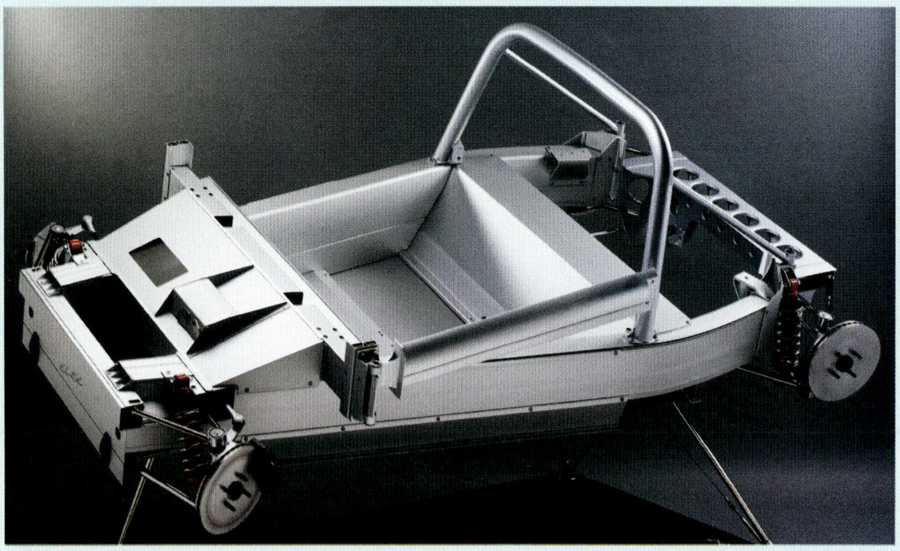

Basis for all Elise and Exige models – and derivative cars – is the extruded aluminium chassis, made from lengths of extruded aluminium, bonded and riveted together. The original chassis was made by Hydro Aluminium in Denmark, then production shifted to Hydro Raufoss in Worcester, taken over by Lotus and renamed Lotus Lightweight Structures in May 2008. The chassis provides pick-up points for the wishbone suspension and coil-over damper mounts, while coolant tubes run within the hollow extrusions.
WILLIAM TAYLOR

car is so simple, and b) it's so well engineered, right from the start. It's a great survivor, where all the attempts to do other stuff, such as an Esprit replacement, have fallen by the wayside. It has captured people's imagination; it is true to the philosophy of Lotus, and it is a great car. The brief for that car was 3,000 units over a four-year period – little race cars for the road – and if the brief car had been selling a few thousand per annum, with the practicality to attract that number of people, it would have been a different design. It is amazing that it's managed to survive with all its shortcomings of noise, stiffness and austerity. Nobody sets out to say, 'I'm going to design an icon,' but actually it is just right, it's hit the spot, and the fact that it's been going for so long pretty much unchanged is testimony to the rightness of the original design.

JT: How do you see it having evolved, then?

RR: By design, it was originally not the car it's been forced to become; it's become the car it's become because of the greater need for utility in the car, and to make the car more everyday usable, and that's not a bad thing. It's just that it's very compromised today. In the past, we've tried to backfill it with something less compromised, but because of the ownership of our company prior to Geely there was never consistency of budget or management to enable a three- or four-year car creation programme to exist; it just couldn't happen. We'd start building prototypes, and then they would be switched off; I personally was involved in three programmes where we were actually building prototypes that got switched off, after tens of millions of pounds had been spent, which was incredibly frustrating. The compromise level is a relative thing; the Elise from Series 1 to where we are now, has involved a lot of compromise, but it is still the purest sports car on the market. The closest now is probably the Alpine A110, but that's Cayman weight, isn't it?

JT: Surely the Exige is rather less compromised?

RR: The Exige was obviously built on the Elise platform with a full roof and a higher performance, and looked great. It's got loads of technical content, different engines, different engineering requirements – it's the ultimate Elise, if you like, as far as embodying the original concept is concerned. The idea of a race car for the road has gone soft in the Elise, and it has gone hard again with the Exige. It is still a great car; it's still beautiful, and nothing else drives like it. Everything is right: the steering is nicely weighted, the power response is beautifully delivered, and it just does what you want it to.

JT: And the future?

RR: We are now in a position where we've got a really long-term plan, including new buildings and manufacturing facilities for major projects. We're rebuilding a new assembly line for new models, a staff restaurant, heritage centre, and general management site with tightened security and IT infrastructure – everything that will combine to make Hethel the centre of the Lotus brand worldwide.

Lotus Elise Type 111 (1996–2000)

Layout and Chassis
Two-seater, Lotus-designed epoxy-bonded aluminium-alloy extrusions with integral steel rollover structure and lightweight steel rear subframe

Engine

Type	K-series, transverse mid-engine
Block material	Aluminium
Head material	Aluminium
Cylinders	4 cylinders in line
Cooling	Water
Bore and stroke	80mm × 89.3mm
Capacity	1796cc
Valves	DOHC, 16 valves
Fuelling	Multipoint sequential fuel injection
Engine management	Lotus Motorola electronic ignition system, mapping unique to Lotus 85A
Max. power	118bhp at 5,500rpm
Max. torque	122lb ft at 4,800rpm

Transmission

Gearbox	Close-ratio 5-speed transaxle driving rear wheels
Clutch	Hydraulic
Ratios	1st 3.167
	2nd 1.842
	3rd 1.308
	4th 1.033
	5th 0.765
	6th 3.000
Final drive	3.938

Suspension and Steering

Front and rear	Double wishbones, coil springs over gas-pressured monotube dampers, front anti-roll bar. Lotus-patented uprights of extruded aluminium, made by Alusuisse
Steering	Rack and pinion, non-assisted
Wheels	Front: Alloy Wheels International 5.5in × 15in cast alloy 5-spoke Rear: Alloy Wheels International 7.0in × 16in cast alloy 5-spoke
Tyres	Front: Pirelli P-Zero 185/55 R15 Rear: Pirelli P-Zero 205/50 R16

Brakes

Type	Aluminium-metal matrix ventilated discs made by Lanxide Brembo, mounted outboard. Non-servo split hydraulic system supplied by Automotive Products, including unique Lotus/AP Racing opposed-piston front calipers
Size	282mm diameter

Dimensions

Track	1,440mm (56.7in) front, 1,453mm (57.2in) rear
Wheelbase	2,300mm (90.6in)
Overall length	3,726mm (146.7in)
Overall width	1,701mm (67in) excluding door mirrors
Overall height	1,202mm (47.3in)
Dry weight	675kg (1,488lb)

Performance

Max. speed	124mph (201km/h)
0–100km/h (62mph)	5.9sec
0–100mph (160km/h)	18.0sec
Fuel consumption	Urban 28.9mpg (9.6ltr/100km) Extra urban 49.9mpg (5.7ltr/100km) Combined 39.4mpg (7.1ltr/100km)

CHAPTER ONE

THE SERIES 1 ELISE AND EXIGE

The Elise was designed and built by a focused and dedicated team within two fraught years. From the outset, it embodied the core values laid down three decades earlier by marque founder Colin Chapman: high performance through light weight, a radical chassis made of extruded and bonded aluminium, race-derived suspension, and efficient though relatively modest powertrains, clad in aerodynamic fibreglass bodywork.

While it was only planned to make a few hundred units a year, that figure had risen to 3,000 a year by 1998. The Elise flourished, although it was actually sister company Lotus Engineering's pioneering consultancy work, honing and fine-tuning products for other car makers worldwide, that proved to be the most profitable part of the business. It was this depth of in-house expertise as much as the efficiency and adaptability of a small volume production operation that allowed the Elise's gestation to come to fruition so quickly.

The original Series 1 Elise was an affordable, individualistic sports car, ideal for the enthusiast who was not overly concerned with creature comforts and appreciated the finer points of the driving experience. It was the only model available until the Sport 135 came out late in 1998. As is typical with model evolutions, the original Elise, built between 1995 and 2000, became known retrospectively as the Series 1 when its successor, designated the Series 2 – or S2 – arrived, five years later.

The Elise S1 was styled by Julian Thomson, then head of design at Lotus; since 2000 he has been chief designer at Jaguar. In fact, he left Lotus in 1998 to work for Volkswagen in Spain. Julian explained the philosophy behind the Elise:

> The whole idea behind the car as a lightweight Lotus has to be credited to Colin Chapman. You can see a whole book full of them. It's just that we drifted away from them, and then we thought we should be doing what we've always done. So, I think

Reflecting Lotus's seven decades of competition history, the red, white and gold livery of the Elise Type 49 celebrates the Team Lotus F1 car that won the Constructors' World Championship in 1968, and contributed to similar success in 1970.

ANTONY FRASER

The Elise was launched at the Frankfurt Show in 1995. The extruded aluminium chassis is also displayed on the Lotus stand.
WILLIAM TAYLOR

HISTORICAL CONTEXT

The Elise is the culmination of Lotus's seventy years' competition history: it used to be said that (like Enzo Ferrari) Colin Chapman built road cars to finance his racing cars. Achievements can be summarized as seven F1 World Championships, seventy-nine Grand Prix victories and innumerable race wins in the 1960s and 1970s. Though a spent force in F1 by the end of the 1980s, the marque survived as a road car producer after Chapman's death in 1982 under the umbrella of General Motors, before being taken over by Bugatti owner Romano Artioli, who had the majority share in Lotus from 1993 to 1996, when he sold out to Proton to pay his Bugatti debts.

By 1997, 80 per cent of Group Lotus belonged to the Malaysian HICOM Group, who also owned Proton. The Perusahaan OtomoMi Malaysia – or Proton – group took a big step onto the international stage in 1996 by acquiring a majority stake in Lotus, and, despite a downturn in the far eastern economy, in June 1998 the Malaysian parent increased its stake in Group Lotus from 64 to 80 per cent, claiming it was consolidating its investment. The extra 16 per cent stake bought by the Proton group was that previously held by former chairman, Tan Sri Yahaya, who invested some of his own cash alongside Proton's, but who died in a helicopter crash in 1997. Artioli retained 20 per cent and continued to act for Lotus as a consultant.

Elisa Artiolo was lent a motorsport-oriented Sport 260 model during her factory visit in 2018. In association with Delightful Driving, she led the celebratory cavalcade up northern Italy's legendary Stelvio Pass in September 2020, negotiating its seventy-five relentless hairpins up to 2,757m (9,045ft) in her own car to commemorate the twenty-fifth anniversary of her namesake, the Lotus Elise.

Lotus Cars' press officer Alastair Florance provided me with an Elise S1 to sample for a week in 1998, posed for a riverside snapshot opposite Norwich's old Ferry Boat Inn.

Part-way through the design process the Elise takes shape as a full-size clay model in the design studio.
WILLIAM TAYLOR

> the Elise is a Colin Chapman car. But I don't think anyone can take the credit for coming up with the idea, because basically the Elise defines what a Lotus is. That's down to our founder, but the interpretation of it is down to people like Richard [Rackham].

The Elise's ground-breaking chassis was designed by Richard Rackham, Lotus's then chief engineer and now its chief vehicle architect. Thomson was influenced by a number of automotive icons from the 1960s, including the Ferrari 330P4 Le Mans car and its little sister, the 246 Dino, as well as Lotus's own Type 23, though he also cited the Ford GT40 and Lancia Stratos as significant. My own references, visually at least, are the Ginetta G12 and the Porsche 910, both mid-engined sports prototypes from 1966 and 1967. For his part, chassis

The Lotus Design Studio, late 1990s, with Julian Thomson, Andrew Hill, David Brisbourne (standing), Steve Crijns and Andrew McLachlan progressing new styling concepts.
WILLIAM TAYLOR

A number of classic racing cars were influential in Julian Thomson's styling for the original Lotus Elise, primarily the Ferrari Dino 289; my own preference is the Porsche 910, photographed here at Brands Hatch during the 1967 BOAC 500km, shared by Graham Hill and Jochen Rindt, who went on to be team mates at Team Lotus in 1969.
IAN CATT

The S1 Elise was fitted with the Rover K-series 4-valves-per-cylinder, 4-cylinder, aluminium-cased 1.8-litre (1796cc) twin-cam engine, mounted transversely amidships, developing 118bhp at 5,500rpm. Derivatives like the Elise Sport 111were rated at 135bhp, and the Type 49 pictured here at 143bhp.
WIM TE RIET

The Series 1 Elise cockpit is a basic environment, but it is driver-focused, and everything necessary to control the car falls neatly to hand.
WILLIAM TAYLOR

For almost a decade, from launch in 1995 to 2004, the Elise was powered by the 1796cc Rover K-series engine, developing 143bhp in untuned format. WILLIAM TAYLOR

BELOW: **The Elise pedal-box assembly features the three extruded aluminium pedals, an absolute work of art, as well as elegantly functional.** WILLIAM TAYLOR

man Rackham identified the Ducati 916 motorcycle as a principal influence on the Elise design, an example of what was at the time a bike at the cutting edge of design technology.

The powerplant chosen initially was the well-proven Rover K-series unit, with the 4-valves-per-cylinder, 4-cylinder, aluminium-cased 1.8-litre (1796cc) twin-cam unit selected for the Elise. Mounted transversely amidships, like halcyon predecessors such as the Types 19, 23, 30 and 47, it developed 118bhp at 5,500rpm in the launch model (165Nm torque at 3,000rpm), with derivatives like Elise Sport 111 rated at 135bhp. The K-series engine was mated to Rover's R65 close-ratio five-speed gearbox with central shift tunnel running through the cockpit and handily placed gear lever.

REVOLUTIONARY CONSTRUCTION

In accordance with founder Colin Chapman's maxim 'add lightness', Lotus has tended to use lightweight materials and construction rather than brute power to optimize performance, and the Elise conforms to type. The Series 1 Lotus Elise weighs only 675kg (1,485lb); compare that, for example, with a Porsche Boxster at 1,250kg (2,756lb), 74 per cent heavier. It can accelerate from 0 to 60mph in 5.8 seconds despite its relatively modest power output of 118bhp from the standard Rover 1.8 L K-series 118bhp straight-four unit. The double wishbone, coil-over-damper suspension layout remained refreshingly unaltered over the model's lifetime. The Koni monotube shocks were mounted upside down, and a front anti-roll bar

On the Lotus Cars stand at the 1995 Frankfurt Show for the launch of the Elise are senior development engineer Tony Shute and PR officer Patrick Peel.
WILLIAM TAYLOR

was fitted, while extruded aluminium uprights were made by Alusuisse. Steering was non-assisted rack and pinion.

Braking, cornering and fuel consumption were also improved by the car's low weight. This was a revolutionary car: no one had ever done an extruded aluminium chassis with bonded joints before and then clad it in lightweight fibreglass panels. When Richard Rackham designed the chassis there was no industry standard for bonding aluminium; the new process was developed in house by Lotus technicians in association with Hydro Aluminium in Denmark, a company subsequently bought by Lotus and now operating as Lotus Lightweight Structures in Worcester. The fundamental base for the Elise and its derivatives, from the word go, and right up to the present, is the extruded aluminium chassis. It consists of two high-sided members running down either side of the car, connected front and rear by torsion boxes, which provide its structural integrity. To provide for passenger occupation, the rear torsion box incorporates a roll-over structure, the rear of the seat mounting, and a larger section with a sliding joint and the crumple zone where the rear subframe bolts on. At the front is the front of the seat mounting and the top of the steering column mount, where the crash structure goes on.

Elise project manager from the outset was the highly knowledgeable and amiable Tony Shute. The original challenge was to produce an efficient chassis structure, and he drew a comparison between an archaic Austin Seven chassis, with very low stiffness and therefore a very inefficient structure, and at the other extreme, a 1980s Group C WEC racing car with a carbon tub, which is very light and very stiff. The target was to create a chassis with 10,000Nm per degree stiffness at a weight of about 700kg (1,540lb). Such a chassis would be some seven times stiffer than a Lotus Seven, or three times stiffer than the Esprit. Research indicated this target was world class for an open-top car.

The next decision Lotus had to make was whether to weld or to bond the chassis components, and much research was done into both methods. The bonding-only method would absorb very high loads, but once those loads were exceeded the structure had nothing left to rely on. In other words, in an impact situation the joints would tolerate a great deal of stress and then suddenly fall apart. A welded joint, on the other hand, doesn't have a very high peak load, but it does have very good elongation: it doesn't give up like a plain bonded joint. Lotus discovered that the trick is to use a mechanical fastener along with the bonded joint, which not only stops the joint peeling apart, but holds it together during a period of elongation.

The Ejot thread-forming fastener is commonly used in the building industry, and these fasteners were selected for the Elise. They were thought to be so effective that the car could even be driven without bonded joints. The bond is created by an epoxy adhesive, which doesn't actually cure until the chassis has been in the oven. This meant that the component parts could be disassembled and moved around, and adjusted during the experimentation stage.

The doors were extremely compact units and contained aluminium beam extrusions, which featured the only aluminium weld in the whole car where the hinge rotor was welded on. The Elise thus had two side impact beams, one at the height of the sills, and another a little higher up with the dash cross-beam and the roll-hoop around the back giving it support. The door beam ran right through the length of the door and supported the rest of the window mechanism.

Built on site at Hethel in a long-standing factory, the Series 1 clamshells and body panels were made using the traditional hand-laid matting/resin/mould methods that are still used on site for lower-volume Exige, Europa and circuit racing cars.

With its unique construction, based on a super-strong extruded aluminium chassis and clothed in curvaceous panel work, this was no mainstream sports car model of the sort exemplified by the Mazda MX5/Miata, or even the more exclusive Porsche 986 Boxster that appeared a year later in 1996. From a specification point of view, the Series 1 is easy to quantify and categorize because there were only five main options: metallic paint, leather seats, a Category 1 alarm, auxiliary driving lamps and radio fitting kit. When they were in production, an Elise Series 1 with four out of five of those items was considered more desirable, while a cloth interior and no driving lamps was seen as a basic car.

In 1998, the Elise Sport 135 was introduced, making 130bhp as opposed to the standard K-series' 118bhp, while the Elise Sport 190 produced 190bhp, powered by a VVC Rover K-series engine with a modified head and VVT (variable valve timing) technology, producing 143bhp, along with a closer ratio manual gearbox and lower ratio final drive. The 111S had headlamp covers, rear spoiler, cross-drilled brake discs, alloy window winders and a six-spoke road wheel design, plus a touch of comfort – extra padding in the seats. With more power for less money – the 111S was cheaper than the standard Series 1 – it had to be a bargain, which upset a few people at the time. The 111S is now quite a desirable version because it was only around for the last eighteen months of Series 1 production. The final variant on the hotted-up S1 theme was the Elise Sport 190, introduced in 2000.

A trio of Elise S1s battle for second and third podium places in a Modified Elise race at Snetterton in 2009, featuring Steve Williams, Steve Owen and Ben Pitch.

Lotus Elise 340R (2000-1)

Layout and Chassis

Two-seater roadster, comprising composite body panels with detachable one-piece top shell and integral fixed faired headlamps. Lotus-designed spaceframe structure of epoxy-bonded sections of aluminium extrusions (built by Hydro Aluminium) incorporating dedicated integral occupant roll-over protection

Engine

Type	K-series, transverse mid-engine
Block material	Aluminium
Head material	Aluminium
Cylinders	4 cylinders in line
Cooling	Water
Bore and stroke	80mm × 89.3mm
Capacity	1796cc
Valves	DOHC, 16 valves
Fuelling	Multipoint sequential fuel injection
Engine management	Lotus Motorola electronic ignition system, mapping unique to Lotus 85A
Max. power	170bhp at 8,000rpm
Max. torque	105lb ft at 5,000rpm
Fuel capacity	40ltr (8.8gal)
Fuel grade	98 RON

Instrumentation

Type	Stack analogue electronic unit with DAS (data acquisition system) comprising speedometer and tachometer with multifunction LCD readout incorporating fuel and coolant gauges

Transmission

Gearbox	Close-ratio 5-speed transaxle driving rear wheels
Clutch	Hydraulic
Ratios	1st 3.167
	2nd 1.842
	3rd 1.308
	4th 1.033
	5th 0.765
	Reverse 3.000
Final drive	3.938

Suspension and Steering

Front and rear	Double wishbones with single coil springs over two-way adjustable Koni monotube dampers all round. Lotus-patented uprights of extruded aluminium, made by Alusuisse
Steering	Rack and pinion, non-assisted
Wheels	Ultra-light 10-spoke magnesium, specially made for Lotus by OZ Racing, 7.0in × 16in front, 8.0in × 17in rear
Tyres	Front: Yokohama A038 195/45 × 16
	Rear: Yokohama A038 205/40 × 17

Brakes

Type	Non-servo split hydraulic system Front: four-pot AP Racing calipers, drilled and ventilated discs Rear: AP Racing calipers, drilled and ventilated discs
Size	95mm diameter (front), 82mm (rear)

Performance

Max. speed	133mph (214km/h)
0–100km/h (62mph)	4.0sec
0–100mph (160km/h)	10.0sec

Dimensions

Track	1,440mm (56.7in) front, 1,453mm (57.2in) rear
Wheelbase	2,300mm (90.6in)
Overall length	3,500mm (137.8in)
Overall width	1,702mm (67in) excluding door mirrors
Overall height	1,050mm (41.3in)
Dry weight	500kg (1,100lb)

THE ELISE TROPHY

The Lotus Elise Trophy was introduced in Italy in 1997, and attracted the interest of many Italian drivers. Peroni Promotions were responsible for all the organization and attracting substantial press and television coverage, as well as paddock hospitality. There were nine races altogether in the 1997 championship, eight of which were in Italy and one at Rijeka in Croatia. There were two rounds each at Vallelunga, Magione, Misano Adriatico and Varano. In addition, some Elise Trophy cars raced in the Six Hours of Vallelunga, where the first Elise finished fifth overall. At the Bologna Motor Show, Peroni Promotions organized a demonstration Elise race. There were two half-hour practice sessions before each race, which was either a single 70km (44-mile) race or two one-hour races.

Twenty Lotus Sport Elise race cars battled season-long during the 2000 Lotus Autobytel championship, staged at major UK race circuits plus Spa Francorchamps and the Nürburgring, finishing with fourteen different drivers on the podium and five different race winners. Main contenders included Edward Horner, Ben Devlin, Spencer Marsh, Mark Cole, Simon Hill and Paula Cook, with celebrity drivers Tiff Needell, Gwyndaf Evans and Will Hoy in the fray. The leader here is eventual championship winner Adam Wilcox.
WILLIAM TAYLOR

Ade Wootton's 257bhp Exige Cup 260 pictured in the Snetterton pit lane during a round of the MSVR Lotus Elise Trophy, 2019.
STEPHANIE EWEN

Nineteen drivers registered for the series (average age thirty-four), and an average of fifteen cars participated in each race. Drivers with a grade C CSAI licence were eligible, using a standard Elise fitted with a tuning kit supplied by the long-standing race preparation and tuning firm Conrero. The specification also included standard wheels shod with Avon tyres with a weight limit of 760kg (1,672lb), including driver. As part of the deal, drivers also received fire-resistant overalls and undergarments, paddock waistcoats and quilted jackets.

In 2007, the Elise Trophy was launched in cahoots with MotorSport Vision Racing, and the inaugural race was staged at Brands Hatch in March that year. During its early years, the Elise Trophy was one of the highest-profile club race series in the UK, supporting numerous top-class events such as DTM World Touring Cars and A1 GP, while the championship's own annual event, the Lotus Festival, was supported by the contemporary Lotus F1 team, with Heikki Kovalainen and Jarno Trulli driving classic Lotus F1 cars.

Other guest drivers have included the world's fastest man – Wing Commander Andy Green OBE – and ex-F1 Lotus racer Martin Donnelly, who entered the Elise Trophy in 2007 and has competed in numerous races since.

The Elise Trophy grew from Lotus on Track, the UK's largest track day club, and the series was granted championship status at the end of the 2013 season. The Lotus on Track Racing Drivers Club (LoTRDC) is a race series for Lotus Elise owners, and now runs the FIA International Series – Lotus Cup Europe. From the 2019 season, MotorSport Vision Racing ran the MSVR Elise Trophy; for 2020, Road Race Rally Engineering was nominated official power testers, and the Avon ZZR was set to be the control tyre, just as they are for Lotus Cup Europe. Unfortunately, however, the global Covid-19 pandemic halted proceedings for 2020.

In his debut race in an Elise S1 – indeed, in his first-ever circuit race – world land speed record holder Wing Commander Andy Green finished a laudable eighteenth. These things are all relative: top speed of an Elise S1 is 145mph (233km/h), depending on spec, while the current WLSR is 763mph (1,227.9km/h) achieved by Andy Green in 1997.

LEFT: **At Snetterton circuit for Lotus's sixtieth anniversary celebrations, World Land Speed Record holder Andy Green of Bloodhound fame chats with Clive Chapman of Classic Team Lotus.**

continued overleaf

THE ELISE TROPHY *continued*

Pupils signed up to the Lotus Driving Academy are often tutored by star drivers, such as ex-Lotus Formula I pilot Martin Donnelly, posed here with the 2006 Exige S press car.
JASON PARNELL

OPPOSITE TOP: **Single-make racing inevitably provides close competition: here, a couple of Series I Elises lead a Series 2 Elise and an Exige during an Elise Trophy race at Snetterton in September 2011.**

Dramatic night race shot of Adam Wilcox's Exige during the 2002 Lotus Autobytel one-make championship.
STEPHANIE EWEN

LOTUS CUP EUROPE

By 2020, the Lotus Cup Europe, originally set up as a fun but professionally run motor sport series, had become the world's longest-running Lotus racing championship. As an FIA International Series, adhering to their safety and technical regulations, it has similar status to prestigious race series such as the DTM (Deutsche Touren Meisterschaft) and Blancpain, as well as attracting support from the broader Lotus community, with many enthusiasts attending events. All rounds are broadcast on TV and it also has more than 60,000 Facebook followers. Race weekends start with two free practice sessions, followed by thirty minutes of qualifying, and then there are two or three half-hour races, with standing and rolling starts. It is open to drivers with all levels of experience, provided they hold an international D licence or higher. Whilst the series has grown hugely since its inception over a decade ago, it has firmly remained as a fun and social environment in which to compete.

BELOW LEFT: **By 2020, the Lotus Cup Europe had become the world's longest-running Lotus racing championship. Here is Joe Taylor in his Exige in the Lotus Elise Trophy race.**
STEPHANIE EWEN

BELOW RIGHT: **Front runner Jason McInulty participating in the Motorsport Vision Racing (MSVR) Lotus Elise Trophy in 2019: note the additional aero and hefty cage inside the cabin.**
STEPHANIE EWEN

continued overleaf

LOTUS CUP EUROPE *continued*

Entries are split into three classes: the V6 Cup for the Exige V6 Cup and Evora GT4; the 2-Eleven/Open class for the 4-cylinder, supercharged, open-top 2-Eleven, 4-cylinder Exige Cup cars and most other Lotus cars that are not eligible for the other categories; and third the Production category, containing Elises such as the Elise Cup R. Points are scored according to class position, with bonus points added for the number of cars starting races in each class, and therefore drivers from all classes have an equal chance of competing for the overall championship victory. Hungarian Bence Balogh won the 2018 title from the V6 Cup class, Belgian John Rasse raced a Production car to take the title in 2015, and Frenchman Jérémy Lourenco claimed the 2014 championship with a 2-Eleven.

Organized by Paul Golding, the Lotus Cup Europe calendar features on several of Europe's top circuits, with three of 2020's rounds potentially (depending on the duration of lockdown and rescheduling of events) supporting the DTM rounds at Monza, Brands Hatch and the Nürburgring. The season was meant to kick off at the Hockenheim Historic GPP event, and conclude at the 24-Heures' Camions event at Le Mans in front of 60,000 spectators.

The cockpit of the 2-Eleven 272 'Circuit Car' is the epitome of racing car austerity.
WILLIAM TAYLOR

OPPOSITE BOTTOM: **The MSVR Lotus Elise Trophy provided close, exhilarating competition between S1 and S2 Elises and Exiges: frequently in the leading pack, Dave Carr's Gold Leaf-hued Elise sprouts a taller wing and larger front splitter and rear diffuser.**
STEPHANIE EWEN

THE ELISE SPORT 190

In March 1997, Lotus announced the Sport Elise, destined for the Autobytel race series, which had a centrally located driving position and controls. The Sport Elise was built by Lotus Motorsport department under team manager Chris Arnold, Chris Dinnage (ex-Team Lotus and now racing manager of Classic Team Lotus) and design engineer Greg Taylor, with Myles Lubbock, Steve Hardy and John Danby as race engineers. A total of sixty-five centre-seat customer cars were built to contest the one-make 2000 Autobytel Championship, also prefiguring the Series 1 Exige. Lotus Motorsport who undertake setting-up and transporting the Sport Elise racing cars to and from circuits, as well as sourcing major sponsors and suppliers for the series. Stylistically, this car was the harbinger of the hardcore Motorsport Elise, announced at the 1999 Earls Court Show and the basis of another one-make series that was part of the BTCC package doing the rounds of UK circuits in 2000; unquestionably, it also set the stage for the Exige, launched in April 2000. The Sport Elise was a logical evolution of the original model and successfully combined the performance and sensation of a competition car with the usability of a road car. The idea was that it could be driven to the circuit

ABOVE LEFT: **The 2-Eleven prototype was the 272 'Circuit Car', which weighed just 650kg (1,433lb), 20kg (44lb) less than the production 2-Eleven. Powered by the supercharged 1796cc Toyota 4-cylinder unit, it was the ultimate example of Lotus's enduring slogan, 'performance through light weight.'**
STEVE BENNETT

ABOVE RIGHT: **Having raced a Honda-powered Exige, Chris Randall won the opening round of the 2009 Elise Trophy with his Hofmann's Racing Type 121 Europa – the first race for this particular model, seen here negotiating Snetterton's Russell complex in September 2009.**

and back and used quite happily in any racing discipline without the need for massive sponsorship budgets. The Sport 190 could have carbon-fibre clamshells, magnesium wheels, lightweight battery, silencer and rear window glass, bringing its weight down to 650kg (1,430lb). Options included an FIA-approved roll cage, a full four-point harness, competition springs, dampers, anti-roll bar, competition Stack instrument pack with data-logging facility, a closer ratio gearbox and competition silencers. A tonneau cover was a sensible option.

The Sport 190 Motorsport car was tested at Prescott hillclimb and the Brighton Speed Trials in 1997, driven by senior development engineer Tony Shute and attracted seventy-five orders before the year's end. This initial batch was built up in one of the workshops off the main production line because of the difficulties of installing special components and possibility of interfering with the tight schedule on the line. The optional carbon-fibre clamshells were made by ex-Lotus F1 crewman Arthur Birchill, and could have a paint finish that would show off the material. Several of the cars were destined for Australia and the USA to compete against 911s in the Bathurst sports car event, and these were fitted with the hard-tops that were mandatory in Australia.

The Elise Sport was released in February 2000 as a high-performance version aimed at enthusiast buyers requiring a slightly higher level of dynamic handling and performance for use on road and track. WILLIAM TAYLOR

BELOW LEFT: **Introduced in January 1999, the 111S was the first model in the Elise range to be equipped with the 1796cc 143bhp MG-Rover Variable Valve Control VVC engine, as fitted in the premium version of the MGF. All together, 1,487 units were built up to 2001.** WILLIAM TAYLOR

LIMITED-EDITION VARIANTS

Lotus also released some limited-edition models, including the Sport 135 (1998/9), with approximately 145bhp and available in different colours and steering wheel; the Sport 160 (2000) with 150–160bhp; and the Sport 190, released in 2000. These were more competent on track with their differently rated sports suspension, wheels, tyres and seats according to model. A range of special editions paid testament to Lotus's racing pedigree, such as the 50th Anniversary Edition (green/gold) celebrating fifty years of Lotus cars, and the Type 49 ('Gold Leaf' red and white two-tone with gold stripes – reminiscent of the similarly liveried Lotus Elan Sprint) and Type 72 ('JPS' black and gold), which referred to the company's successful F1 Grand Prix car type numbers.

The cognoscenti view the Sport 160, brought out towards the end of Series 1 production, as the most desirable car of the entire Series 1 line-up. Originally it was just going to be a fifty-units-only special produced under the single vehicle rules that applied at the time, although subsequently Lotus got the whole vehicle approved and built more cars. But the first fifty only had to comply with SVA regs and were probably in excess of 160bhp. Performance had to be stifled a little bit by a change of exhaust to obtain the whole vehicle type approval. This was the first real special edition model in the range. It had a bit of characteristic popping and banging and burbling built in, a nice set of wheels and an even bigger wing on the back, so it was a car with attitude. But for everybody that liked the way it burbled and banged, there was somebody else who said it was ridiculous, give it 160bhp but make it perfectly smooth. So, a few people missed the point.

The Type 115 GT1 was an Elise-based sports prototype racing car, using a widened Elise chassis and carbon-fibre bodywork. The works racing team rejected the in-house 3.5-litre turbo V8 from the Esprit GT1 in favour of the GM 6.0-litre Corvette V8 engine. Altogether, eight Elise GT1 race-car chassis were built; Fabien Giroix's First Racing ran cars for

the Lotus factory, with privateers GBF UK and Martin Veyhle Racing running the others. The Elise GT1s were campaigned in the 1997 FIA GT championship alongside proven GT1 offerings from Porsche, Mercedes-Benz, McLaren, Ferrari and TVR. After alternator and gearbox teething troubles, the three Lotuses acquitted themselves well enough in the hands of Jan Lammers, Alex Grau and Mike Hezemans, Jerome Polican and Ratanakul Prutirat, Luca Badoer and Domenico Schiattarella, but though points were scored they failed to build on that modest success. When Proton acquired Lotus Cars in 1998 the GT1 project was dropped. The factory had a third car in hand, intended for use in the British GT championship, which got as far as scrutineering for the Silverstone round in 2000. Toine Hezemans (Mike's father and winner of multiple 1970s ETCC championships) drove it on the Supercar Rally 2001 from Paris to Monaco.

Another car based on the Elise S1 platform was the 340R, an attractive proposition for prospective Caterham or Ariel Atom purchasers, though bearing in mind that technology had moved on, the 340R, delivering 190bhp through a K-series engine, was operating near the edge of the envelope.

Launched in 2000, just 340 units of the roofless car were produced, and their name and number refer to the 340bhp per tonne power-to-weight ratio of the original 340R prototype, which delivered 177bhp while weighing just 500kg

ABOVE: **In 1999, Lotus released the Type 49, first of a succession of special edition Elises, referencing Team Lotus successes, in this case the 1968 World Championship-winning F1 car, liveried in the colours of its sponsor, John Player's Gold Leaf cigarette brand. Here at Goodwood House, Lord March knows a thing or two about projecting one's heritage.**
ANTONY FRASER

Team Lotus's black and gold era spanned a decade and a half, from 1972 to 1986. The JPS livery was classy and refined and, most of all, distinctive. The layout of the cigarette packet design was applied to the Type 72 Formula 1 car by promotions agent Barry Foley ahead of the switch from Gold Leaf to John Player Special brands in 1972, and in 2002 Lotus applied it to the heritage edition Type 72 Elise S2.
WILLIAM TAYLOR

The Type 115 Elise GT1 is one of seven road-going versions of the one-off GT1 race car developed by Neil Lloyd and Richard Rackham, mainly constructed at Ketteringham Hall (Team Lotus's former HQ). Wheelbase is 15in (380mm) longer and the aerodynamically evolved body 15in (380mm) wider than the standard Elise, and the power unit is the 350bhp 3.5-litre Lotus 918 V8. Pictured at Silverstone in 2006, also in shot is Miss Zoë Tipler.

Released in 2000, the Elise 340R was so-called because its stripped-to-the-bone nature enabled a power-to-weight ratio of 340bhp per tonne, attained by the 190bhp track-only version late in the year. It was no coincidence that production was limited to 340 units.

The Lotus Exposé, based on an Elise 340R, with transparent bodywork made from Vacuum Formed Polycarbonate, powered by the 1.8 Rover K-series engine in 190bhp tune, and equipped with active adjustable suspension by Dynamics Suspension of Thetford. It was used in 2001 by senior development engineer Tony Shute to compete successfully in hillclimbs such as Harewood and Llandow.

WILLIAM TAYLOR

(1,100lb). The final production versions, however, weighed 568kg (1,250lb) in race trim. It took the performance through light weight paradigm to its extreme in an optional 190bhp version that everybody went for, in a car with no doors, no windows and no heater. Born of a design study, the 340R's futuristic looks were those of a concept car that found its way into production, and it proved a hard sell at £33,000.

THE EXIGE S1

The Exige was launched in April 2000 at Brands Hatch, to coincide with the first practice for the opening one-make Autobytel Race Championship race of the season. It remained in production until the Series 1 Elise was phased out. Bristling with on-track attitude, the Exige was like an

Elise on steroids, heavily reliant on elements of the Sport Elise parts bin, with purposeful beetle-back coupé bodywork, coxcomb overhead engine air intake, rear wing and front splitter, though in normal format it shared its soft-top sibling's normally aspirated 1.8-litre Rover K-series engine, albeit in VHPD (very high performance derivative) tune like the 340R. It produced 177bhp (132kW or 179PS) in standard form and 192bhp (143kW/195PS) in the 'track spec' version. The Exige Series 1 proved fairly difficult to sell at the time, coming in the dying days of the Series 1's lifecycle, and customers had to be incentivized by limited editions, including a Millennium Edition in 2000. Of the 700 Exiges made in Series 1 format, around 400 stayed in the UK. It made way for the S2 model in 2004.

Sixteen motor sport Elises and S1 Exiges line up on the Brands Hatch grid on 4 April 2002 for a round of the one-make Autobytel Lotus Championship. Sponsors also competed and earned points in a dedicated 'Constructors' Challenge', which ran alongside the main drivers' championship.

STEPHANIE EWEN

ABOVE LEFT: **Instigated by Lotus Motorsport, the Autobytel Lotus Championship regularly saw grids of up to twenty motor sport Elises and S1 Exiges, as here in April 2002, swarming out of Druid's Hairpin and down towards Graham Hill Bend at Brands Hatch.**

STEPHANIE EWEN

RIGHT: **Contemporary Lotus press advert from 2000 for the Series 1 Exige.**

WILLIAM TAYLOR

CHAPTER TWO

THE SERIES 2 ELISE AND EXIGE

The twenty-first century ushered in the new second-generation Series 2 version of the Elise – the S2 – with heavily revised body and interior, revised soft-top, lowered chassis side-rails, suspension, hubs and hub carriers. Power unit was the 1796cc MG-Rover K-series.
WILLIAM TAYLOR

Announced on 9 October 2000, the Series 2 Elise was a substantially redesigned Series 1, using a slightly modified version of the Series 1 chassis and the same K-series engine with a brand-new Lotus-developed ECU. Initially, Series 1 (S1) and Series 2 (S2) cars shared many parts, including the chassis, although they came to have totally different drivetrains when Lotus embraced the Toyota powerplant in 2004. The S2 Elise ushered in much-improved build quality, insisted upon by its General Motors clients when Lotus undertook construction of the Elise-based Vauxhall/Opel/Daewoo VX220 Roadster.

With Russell Carr now heading the styling studio, this was the first Lotus to be designed on computer. The new body design paid homage to Lotus's stillborn M250 project and has a much more aggressive demeanour than the classically inspired Series 1 with its cheeky front façade. To achieve the desired effect, tiny modifications were made to the chassis. Lotus pruned the side sills away to make entry and exit a bit easier, while the body contours were sharpened up with much more edgy styling cues, especially in the almond-esque headlight clusters and knife-edge front wing tops and side air intakes.

Here's the great divide in the world of the Elise: in single-marque terms, the Series 2 is a quantum leap from its forebear. For a start, it is much better built. Warranty statistics prove it – not far into S2 production, the cost of parts and time spent in rectification was halved compared with the S1. Constructed in a new factory building on a production line alongside the VX220/Opel Speedster (dropped in 2005), the whole plant was geared to build a General Motors product, and all manufacturing systems had to comply with General Motors' rigorous quality-control standards. There was a slight price to pay, because to a small degree it compromised the car's performance through light weight, as the S2 was slightly heavier, although there was much more scope for tailoring performance.

An innovation was that the bodyshells – clamshells, in Lotus parlance – themselves were supplied by SOTIRA, succeeded by Faurecia, headquartered at Nanterre, France, who have produced all Lotus clamshells and certain other panels for the last few years using the RTM (resin transfer moulding) process that is basically a variation of the VARI (vacuum-assisted resin injection) system Lotus used to use for the Esprit. The advantages of this method are that woven or random fibreglass mat can be moulded in a low two-minute cycle time, giving constant thickness of material and the facility to produce undercut lips or rims.

When the Series 2 Elise went on sale in 2001, two option packs were available – a first for Lotus: Race Tech, a bare aluminium style statement, and Sports Tourer, a more comfortable version with leather interior and sound baffling. Lotus specialist Guy Munday was sales manager at the Stratton Motor Company dealership at the time, and was surprised by the take-up:

> I remember going to a dealer meeting when the car was launched, and Lotus explained the differences between the two option packages, and we assumed 80 per cent of customers would go for Race Tech and a few softies would choose the less hard-core version. Race Tech came along first, but although we had a queue of people waiting to buy the car, they all said, 'Well, actually, we will wait till the Sports Tourer comes out.'

The Series 2 Elise cockpit from 2004 was functional, with just enough comfort but no frills – like electric windows.
WILLIAM TAYLOR

It was the complete reverse of what had been expected; about 80 per cent were specified as Sports Tourers and about 20 per cent were Race Tech. With carpets, sound-deadening and a stereo in an Elise, Mazda MX5, Honda S2000 and Boxster devotees could be tempted into the Lotus fold. So, although the S2 is visually harder-edged than the S1, it is easier to live with because of cockpit access, materials, fixtures and fittings and creature comfort options.

In production from May, the Elise Type 111S retained the Rover K-Series VVC engine, revised transmission ratios, round tailpipes with flap valve, three-tier rear diffuser, larger radiator, and polished nickel finish eight-spoke wheels. Lotus observed that most customers were improving the specifications of the standard car to 111S standard, so the base model was dropped at the end of the year.

The Series 2's specification remained untouched until 2004, when Lotus fitted the Toyota 2ZZ-GE 1.8-litre twin-cam engine in the top-of-the-range 111R. That still left the Elise 120 and 160 Rover-powered cars in the line-up, and the two engine makes ran concurrently in the range for just over eighteen months, from March 2004 to the end of 2005. However, the mooted Toyota-powered 111RS flagship car caused a certain amount of shenanigans with Rover. There hadn't been a problem with engine supply or reliability issues, but customer perception of the Rover product fell through the floor to the point where there was a real fight to get customers into Rover-engined cars. But without the K-series powered cars, in 2005 and 2006 Lotus would have been left with just a single model line-up.

There was a considerable price hike with the first Toyota-engined cars, with the standard Elise 120 up to around £24,000, while a 111S with 160bhp cost about £28,000 and the 190 with a Toyota engine coupled to a six-speed gearbox was on sale at £32,000. From 2007, the Toyota 1ZZ-FE 1.8-litre engine replaced the K-series Rover engine, developing 134bhp at 6,200rpm. The 218bhp supercharged SE version was released in 2008, and the entry-level 1.6-litre version announced for 2011. The Toyota driveline included the Japanese firm's six-speed gearbox.

In 2004, the Toyota 2ZZ-GE 1.8-litre twin-cam engine was installed in the top-of-the-range Elise 111R, though the Rover-powered cars ran concurrently for just another eighteen months up to the end of 2005.
WILLIAM TAYLOR

A major evolution in the Elise and Exige specification came about in spring 2004, when the 1796cc Rover K-series engine was dropped and the similar-capacity Toyota VVTL was introduced. Although heavier by 3 per cent, performance was 18 per cent better, producing 189bhp.
WILLIAM TAYLOR

Lotus Sport Elise 135R (2003–4)

Layout and Chassis

Two-seater, Lotus-designed epoxy-bonded aluminium alloy extrusions with integral steel rollover structure and lightweight steel rear subframe

Engine

Type	K-series, transverse mid-engine
Block material	Aluminium
Head material	Aluminium
Cylinders	4 cylinders in line
Cooling	Water
Bore and stroke	80mm × 89.3mm
Capacity	1796cc
Valves	DOHC, 16 valves
Fuelling	Multipoint sequential fuel injection
Engine management	Reprogrammed Lotus K4 engine controller
Max. power	135bhp (100kW) at 6,250rpm
Max. torque	126lb ft at 4,800rpm
Fuel	95 RON ULG minimum
Emission control	Three-way catalytic converter Active on-board diagnostics – Euro III emissions compliant CO_2 emissions 184g/km

Transmission

Gearbox	Close-ratio 5-speed transaxle driving rear wheels
Clutch	Hydraulic
Ratios	1st 2.923 2nd 1.750 3rd 1.307 4th 1.033 5th 0.848 Reverse 3.000
Final drive	4.200

Suspension and Steering

Front and rear	Double wishbones, Eibach coil springs over Bilstein gas-pressured monotube dampers. Adjustable ride height and adjustable front anti-roll bar
Steering	Rigidly mounted rack and pinion; 2.8 turns lock to lock
Wheels	Front: OZ 6.5in × 16in cast alloy 16-spoke wheels Rear: OZ 7.5in × 17in cast alloy 16-spoke wheels
Tyres	Front: Yokohama A048 195/50 R16 Rear: Yokohama A048 225/45 R17

Brakes

Type	Cast iron, cross-drilled and ventilated discs. Non-servo split hydraulic system, including unique Lotus/AP Racing opposed piston aluminium front calipers
Size	282mm diameter

Dimensions

Track	1,457mm (57.4in) front, 1,503mm (59.2in) rear
Wheelbase	2,300mm (90.6in)
Overall length	3,785mm (149in)
Overall width	1,719mm (67.7in) excluding door mirrors
Overall height	1,143mm (45in)
Dry weight	710kg (1,565lb)
Kerb weight	757kg (1,669lb) including full tank of fuel
Luggage capacity	115ltr

Performance

Max. speed	129mph (207.6km/h)
0–100km/h (62mph)	5.3sec
0–100mph (160km/h)	14.2sec
Fuel consumption	Urban 27.2mpg (10.4ltr/100km) Extra urban 45.1mpg (6.3ltr/100km) Combined 36.2mpg (7.8ltr/100km)

LOTUS SPORT ELISE 135R

Available at UK dealerships from 1 May 2003, the Lotus Sport Elise 135R was a special edition, denoted by the Lotus Sport chassis plate fixed in the passenger footwell, and only 123 units were built. Developed by Lotus Sport and Performance in conjunction with the Lotus Ride and Handling team, the Lotus Sport Elise 135R was designed to provide ultimate performance both on and off track. Engine, suspension, wheel and tyre upgrades all contributed to what was, at the time, the ultimate Elise road racer. Demonstrating a more direct feel than standard, the 135R gives the enthusiast driver sharper responses and enhanced feedback. The sports-suspension set-up allows full control over ride-height settings to maximize performance and handling, while Lotus Sport and Performance redesigned the flow characteristics of the cylinder head to provide greater flexibility throughout the rev range. The three-piece F1-style diffuser and exhaust system have also been optimized to further enhance the performance and character of the car, visually and aerodynamically.

Power output of the 1796cc Rover K-series engine was 135bhp, which was achieved by modifying the ports of the cylinder head to improve gas-flow mixture and cylinder filling. The standard intake manifold was replaced by a cast-alloy version as used on the 111 range. Alongside a reprogrammed ECU, these modifications improved engine breathing, permitting the driver to explore maximum engine revs in all gears, especially during track use.

Lotus's ride and handling team developed an optimum set-up for both road and track use, involving Bilstein dampers that were recalibrated to give stiffer bump and rebound settings. The dampers were also fitted with adjustable upper spring platforms threaded onto the damper itself, providing a wide range of settings for any use. A stiffer motor sport adjustable anti-roll bar was also fitted to provide optimum steering response.

The Sport Elise 135R was fitted with OZ Racing one-piece lightweight cast-alloy sixteen-spoke wheels. While the rear wheel size remained unchanged, the front wheel rim size increased from 5.5in to 6.5in to give a more positive turn-in during track actions. The OZ wheels were fitted with Yokohama A048 tyres, developed in conjunction with Lotus with special emphasis on track use.

Externally, the 135R could be identified by its striking finish and decals: available in just two colours – Silver Mica and Blue Mica – the model's designation was also resplendent on the flanks above each side repeater lamp, with a larger decal at the rear. As befitted its special edition status, the 135R had a bespoke interior, with the instrument binnacle and column cowlings trimmed in blue Alcantara, just like the seats, with additional carbon and leather trim and unique embroidery. The blue footwell carpets were embroidered with the 135R logo, and could be removed for track days.

LOTUS SPORT EXIGE 240R

Lotus Sport, the performance division of Lotus Cars, developed the Lotus Sport Exige 240R in spring 2004 as a limited-edition model, with total global volumes kept strictly to fifty cars. All fifty examples were built to order, and painted in a high-metallic-content paint, in either Sport Yellow or Sport Black, both hues specifically blended to denote the brand colour scheme of Lotus Sport. Performance enhancements were made by increasing engine power without significantly increasing the weight of the engine, and therefore the overall weight of the car.

The standard Exige uses a 189bhp Toyota 2ZZ-GE 1.8-litre VVTL-i unit, governed to a maximum speed of 8,500rpm with a switchover between high-speed cam and low-speed cam occurring between 5,800rpm and 6,200rpm, depending on operating circumstances. The Lotus Sport Exige 240R used the supercharged version of the engine, with charge-cooler, and had a maximum power output of 243bhp at 8,000rpm and a torque figure of 174lb ft at 7,000rpm. The 240R suffix indicated approximate horsepower, conservatively rounded down from the actual figure of 243bhp. The lightweight 2ZZ-GE engine with its compact metal matrix composite alloy cylinder had a very high compression ratio of 11.5:1. The Roots-type Eaton M62 supercharger had a sealed-for-life internal mechanism, meaning that it didn't need to use the engine's oil. It ran from the crankshaft, and had an integral bypass valve for part load operation. Charge air, which is the air under pressure from the supercharger, was cooled through a Lotus Sport air-to-air intercooler; the cooling air entered via the roof scoop before being fed into the engine itself.

The vast amount of extra power and torque available meant that the cam change between low-speed cam and high-speed cam now happened at around 4,000rpm, releasing a smooth and linear surge of power from 4,000rpm all the way to the maximum 8,500rpm. The Sport Exige 240R reached 60mph in less than 4 seconds, and 100mph (160km/h) in less

Lotus Exige S2 2004–7

Layout and Chassis

Lotus-designed lightweight structure of epoxy-bonded and riveted aluminium alloy extrusions with integral steel seatbelt support structure and lightweight steel rear subframe

Engine

Type	Toyota-based 2ZZ-GE, transverse mid-engine
Block material	Metal matrix composite (MMC) and aluminium lightweight compact construction
Head material	Metal matrix composite (MMC) and aluminium lightweight compact construction
Cylinders	4 cylinders in line
Cooling	Water
Bore and stroke	82mm × 85mm
Capacity	1796cc
Valves	16 valves, VVTL-i (variable valve timing and lift with intelligent system), hydraulic tappets, 4 valves per cylinder
Fuelling	Multipoint sequential fuel injection, electronic ignition
Engine management	Lotus T4 engine control unit
Max. power	189bhp (141kW) at 7,800rpm
Max. torque	133lb ft at 6,800rpm
Emission control	Three-way catalytic converter Euro IV emissions compliant with full on-board diagnostics (OBD) CO_2 emissions 208g/km

Transmission

Gearbox	Close ratio 6-speed transaxle driving rear wheels
Clutch	Hydraulic
Ratios	1st 3.116 2nd 2.050 3rd 1.481 4th 1.166 5th 0.916 6th 0.815 Reverse 3.250
Final drive	4.529

Suspension and Steering

Front and rear	Unequal-length double wishbones, Eibach coil springs over Bilstein gas-pressured monotube dampers. Adjustable ride height and adjustable front anti-roll bar
Steering	Rigidly mounted rack and pinion; 2.8 turns lock to lock
Wheels	Unique black lightweight 8-spoke wheels, 16in front, 17in rear
Tyres	Front: Yokohama A048 LTS (W rated) 195/50 R16 Rear: Yokohama A048 LTS (W rated) 225/45 R17

Brakes

Type	Cast iron ventilated and cross-drilled discs front and rear. Servo-assisted track tuned 4-channel ABS with Lotus/AP Racing twin-piston fixed aluminium alloy front brake calipers, Brembo single-piston sliding rear calipers
Size	282mm diameter, 26mm thick

Dimensions

Track	1,457mm (57.4in) front, 1,507mm (59.3in) rear
Wheelbase	2,300mm (90.6in)
Overall length	3,797mm (149.5in)
Overall width	1,727mm (68in) excluding door mirrors
Overall height	1,159mm (45.6in)
Dry weight	875kg (1,929lb)
Kerb weight	916kg (2,019lb) including full tank of fuel

Performance

Max. speed	147mph (237.6km/h)
0–100km/h (62mph)	4.9sec
0–100mph (160km/h)	13.2sec
Fuel consumption	Urban 23.3mpg (12.1ltr/100km) Extra urban 41.5mpg (6.8ltr/100km) Combined 32.1mpg (8.8ltr/100km)

Pictured in the back regions of Ketteringham Hall, the Sport Exige 240R was released in 2005 as a limited-edition model, totalling fifty examples, powered by the supercharged Toyota 2ZZ-GE 1.8 litre VVTL-i 4-cylinder engine, developing 243bhp at 8,000rpm (hence the 240R designation) and 174lb ft torque at 7,000rpm.
JASON PARNELL

than 10 seconds, before topping out at 155mph (249km/h). At top speed, the aerodynamics produced 113kg (249lb) of downforce, ensuring grip, stability and safety. Unladen weight was approximately 930kg (2,050lb), and the power-to-weight ratio was 261bhp per tonne.

Aerodynamics are always part of the Exige package. The flat underside of the extruded and bonded aluminium tub promoted ground effect downforce, aided by the anodized rear diffuser that helped promote the Venturi effect underneath the car, and the front splitter, which sits 98mm (minimum) to 108mm (maximum) from the ground, giving just enough ramp angle clearance whilst maintaining the aerodynamic properties and the aggressive stance. The fixed rear wing was set at the optimum 11.5-degree angle for the best compromise between downforce and drag. The downforce ratio between front (47 per cent) and rear (53 per cent) remained constant at the speeds of which the Exige was capable.

Priced at £43,995 (€62,000) new, the Sport Exige 240R had a unique cabin interior, trimmed in black with Lotus Sport Yellow highlights in leather. A specially numbered Lotus Sport build plate was fitted to the aluminium chassis member on the passenger side. The cockpit also featured sports seats, driver and passenger four-point harnesses, fitted to a transom

The Sport Exige 240R was the product of Lotus Cars' performance division, Lotus Sport. It was introduced at the Geneva Show in February 2005, helmed here on the factory test track by the firm's ride and handling expert Matt Becker.
PAUL HARMER

that was part of the motorsport-specification T45 roll bar. Its new, lightweight five-spoke forged alloy wheels had a slightly wider section than the standard Exige wheels, in order to accommodate the optional track-only specification slick tyres, as well as the Yokohama A048 tyres fitted as standard. These wheels were painted in Satin Black for the Sport Yellow version, and High-Power Silver for the Sport Black edition.

The Sport Exige 240R also incorporated specially developed Lotus Sport parts, including upgraded brakes with sport pads, high-grade silicon brake fluid, metal braided brake hoses and Sport Yellow-painted brake calipers. It also came with stiffer springs and two-way adjustable Öhlins dampers with ride-height adjustment capability, from 130mm to 120mm, plus a mind-boggling twenty-two compression and sixty rebound settings. There was also an adjustable front anti-roll bar, twin oil coolers, and an Accusump – a reservoir that stores oil at pressure, ready to release the oil before the engine is started, or when the oil pressure drops whilst in use, for example during ultra-high-speed cornering.

The Lotus T4 engine management system was developed for the Elise 111R and the Exige, and was also employed in the Lotus Sport Exige 240R. This T4 system was reprogrammed to optimize the supercharged engine, with two additional functions to control a fifth injector – located downstream of the intercooler – to add additional fuel flow under hard acceleration or high-speed driving, and to control the bypass valve. The C64 six-speed gearbox with lightweight aluminium casing was fitted with the closest possible ratios and gearset afforded by the transmission, enabling a fast, precise and light-to-the-touch gearchange.

Prior to sign-off, the Sport Exige 240R was tested extensively at Lotus's Hethel test track, as well as on test facilities around Europe. With a 0–60mph time of 3.9 seconds and a 0–100mph time of 9.9 seconds, it was one of the fastest accelerating production cars in the world. Of course, as we know, straight-line speed is not what a Lotus is about, though it was capable of reaching a top speed of 155mph (249km/h), largely thanks to a 22 per cent increase in power and a 23 per cent increase in torque with just a 1.5 per cent increase in weight, giving it a power to weight ratio of 261bhp per tonne. In short, this was a true Lotus in the Chapman tradition: performance through light weight.

THE ELISE 111R

Launched in February 2004, the Elise 111R, was at that point the most powerful and highest-performing production version of the model, thanks to the incorporation of its new powertrain, Toyota's 2ZZ-GE 1.8-litre, 4-cylinder, 16-valve engine and C64 six-speed gearbox. The all-aluminium lightweight Toyota C64 six-speed gearbox was fitted with an all-new Lotus designed and developed shift mechanism. Lotus engineers and development technicians subjected the 2ZZ-GE to a rigorous testing programme, covering a wide range of extreme climate conditions from the Arctic Circle to the Arizona and Nevada deserts, and at altitude in Colorado. The bifurcated exhaust downpipe and bespoke gearshift mechanism had been designed and developed in house, together with a brand new, custom-engineered Lotus T4 engine management system (EMS), with software specifically for the 111R.

With the VVTL-i (variable valve timing and lift-intelligent) motor producing 189bhp and 133.5lb ft torque, the Elise 111R reached 100km/h in 5.2 seconds (60mph in 4.9 seconds) and 160km/h (100mph) in 13.0 seconds, topping out at 241km/h (150mph). Its fully Euro IV emissions-compliant spec enabled it to return 32.1mpg (8.8ltr/100km) on the combined cycle, and 208g/km of CO_2 emissions. The Elise 111R weighed in at 860kg (1,892lb) – unladen with no options – giving a power to weight ratio of 223PS/tonne (220hp/tonne or 164kW/tonne).

For the first time, servo-assisted ABS was standard equipment, along with Eibach coaxial coil springs and Bilstein high-pressure monotube gas dampers. Tyres fitted were bespoke Bridgestone Potenza RE040 – 175/55 R16 front and 225/45 R17 rear, carried over from the Elise and the Elise 111S.

Standard equipment included half-leather cockpit upholstery, sun visors, central door locking, Blaupunkt Lausanne radio CD-R/W player and Blaupunkt high performance front and rear speakers. Optional equipment centred on a touring pack, which provided auxiliary front driving lights, a choice of either full leather or Alcantara trim, a soft-top with sound and thermal insulation, electric windows, an upgraded Blaupunkt Woodstock DAB radio, CD-R/W and MP3 player, interior stowage net, sound insulation, and full carpet with a lightweight aluminium passenger footrest, metallic paint, air-conditioning and body-coloured hard-top.

Introduced in spring 2004, the Elise 111R was equipped with the 1796cc Toyota VVTL-i 16-valve 4-cylinder driveline, effectively swapped for the original Rover K-series engine – though the Elise 120 and 160 models retained the old powertrain until 2005. Some 8,000 examples of the 111R were built up to 2008, and here's one at a track day at Abbeville Circuit, northern France.

GAVAN KERSHAW INTERVIEW

Executive director of sports car engineering at Group Lotus, Gavan Kershaw is also synonymous with racing and the marque's contemporary motorsport strategies. Gavan joined Lotus in August 1988 as an appentice, on the same day as Matthew Becker.

GK: I was always into racing – go-karts, oval racing, and by pure luck I was racing a Super Stock car, one of the 'contact' ones with a live axle, and someone said I should speak to John Miles because I was interested in getting better traction on shale. I had the stock car in the factory car park, and John asked, 'What do you want to know?' I said I was thinking about putting a Watts linkage on it and he said, 'You must be the only eighteen-year-old who knows what a Watts linkage is!' And from that day on, John and I got on really well and he mentored me all the way through. Then, under Dany [Bahar] I moved over as technical director of Motor Sport, and we went to Le Mans and Indianapolis and all the big circuits.

JT: But nowadays you're more involved with defining the actual road cars, aren't you?

GK: Yes, more recently Jean-Marc [Gales] put me as engineering director and I looked after all the product that's going down the line now. But I wanted to become more of a product man again, so I'm currently director of attributes and product interior, which is about the way they drive and the way they feel, and that's all signed off by me. All the cars of the future, the ten-year plan, and that means defining the size of them and what technology they have on board. I'm part of that working committee, which consists of five people including Russell Carr, saying what the cars need to be like in the future: how do we keep the Lotus-ness in, what bits do we have to improve on, what bits do we have to trade a little bit, so it's a really interesting place to work at the moment.

Gavan Kershaw is currently executive director of sports car engineering at Group Lotus, though his reputation is also synonymous with racing and the marque's contemporary motor sport strategies.
LOTUS CARS

JT: And in the course of which you're driving and fine-tuning the cars.

GK: Yes, absolutely. I get to drive the Evija, I get to drive every car, and I've probably driven 50 per cent of Clive's Formula 1 cars. I race a [Type] 30 at the various revivals and Silverstone Classic, and one of my proudest memories is winning the trophy at the Birkett Six Hours at Silverstone. I did the whole stint on my own because it was raining heavily, and I got out of the car and Bob Dance put his arm round me and said, 'The old man would be proud of you!' And that's one of my best moments, because I thought, 'If Bob can tell me this, I must be doing all right.'

JT: You've also driven 2-Elevens in British GT and so on, haven't you?

GK: Yep, I've raced Lotuses in British GT, won all the championships in British GT with 3-Elevens, 2-Elevens, the Nürburgring lap records. It was always Matt [Becker] and me, working together all the way through, developing all the variants in Elises, Exiges, the 340R. Even when we first went to the Toyota engine with the Speedster, Matt and I did the Speedster programme, and the Elise went side by side. We spent months tyre testing and things like that.

JT: With John Miles behind you to start with you couldn't have had a better guru, really.

GK: With people like John and Bob Dance you just have to listen and say very little yourself! They understood the physics of handling, and tyres and springs, and that hasn't changed. It doesn't matter that we were doing cars twenty or so years ago with John, the philosophy that he had towards ride and handling, and the methodical steps in tuning work just the same today, and he's trained some of the best in the world. Lotus has filtered out across all the industries. We were in awe of people like Roger [Becker] and John. Roger was a different personality to John: he was quite flamboyant, while John just had a complete understanding of the matrix that makes the car work. He taught us all: Tony Shute, Alistair McQueen, Dave Minter – everyone learned something from John Miles. We've just been his disciples, he was the nucleus that understood it, and if he was prepared to let you have the little bits of his knowledge it was because he realized how hard he'd had to work himself to understand it to that depth. I think all of our products became as good as they were because of his dedication. He used to say that the M100 [Elan] cost him a wife and the Elise cost him a heart attack. Basically he was working tirelessly and methodically through the night, which meant that, when you got the result, you knew he'd gone to all four corners and found the boundary, and what you ended up with was the best solution. I think that's stood us all in good stead, really.

JT: Of course, he came into it with a motor racing background, which is what you came into it with, so obviously you'll bring that into the Lotus road cars as well.

GK: Understanding the dynamics is crucial, because ultimately, even with the electronics in the cars and what your engineer tells you, the more you understand the more you can fix the problem. Sometimes it's not about car control or bravery, it could be all sorts of things, I think that was where John's turmoil was. John was such a smooth driver, but he always said his team mates didn't have his level of understanding; they were better drivers, they were braver, they were more relaxed, they were easy-going, but he always found that a bit difficult. He was always the one scratching his head, staring at the suspension system, while they were running, jogging, meeting the ladies or whatever.

JT: But he stayed alive, not only because he had a strong sense of self-preservation, but also because he wouldn't drive a 72 without a rear wing.

GK: Yes, and that's also the thing as well. John always instilled into us that the handling has to be forgiving. Alistair McQueen is a smooth driver, and although his level of the suspension understanding isn't the same as John's, they came to the same conclusion by totally different assessments. They were the guys who drummed into us that the handling has to be calm, it has to be confidence-inspiring. It's not all just about grip and aggression – the car has to have finesse; and when you look back, the Elite, the Elan, the Seven were all that – they were fun, they were confidence-inspiring. The motor racing cars were something different – they were designed to win – but these road cars were always compliant, composed, fun, not intimidating, and we're trying to instil that in the cars today.

JT: Yes, there are some fundamental as well as some subtle differences between a competition car and a road car.

Lotus's ride and handling expert Alistair McQueen demonstrates how to slide a Series 1 Elise on the test track. He and Dave Minter were instrumental in setting up the Lotus Driving Academy in 1998.
TOM WOOD

GK: A competition car has one job to do. You have to find ultimate grip, and that's all you're challenging for. When you drive a circuit, you just have to keep digging deeper – why can't I go quicker through there, why do I have to brake for that corner, why am I only able to put the throttle half-way down? Those are all the questions you're asking yourself. Even now, when we work with the data-logging engineers, they are asking me why I'm not going flat out through a particular corner, but something in my veins is telling me I daren't go through that corner flat, so we check to see what the data's telling us: why is the car on the limit, what's the 'G' circle look like, can we get more downforce, what do I lose down the straight? And that's why the working relationship between the engineer and the driver is the strongest of all.

Elise rear suspension consists of cast iron vented disc and Brembo caliper, hub and wheel bearing, Eibach coil-over Bilstein damper, and double wishbones.
WILLIAM TAYLOR

JT: And talking of grip, presumably you're working with the tyre guys as well.

GK: Every single system will work with the tyre engineers: springs and dampers, steering and gearing, obviously. Typically, the way that any car, including the Elise, is developed is that someone like Tony Shute will come up with the concept of a basic architecture – how long the wheelbase is, how wide the track is (and that's often driven by the market), driver and passenger spacing in the cockpit, the width of the car, how much power it's going to have, what powertrain you're going to employ, whether it's going to be positioned in the front, the middle or rear – and then you start to work out whether this car is going to be highly track-focused or whether it's going to be ride-focused, so are we going to have double wishbones or are we going to have MacPherson struts, are we going to have a live axle on the back? Based on the answers to those questions, from what we've learnt as vehicle dynamics engineers, we go through iterations of tyre behaviour. The tyre has certain control characteristics, which we can use to influence how the car is set up – aspects like toe-in, toe-out, tracking and camber.

JT: Presumably that accounts in part for the difference between an Elise and a VX220 Speedster – why when you drive them, they feel like completely different cars, even though fundamentally they're probably around 80 per cent carry-over?

GK: Yes, although officially there was only 8 per cent carry-over, because while the chassis looks identical apart from a couple of extra bolts in it, it has a different part number. The Elise has spawned so many innovations – to start with, the race Exige. People couldn't believe they had a car that was that aggressive, that focused in aero, because it was so closely related to something they were driving around in the sunshine in, with only a few minor changes. We even went central-seat with that car.

Then came the Speedster, the Tesla, and the remarkable thing was how little we had to change the chassis to put a V6 in the back of it, and because of that, people believed that they are all completely different architecture, whereas, fundamentally, the dimensions within the cockpit are very similar. We add stiffness where we want stiffness, and a lot of it the track width is influenced by the geometry of the suspension, so the cars have so many different characteristics. It's also expanded the aftermarket world as well, because car tuning became less and less of a thing in the UK compared with what it was forty or fifty years ago, as people weren't spending the money with the availability of all the off-the-peg Japanese stuff. I think the Elise gave garages and specialists the opportunity to develop parts for race cars, which is really how it's been for twenty-odd years.

JT: Talk us through the evolutionary staircase, then.

GK: Right, well, first there was the launch model, then there was the 135, then the Sport 190, which was the first development car, running the K-series with the twin-cam heads, different cams, different dampers, lower ride height, which spawned the development tool for the Exige. Then we went to Sport 160, then we had the S2, with the 111R and the 111S with the extra wing on it, as well as the run-out model S1s. The highlight of the S1 was the 111S. Then we progressed to the 111R, which was the S2 with the K-series engine, and that transitioned to the Toyota-powered car. In the middle of that was the 340R, and then the 111R with the Toyota engine became the 240 and Exige. The S1s were on an off-the-shelf Michelin tyre; then we put the S2 on bespoke Bridgestone tyres, and we changed the rear suspension characteristics and altered the aero, and we started to introduce some ABS functionality.

Then we went from the Rover engine to the Toyota engine; Series 1 and early Series 2 were K-series engines. With the transition to the 111R, we went to the Toyota 1.6 and 1.8. Some of the variants had the supercharger – the Exige 2.0 and the 240R – and once we'd found the supercharger it opened up a lot more opportunities for the Elise as well as the Exige. Obviously the first Exiges were 4-cylinders as well, so the Elise and Exige were much more closely related; it was a body set, really. And then, when we introduced the V6, that's where it found its own fork in the road. There's not a 4-cylinder Exige anymore – it's all V6, with a longer wheelbase and wider track. Up until the last of the 4-cylinder Exiges, the Elise and Exige were fundamentally the same state of tune and componentry. And then, all of a sudden, the V6 Exige became a completely new monster. Also, the 2-Eleven was effectively walking back towards some of the S1 criteria, and even with the 3-Eleven, which we've only just stopped building, we went back to a high-sided Series 1 Elise chassis to get some of the mass out of it and some of the stiffness back in.

ABOVE LEFT: **The General Motors VX220 – seen here at Edinburgh sports car specialist Kenny Dunn's – was built at Hethel on the Elise chassis, which looks identical, but has a different part number.**

A wonderful line-up of Elise S1s at Snetterton during Lotus's sixtieth anniversary celebrations in 2011.

THE SWITCH FROM ELISE SERIES 1 TO SERIES 2

Some of the fundamentals of the Series 1 were a compromise for various reasons, so when the Series 2 came out we said, well we've done the S2 like this, for a number of reasons: different body, different cockpit, different suspension set-up because we now had bespoke tyres instead of off-the-shelf tyres, as well as better buying power within our supply chain. For example, we could go to a headlight manufacturer, and instead of four headlights on the Elise S1 have a proper bespoke one, because by the late 1990s the rest of the industry effectively said, 'We will do business with you, we can see what this car is all about.' Apart from complying with some foreign legislation, the S2 chassis was actually changed a lot less than the other parts; as a true Lotus, there was always a real focus on the chassis and our own unique suspension systems, working with Koni on bespoke dampers with no compromises.

Some of the issues with the S1 were that it was a little bit edgy to drive, and we wanted to improve the brakes, because although the MMC (metal matrix composite) brakes were great, as soon as we started to increase the power they started to struggle with the thermal capacity, even the wet braking; if you'd been travelling on a wet road and you touched the brakes, they didn't have enough bite. Customers were struggling because they had to put too much effort in, which prompted our decision to go to a booster system.

Where the Elise also gained was in all the peripheral parts – locks, latches, headlights, things that the customer feels and sees; he doesn't feel a wishbone every time he drives it, he just gets the result from it, but when he unlocks his car and uses his headlights, he directly sees what he is getting. The volume forecasts predicted that more people were going to own the S2 than the S1, maybe people who were getting back into sports cars having owned one several years ago, who would weigh up the soft-top seal, looking for wind noise, ingress and egress. Just climbing over the chassis sills felt an event for some people, and what was part of the experience for some became an annoyance to others. Race car-like brake feel with modulation through just squeezing your toes to acquiring an ABS system – little changes like that happen where you open it up to the masses. But opening it up to the masses is what caused it to become an icon.

JT: In terms of production, the Elise clamshells haven't been made on site since the S1 days, have they?

GK: No. Factory volume peaked, and we couldn't produce that many parts. The traditional technologies we used for cars like the Esprit, which were hand-laid, involved lots of guys, big moulds, stinky machinery and stinky glues. That was the VARI process. Then we went over to SMC, so we got much better panel quality – lighter and very accurate in dimensions – but the process involves high pressure and big moulds, very like diecasting for fibreglass, and we weren't going to invest in that. Also, if we were planning on building 5,000 cars a year we couldn't expect that to be done, hand-laid, in the factory. In fact, some carbon fibre components are, because they are single components, such as the front access cover, and we know we're only going to need 300 of those for the race cars. We'll build them in house, or we'll take them to a small business, through to where we'll order 2,000 or 3,000 of something.

JT: Where are the chassis built now?

GK: They're all done at Wellingborough, where Lotus Lightweight Structures is based. The extrusions go there, where they're cut, machined, bonded, glued, then anodized, and when it's a complete chassis that you would recognize as an Elise, it's transported here, and that's where we start the assembly process. None of our chassis are right- or left-hand drive when they arrive; it's not until they get a VIN number that they become a car, and then it's designated right-hand drive or left-hand drive, market-specific, and that's where it goes down the line.

JT: The build sheet starts with the chassis?

GK: The build sheet starts when it arrives at Hethel. Really, up until that point, it's an anonymous vehicle: it could be a race car, a right-hand drive, left-hand drive, 1.8, 1.6, red, yellow, green, whatever. But at the point when it gets its stamp, it gets its build book, it's got a customer, it's got its full specification and we know what engine, gearbox and dampers, wheels, tyres – everything that's going into that one car.

GAVAN KERSHAW INTERVIEW *continued*

JT: And if it's going to be an Exige?

GK: The Exige chassis is dimensionally the same, and inside, where you sit, is very similar, but the rear subframe is different, and that bolts on differently. We have pusher blocks for some of the crash intrusion and mounting systems, so an Elise is an Elise chassis and an Exige is an Exige chassis, likewise a 3-Eleven is its own, and Evora is its own. The 410 and the Evora chassis is always the same. There's a US chassis that has some slight changes to it for crash regulations. But it's quite a simple system, and it's very adaptable for us, and that's what's kept the Elise alive so long – it could morph into other versions as the market changed. For instance, the customers wanted easier ingress so we had to cut the sill down; we could just add a stiffening prism inside and we maintained that stiffness, but all of a sudden it felt like a new car, because the sills were much lower. We could add a V6 by changing the mounting point system, so it had stretch and growth potential, and really the Evora was always the more practical bigger Elise.

Launched at the 2015 Goodwood Festival of Speed, the Elise 3-Eleven can be specified in road or race format, as demonstrated here at Brünnchen on the Nürburgring Nordschleife.
WILLIAM TAYLOR

THE ELISE'S COMPETITION

In 2020, *Fifth Gear* ran a back-to-back on the Hethel test track between the Elise and the latest Renault Alpine. It was a little bit like when people said the Renault Spyder was going to kill the Elise, and then the Caterham 21 was going to kill the Elise, and the Boxster and the Audi TT, which were almost 500kg (1,100lb) heavier and less wieldy – and actually the Elise is still the best car to drive. The Alpine is good in a fun way, in an 'I'm not an experienced driver' type way. It's sort of Cayman-esque; you can saturate its performance very quickly, and if you're an able Elise driver you'll recognize all its strengths, but you'll go away saying 'I wish I'd had the Elise here.' And that's what gave us the confidence to go and take it on head to head.

JT: With Jason Plato helming both cars, the Elise beat the Alpine by 0.2 seconds. Another obvious adversary is the Alfa Romeo 4C, equally as competitive as the Alpine in terms of performance handing and ergonomics. It's a close-run thing, then, and maybe aesthetic appeal plays a part in final choice.

An Elise 111R on the Grand Corniche above Monte Carlo in 2004: it delivers comfort, fun, efficiency, and is also remarkably economical even when driven hard.
WILLIAM TAYLOR

BELOW RIGHT: **Cabin of the Exige Cup 360, sparsely appointed but totally functional, with seat squabs, door panels and gearshift gaiter detailed in red. Austere it may be, but it does have electric windows.**
WILLIAM TAYLOR

JT: Where are we at in volumes, then?

GK: Around 2,000 cars a year, combined across the range, but there's a much higher desire for growth over the coming years.

JT: Meanwhile, we're still talking Toyota engines? The 2ZZ-GE?

GK: Yes, we're still talking HiAce engines for the next phase, and the next car coming will have a HiAce engine as well.

JT: What's the public perception of the current Elise?

GK: We held a driver event, with competitive cars from other brands ranged against an Elise, an Exige and an Evora, and drivers of all shapes, sizes and genders, and people thought that the car that was very clearly uncompromised and enjoyable was the Elise. They could really see themselves jumping in that on a sunny day because it delivers everything you want – comfort, fun and efficiency. People were amazed by the mpg because they are used to 18–22mpg (13–16ltr/100km) in some of these fast cars, whereas the Elise fuel gauge never moved and we were driving it hard all day. And it was more spacious than they thought, even though there's no adjustment in the cockpit: the steering wheel doesn't go in and out or up and down, and the seats don't rake back, but everyone got in it and felt quite comfortable. That was a big step forward for us, and a big confidence boost that Lotus was producing the right sports car; understanding what it's delivering means that product will have longevity.

JT: How did you arrive at those ergonomics that are apparently perfect for everybody?

GK: When we were doing the Elise, we used a traditional method of establishing the cockpit layout: we have a pattern shop, we mount seats in full-size models blocked up using polystyrene and wood, with steering wheels, gearshifts and pedals, and everything adjustable, and there's a panel of driving experts that go through all the permutations because we're all different shapes and sizes. Then, independently, you put the steering wheel where you like it, you put the gearshift height where you want it, the pedal offset to suit you – things which aren't necessarily governed by some other factor. And then we go through all the different iteration loops. Our mindset has always been that the controls have to be intuitive and there shouldn't be any distraction – you shouldn't have to move your head to see that you've put your hand on the gearshift, your hand should automatically fall to it, so you feel it with your little finger and then you shift the gear. Same with the pedals, what you call the step-over, that is the height between the brake pedal and the throttle pedal. We now know what that dimension feels like, and Lotus has been getting it right for many years. Our mentors would explain that you hold the gearshift and you have the steering wheel at quarter-past-nine, and that's where you should roughly be. If you look at an Elise, that's where it is. When you go away from that dimension it just feels unnatural – if your hand drops too much or if it's too level it feels weird, so that you put stress into your shoulder.

JT: That seems pretty straightforward methodology.

GK: The only time we can't get that absolutely to perfection is where another factor has an influence. The Elise chassis is very tapered and the pedals are slightly offset at the centre. That's because the wheelbase is short, and we wanted the front wheel enveloped to allow us to have back-lock angle, which means our clutch pedal would be typically where the inside face of the tyre would be. So, at that point we go into trade-offs: do we want a car that's this narrow, with this back-lock angle and this wheelbase, or do we want the pedals not to be slightly offset? And if that's the styling then we'll work around it. In the Elise the seats are on a slight angle – the driver's is not quite square with the steering wheel – but you hardly notice. It's those compromises and those trades that make it all feel natural, and when you get in, it feels like putting on an old coat: you feel at home in it.

JT: Was this the Series 1 Elise, and did it apply to the Series 2? Is that how it's always been done?

GK: The floor, the footwell position, your seat and where the steering column sits within it hasn't changed from the earliest cars. What has changed is some of the throttle pedals and braking systems where we've had to use ABS and the vacuum boosters, electronic throttle pedals, gearshift selection systems... actually they've always got better – the gearshift in a modern Elise is absolutely rifle-like in action. There's no slop in it, and that's what contributes so much to the driving pleasure; there aren't many cars where you can actually shift gear, so we want that attribute to be perfect.

JT: And brake feel too?

GK: The brake feel on all of our cars – the Elise, the Exige, the Evora – is still the benchmark; and that's not total braking and stopping distance, it's to do with the amount of pressure you need to apply when you come up to a T-junction at 40 or 50mph, when you want to do 'chauffeur stops', where you don't want your bottle of drink to roll off your seat or your passenger to be made to lean forward.

JT: And I suppose you deliberately go for the minimalist approach?

GK: Quite. We don't have multiple switches on our steering wheel; our steering wheel is quite pure. But also, we mustn't be backward, and one of the things that's coming in is these massive tablets in cars. If that was to be a Lotus feature in the future, we'd have to think, how do we give that Lotus-ness? Perhaps we don't want an iPad-sized one, we only want an iPhone-sized one. We've been conventional with what the gauges display and we've been analogue for quite a long time, but now with what the TFT (thin film transistor) screens can do for you, the level of information you can bring to the driver and the clarity at night time (when you can dim it), things have moved on. You have to embrace this technology, but we do it slowly. For instance, the Elise is still a completely non-hydraulic manual-steering car, so it's the least corrupted in that respect. But people who are not used to that level of control, because they've driven an electric power steering or column-assisted car, where they are completely disconnected from the road, so they can feel a bit nervous when they go down a B road and the steering is just shimmying in their fingers, telling them the road is uneven. But we have to embrace change and adapt as the customers' expectations increase and tech like this evolves.

JT: So, you haven't just written down a list of kind of potential attributes, and said, 'We've got to go for that,' or gone out on the test track with a car and thought, 'We can do a bit more with that'?

GK: It's a bit of both; now, it's becoming very objective. It's still a subjective sign-off, just like we've always done historically, where our project experts in the frame sign off. So, our vision, say, for ergonomics, is that we want the hip-to-heel to be within a certain dimension because we know that if you sit flat in a car, if your heel is x amount lower than your hip point, that will feel like a sports car, and we want the upward vision angle to be y because any lower

Driver's-eye view: the steering wheel with its sculpted bound rim, gauges and controls of the Elise Sprint 220.
WILLIAM TAYLOR

than that and it will feel like a letterbox and any more than that, it feels too open and you don't feel engaged with the road. We want to have the downward vision because we want to be able to see z amount of the fender because that brings the road surface and the bodywork into the cockpit, so that you can place the car accurately on the road.

With the pedal position, spacing, height, we've got our manual of what makes a good car, and then that continues into the dynamics: we want the car to be able to decelerate at 11 metres per second, we want the lateral g to be at a peak of 1.1–1.2, but we want the roll rate to lateral g to give us x roll per g.

So, we have all these criteria, which we then give to the engineers, people like Richard Rackham, who understand all the vision angles and the optimum spacing. He's never going to deliver us a car where it's like we're sitting in a Transit, or we're lounging on a bed, and that's how we start to morph all that. The first thing we do is build interior butts, so Russell's team will be doing the exterior; they go through their volume models, they go through their clays, and then produce a full-sized clay. All of those iterations are fed back through to the headlamps, so we can check: are the headlamps at the right height, are the door mirrors at the right size, have we got enough travel within the wheels that the wheels are not going to clash with the bodywork? He's not just looking at the function, he's looking at the function and the form.

JT: And similar strictures and permutations go for the cockpit?

GK: Yes, looking at ergonomics within the interior, we're making sure the fiftieth percentile and the ninety-fifth percentile can reach the pedals and can get in and out of the car easily enough. The interior mirror is in the right place, the gearshift and switchgear falls easily to hand. Are the occupants confronted with glare, and are the seat cushions comfortable? If you're going to have an adjustable seat, how much does it need to be adjustable? And then we look at targets for stowage – how big does the glovebox need to be, do you want a net there, do you want to be able to put a bottle here? All of these boxes have to be ticked, and once that's been put into a 3D model we look at it virtually now, where previously it was all done in the pattern shop, making wooden models and fibreglass and foam.

JT: When did that shift come about?

GK: With 3D printing and virtual reality you can now put a VR headset on, sit in a chair and reach out and physically establish how close or far away objects are. That whole technology is a really useful tool now, because you can evaluate and assess which designs are going to cause you problems with quality. So, if the interior designer has put a stitch line on the door card, say, where it joins another stitch line, you can see that in VR, and you can query what happens if that stitch line across the door card to the dash dips and the other one goes straight, you can picture how it looks and feels in real life. It's strange how quickly your body adapts to going from vehicle simulators through to this VR; all of a sudden, you're in the car, and the more we do that with touch points the more accurately we can define the optimum interior. There's a firmness to the seat, your brain is telling you you're holding the actual steering wheel that you're seeing, and when you move it you get the sensation of its weight, so it's a really important part of design construction now.

JT: And presumably you can use the vehicle simulator to configure the suspension geometry as well?

GK: We go from the simulator to the suspension model so that the CAD guys can run simulation tests, manoeuvres and handling tests, which they do on their PCs. They get a set of results, and they tune the suspension system and make sure the car is stable, and then we'll move that onto a driven simulator. Then we'll build a development mule out of an old chassis, make a new subframe, fit uprights and wishbones, and drive that, working with the tyre engineers and the brakes engineers and constantly feeding back into the simulation. Then we have wind tunnel models, where Richard is going to be in the tunnel, and there's now guys doing CFD (computational fluid dynamics).

JT: Have you got a wind tunnel here?

GK: No, we hire that in. All CFD is done here, but it's a little different from when early Elises were wind tunnel tested. Richard would take the car to the wind tunnel, and if it had lift then he'd add the tail plate to the rear. Now, obviously, we don't find surprises like that because Russell's work is constantly being digitized and he's got a band of CFD engineers advising him when it's generating lift or generating too much front or rear downforce, recommending he tweaks this or that surface, so when we go to the tunnel now it's for confirmation rather than looking for answers. Because it's full size, you can monitor thermals and cooling, so you can see how the air acts through the radiator systems. It's a balance now between CFD and real world. When I drive it on the track, I might suggest that it could do with some more front toe or some rear camber, and the CFD guys might say, 'Oh, that's strange, because we're meeting the target in the tunnel,' and that's as may be, but the wind tunnel doesn't take into consideration that we've got a really good rear tyre, and that's causing some understeer. It's that sort of sophisticated evaluation that makes our cars the best-handling in the business.

JT: So, at what point in the last ten or the last five years did this evolution take place?

GK: Probably ten years ago. I think now, what is happening with the introduction of electric vehicles, is we're cautious with our

While the shape of early Elise models was fine-tuned in the wind tunnel, current cars are designed according to CFD – computerized fluid dynamics – which informs the stylists which elements of the design need adjusting to address downforce and drag, exemplified by the Exige Sport 360 from 2016.
WILLIAM TAYLOR

The bipartite diffuser under the back of the car benefits the aerodynamics by making the air flow away from the rear of the car faster, thereby increasing grip and reducing drag.
WILLIAM TAYLOR

engineers and suppliers. You can't solve everything with electronics. At some point, you have to go back to basics, so when I'm driving the Evija we turn the ESP [electronic stability program] off, all the traction aids, because otherwise, if someone's trying to steer the car by putting 20 per cent more power to the left-hand side than the right-hand side, it's difficult to read what the tyre is doing and what the suspension is doing. So, we still strip it back like an onion, drive the pure physics, drive a tyre that we know is OK and has got wet grip, and then the engineers with the software can now basically change the complete character of the car.

If you imagine when we introduced active ride in the early 1990s, our active suspension and four-wheel steer, you could get the rear wheels to toe out and toe in independently and the car to roll into the corner. That's now in production cars around the world. If you've got a car that perhaps feels understeery, un-agile, if it's got rear steering in it, the software can dictate that above 30mph [50km/h], it's going to make the rear wheels toe out when you turn the steering wheel, so you can physically make it uncontrollable by not changing a single suspension high point, just the algorithm in the rear steer, which means you can get it a long way out as well. So, your sign-off scenarios now have to include thousands of miles of testing on all kinds of road surfaces, algorithm testing and software protection. We drive in systems now where it's steer by wire, so the steering wheel's not even connected to the steering rack. Not on our cars, but in general. The Evora was probably the last of the cars that got developed without all of the software, all of the active suspension, rear steers and things like this. The cars that are coming towards us now have four electric motors, so you can physically have as much torque going independently to each wheel.

JT: Does that mean that all that electronic technology is applied in the Elise now?

GK: No, the Elise is still really, really pure. It has passive dampers, so the dampers don't adjust for speed; they're fixed valves, and there's no wires. The springs are not air, or anything like that, but just standard coil-overs. The steering rack is still manual steer, so it doesn't have an electric hydraulic system. The suspension kinematics are pure, so the suspension link angles are what drives the movement of the kinematics in the wheels, and the bushes control the compliance. Where we've embraced the electronics is in the stability control systems. We're working at the highest level now, so the new Elises have what we call 'Tour mode': when you start the car, it's in Tour mode, and that mode is designed to give you maximum stability and control in the wet and in challenging conditions. That could be your normal commute, or perhaps a wet, icy night. When you drive it in tour mode, if you're going round a roundabout, say, and you put the throttle down too hard and you steer too much it will recognize that the car is understeering, and it will go, 'Come on, you fool, don't put that amount of throttle on, you don't have to steer that much,' and it will actually maintain that radius, irrespective of how much you're stabbing at the throttle or you keep sawing at the steering wheel.

And then we have 'Sport mode', and what happens is that the car anticipates that the driver wants to have a little bit more input. Sometimes you can use understeer to set the car up if you're driving briskly, so we reduce that, and we allow the car to 'yaw' a little bit more before the ABS or the ESP (electronic stability program) kicks in. Then we have 'Race mode', which is actually not looking at the amount of slip between the axles, it's trying to generate as much forward momentum and lateral grip as possible, so it's constantly breaking the system. We're one of the few manufacturers that still allow our cars – the Elise, the Exige and the Evora – to be turned off completely. We keep full ABS, but the ESP system can be completely turned off, and it's then down to the driver. That's when we never want the brakes to be interfered with.

JT: How about if it's in Sport or Race mode when the driver encounters more demanding conditions?

It doesn't get much closer: Gavin Kirby leads Mark Fullalove through Snetterton's Russell complex in their Elise 2-Elevens; they came sixth and seventh in the Lotus Elise Trophy race in September 2009.

GK: The ABS is amazing, but with vehicle dynamics on challenging surfaces you want the car to behave in a slightly different way. If you're on snow or wet grass, if you have an ESP system that won't turn off, it won't pull away, so actually you want it to be able to turn it fully off, because you do want to dig your way out. So, we're constantly looking at that. In tour mode, we want a throttle that's quite progressive, very linear, for when you're driving around city centres or on motorways. But in sport and race modes we want a little less displacement for the throttle. And here, because the throttle is not connected to the engine by cable, we've effectively got the ability to put in as many quadrants as we want, so we could actually have 100 per cent of the throttle to only ever give you 5 per cent of the engine, or vice versa – 5 per cent of the throttle to give you 100 per cent of the throttle at the engine. When tuning that map, we can do it speed-related or lateral gear-accelerated so we can change the character however we want, and that's what's now coming to the Elise: the ability to make it fun and agile, and deliver a power increase too. Just a few horsepower – 10 or 20bhp – changes the Elise's character quite drastically.

JT: This is all being figured out by you and a team of engineers? And how many mules have you got at your disposal?

GK: If it's a model year change, where perhaps we're increasing the power and changing the damper settings, we're running about fifteen cars. Actually, the team that has the most test cars is the engine calibration group, because they're having to pass all the emissions tests. There's not a standard emissions test; there's an American one if we're selling into America, a Chinese one and a UK/European one, so we have to make sure all our cars are compliant, and that's done at different temperatures as well. So, you do it at –6°, +26° and a cold start test, and that's why they've got multiple vehicles – because they'll be working around a particular set of tests. They have to over-check, so that, if they make a slight change in their calibrations, it doesn't affect the result in perhaps the high ambient test.

Emission regs are really stringent now and there's now what they call WLTP – Worldwide Harmonized Light Vehicle Test Procedure – which is a lab test that measures fuel consumption and CO_2 and pollutant emissions. It used to be a set trace, which is how the whole emissions scandal came about: you could teach a car to do an emissions cycle so that it only had to get to a particular rpm in a certain gear and then it would come to rest. That's why stop/start was put in, because if you turned the car off during the rest in the emission cycle, you were getting emissions for free during that phase. So around 8 per cent of the emissions test was turned

continued on p. 60

LOTUS CARS AND TYRE MANUFACTURERS

Lotus Cars' erstwhile ride and handling expert Matt Becker burns rubber on the Hethel loop.
WILLIAM TAYLOR

Historically, we've always had a range of bespoke tyres on our cars. Fundamentally, the Elise was on Yokohama and Bridgestone, but you can really stretch the boundaries of performance when you have bespoke constructions, with sizes and compounds that meet your car's exact requirements. It also depends on how many you want. It's often done because of brand association; for example, if Bridgestone becomes our partner because they're launching a particular tread pattern, it makes good marketing sense to have their tyres on the Lotus and work with our engineers, but they only sell a few hundred car sets a year, whereas if they go on a Transit they sell 200,000 sets a year. So, there's a little bit of trade-off there. We always work with the best manufacturers in the world, so that's Bridgestone, Michelin and Yokohama, because the tyre technology is there, and obviously we make sure that we're on the correct sizes for our car so you're not asking the tyres to do something they're not capable of delivering. We went through a phase with the Elise of putting a 175 on the front, which was a challenge because nobody made that size of tyre apart from Bridgestone, and that can cause problems if the tyre factory stops making that size and model of tyre. In some countries, like Germany, the tyre is legislated to the car, so cars can be taken off the road because you can't get the correct tyres for them.

Over the last few years we've worked closely with Michelin; they've been renowned as one of the best tyre manufacturers in the world for years now, and they have a nice range of tyres. They had an all-weather tyre, the PS4, which we ran on the Evoras and worked well in the wet. With the Elise, we've always worked closely with Yokohama. Yokohama were able to get a tyre to work harmoniously on a light car, and if you look at the race series, they're all on Yokohama control tyres. They gave us the B105, which is our all-season tyre; and they do an A052, which is effectively our performance tyre, and an A048, which is on the extreme cars.

The same goes for shock absorbers and brake pads: the manufacturers want to be associated with Lotus too. Our damper suppliers over the years have been Bilstein, Öhlins, Koni; Bilstein embraced Lotus in the 2000s, when we produced the Speedster and the S2 Elise, then the Evora and the Exige. We re-valve all our dampers here, and they've given us the equipment to do that, plus all the shims, so that we sign off our own dampers and they manufacture them. These partnerships are really good. We have AP Racing for the brake systems, right from the early Elise. AP Racing are a racing brand made to go on road cars, and they are now supplying many road car brakes, which is probably from being associated with us.

LOTUS CARS AND TYRE MANUFACTURERS *continued*

The Exige S was fitted with Öhlins two-way adjustable dampers and Eibach springs, and shod with bespoke Yokohama A048 tyres, helping make it the finest track-day car in the world.
STEPHANIE EWEN

off for stop/start. When the new WLTP system was introduced, a lot of cars failed this, and there are real world driving emissions tests now. The testers can drive a car in any environment, in any conditions, up to a set speed – which is quite high – and it has to correlate to the emissions test.

JT: We're looking down the line at the end of the Elise and the Evora, so what you're telling me about now is going onto whatever is coming next.

GK: Yes, but there is also a run-out phase, during which the car will run out of its parts; some of it is driven by constant changes in legislation and some by parts suppliers; if you're using a carry-over part that Bosch or whoever stopped making six years ago, you're not going to find a manufacturer who is going to keep making that part for you, and if you only need a few hundred a year they're not going to keep running their plant just to keep manufacturing you a sensor. So, some of that comes into the equation. Also, the type of people who buy the Elise probably have it as their third or fourth car; it's not your primary drive, so there's an acceptance that it has enough technology now. It's pure enough, but people still remember it as the Series 1 model, which is great, but if they wouldn't buy it twenty years ago, they don't think there's any reason to buy it today. So we need to broadcast how it's improved substantially since then.

Elisa Artioli relishes the fact that the Elise is named after her. Here she is putting her own S1 model through its paces on the sweeping subalpine hill-roads of northeastern Italy.
RÉMI DARGEGEN

The most significant model to come out of Hethel in recent times is undoubtedly the Elise, which was introduced in 1996 when the company belonged to Romano Artioli, and was named after his granddaughter Elisa. Though she is currently based in Berlin, I interviewed her during a recent visit to Norfolk.

JT: So, Elisa, your own car is the original Series 1 that your grandfather Romano gave you, back at the model's launch?

EA: Yes, it's the silver Series 1 (left-hand drive) that I got from my grandfather. He gave it to me as a present when I was four years old because I presented the car, and also because it's named after me. But the thing is, it stayed in the garage many years till I could drive.

JT: It's a fascinating thing to have a car named after you – every time you see one you must think, 'That's got my name on it!'

EA: It's really crazy, because I don't feel like I'm famous or important because of it, but the weird thing is that for me the Elise is like a sister; I know it's not a person, but for me it has this personal factor. It was named after a person, so let's say a kind of sister, and when I see one on the street I really like that. I'm like, oohh, it's amazing, and, yes, it's fantastic. I really love the car, so it makes me super happy.

JT: Thinking of other cars named after actual real-life women, there's Mércèdes…

EA: Of course, but Mercedes is a brand and the Elise is a model, so I think it is more personal.

JT: It must be a buzz if you go to a Lotus gathering.

EA: I love those meetings, because in the first place I'm a Lotus driver, so I go there for the cars and the driving, not to say, like, 'I'm here', but sometimes they invite me as a special guest, so people know I'm coming and then they take pictures.

JT: These are European events, then?

EA: Most of them were in Europe, and I went just once to the USA; that was LOG56, which was two years ago in Princetown, close to New York. It's so nice; it's really different from the gatherings in Europe because firstly it's really big – it was over three days, so we were doing lots of things, like visiting a museum. I tried a lot of different Elises, and it was interesting because the S1 is not street legal there, there are no S1s in the USA. But I was more there to talk to everybody and to make a speech. I can speak about how much I love the car and a little bit about my story, but the interesting people are really the guys that worked on the car.

JT: Well OK, but you have immortalized the car, and vice versa, and that makes you a figurehead.

EA: Yes, well, we'll see what they do with that! I think Lotus will present a new Elise in 2021.

JT: Some people think the original version of the Elise is the purest, in terms of styling. Which model do you like best?

EA: Actually, I like the way the styling has moved on from the Series 1. It was quite a radical change that they made, especially to the headlights, though of course a new model doesn't have to look the same as the previous one. I really like the face of the S1 – it's like a smiling face – and also the back; I think it's so nice with the

Elisa likes the 'face' of the Series I model: 'It's like a smiling face,' she says.
RÉMI DARGEGEN

curves, and the lines and the side view are really nice. I just love the car. It's beautifully balanced, and the thing is, it looks so modern, but it also looks back to an era when sports cars had those beautiful rounded contours.

JT: Electric cars and hybrids are in the news: what do you think about that?

EA: Well, the Tesla was made on the Elise chassis, and this is also really nice. I saw one at LOG in the USA, but in Europe I've never seen one. It would be nice if they give this option because there are people that want an electric car, so I think it can be the future; I am not so sure about it, to be honest, but at least Lotus has that expertise, having created the Tesla.

While a student in Madrid, Elisa Artioli took her Elise on a European tour, covering thousands of kilometres in the process.
RÉMI DARGEGEN

ELISE S

The Elise S, still with the K-series power unit, was introduced in April 2005 to replace the 120 and 160 Rover-engined cars, which were phased out at the end of the year. At 140bhp, it filled the gap in the range between the 120 and 160. In 2007, the Elise S became the new base model, but now with a Toyota-sourced 1.8-litre engine, the 1ZZ-FE, replacing the K-series Rover. The Toyota unit produced 134bhp at 6,200rpm, an increase over the similar-capacity 120bhp Rover engine. However, it was a heavier engine, and along with the addition of airbags, ABS brakes, electric windows and carpet, weight was increased to 860kg (1,896lb), approximately 85kg (190lb) more than its predecessor.

For 2008, Lotus continued to make a normally aspirated Elise S alongside the supercharged SC. Although the car looked much like other Series 2 models, the cockpit now featured a driver and passenger airbag, and ProBax seats gave proper spinal support and better seat-cushion padding. The dashboard was coated with Sensasoft, a material that gave a sleek finish without resorting to the leather look. A starter button and new instrument cluster (white on black instead of vice versa), were complemented by intelligent progressive

A press shot of the 2004 model year Elise 111R on the Côte d'Azur; the new Federal spec included dual airbags, and the VVTL-i 1.8-litre Toyota in-line 4-cylinder engine, coupled with six-speed transmission was installed. Four-channel anti-lock braking was also a key feature, with twin-piston AP Racing front calipers and single-piston Brembos at the rear.
WILLIAM TAYLOR

Lotus Cars celebrated the fortieth anniversary of production at its Hethel site on 23 September 2007 with an open day at the factory, and the release of the commemorative 40th Anniversary Elise S, presented in Burnt Orange with matching hard-top. Based on the entry-level 2008 Elise, the cockpit also featured leather trim with orange stitching, painted diffuser and wheels. Just fifty were made.
WILLIAM TAYLOR

shift warning lights, which flashed a sequence of three warnings as the 8500 redline loomed on the tacho.

In 2009, three models were available in Europe: the Elise S, with a 134bhp, 1.8-litre Toyota 1ZZ-FE engine and five-speed manual gearbox, capable of 0–60mph in 5.8 seconds and top speed of 127mph (204km/h); the Elise R, with a 189bhp, 1.8-litre Toyota 2ZZ-GE engine and six-speed manual gearbox, doing 0–60mph in 4.9 seconds, and with a top speed of 148mph (238km/h); and the Elise SC, described below. No new models appeared for 2010, though improvements were made to CO_2 emissions and fuel economy.

The 2011 model year Elise range was released at the eightieth Geneva Show in 2010, featuring fresh styling cues incorporating a new front clamshell and new cast and forged wheels. There was a twin-spine engine cover and the diffuser was wrapped by a new bumper design incorporating the rear number plate. All-in-one integrated headlights included LED daylight running lights and LED direction indicators, and aerodynamics were improved by a 4 per cent reduction in drag coefficient. The rear boot could now be opened from the cockpit rather than by a separate key function. Vehicle warranty was increased to three years or 36,000 miles.

The most significant introduction was the new entry-level 1.6-litre Toyota Valvematic engine, developing 134bhp at 6,800 rpm and 118lb ft torque at 4,400rpm, returning 46mpg (6ltr/100km) and CO_2 emissions reduced by 13 per cent, making the Elise the lowest CO_2 producer per performance of any petrol-fuelled sports car in the world. The new engine was mated to a new six-speed manual gearbox, replacing the old five-speed box. For the first time, cruise control was available, operated via a stalk on the steering column.

The 2011 model year Elise range was announced at the eightieth Geneva Show in 2010, featuring fresh styling cues incorporating new front clamshell with individual headlight units instead of pairs. Brett Fraser drives a press demonstrator.
ANTONY FRASER

From 2011, the entry-level Elise was equipped with the 1.6-litre Toyota Valvematic 4-cylinder engine, developing 134bhp at 6,800rpm and 118lb ft torque at 4,400rpm, mated to a new six-speed manual gearbox, superseding the old five-speed box.
ANTONY FRASER

Lotus Elise S 2012–6

Layout and Chassis

Lotus-designed lightweight structure of epoxy-bonded and riveted aluminium alloy extrusions with integral steel seatbelt support structure and lightweight steel rear subframe

Engine

Type	Toyota-based VVT-I 2ZZ-GE, transverse mid-engine
Block material	Metal matrix composite (MMC) and aluminium lightweight compact construction
Head material	Metal matrix composite (MMC) and aluminium lightweight compact construction
Cylinders	4 cylinders in line
Cooling	Water
Bore and stroke	82mm × 85mm
Capacity	1796cc
Valves	DOHC, 16 valves, variable valve timing and lift with Valvematic system, hydraulic tappets, 4 valves per cylinder
Fuelling	Multipoint sequential fuel injection, direct electronic ignition
Supercharger	Charge-cooled Magnuson R900 supercharger utilizing Eaton TVS technology
Engine management	Lotus electronic T4 engine control unit
Max. power	217bhp (162kW) at 6,800rpm
Max. torque	184lb ft (250Nm) at 4,600rpm
Emission control	Three-way catalytic converter Euro IV emissions compliant with full on-board diagnostics (OBD) CO_2 emissions 208g/km

Transmission

Gearbox	Close-ratio 6-speed transaxle driving rear wheels. Bosch electronic differential lock
Clutch	Hydraulic
Ratios	1st 3.116 2nd 2.050 3rd 1.481 4th 1.166 5th 0.91 6th 0.815 Reverse 3.250
Final drive	4.529

Suspension and Steering

Front and rear	Unequal-length double wishbones, Eibach coil springs over Bilstein gas-pressured monotube dampers. Adjustable ride height and adjustable front anti-roll bar. Lotus dynamic performance management. Aerodynamically optimized rear diffuser
Steering	Rigidly mounted rack and pinion; 2.8 turns lock to lock
Wheels	Satin black 14-spoke forged 'Sport' alloy wheels, 16in front, 17in rear
Tyres	Front: Yokohama A048 LTS (W rated) 195/50 R16 Rear: Yokohama A048 LTS (W rated) 225/45 R17

Brakes

Type	Servo-assisted track-tuned 4-channel ABS with Lotus/AP Racing twin-piston fixed aluminium alloy front brake calipers, Brembo single-piston sliding rear calipers. Cast iron ventilated and cross-drilled discs front and rear
Size	282mm diameter, 26mm thick

Dimensions

Track	1,457mm (57.4in) front, 1,507mm (59.3in) rear
Wheelbase	2,298.7mm (90.5in)
Overall length	3,822.7mm (150.5in)
Overall width	1,714.5mm (67.5in) excluding door mirrors
Overall height	1,117.6mm (44in)
Dry weight	924kg (2,037lb)

Performance

Max. speed	145mph (234km/h)
0–60mph	4.2sec
0–100mph	12.9sec
Fuel consumption	Urban 27.3mpg (10.3ltr/100km) Extra urban 47.6mpg (5.9ltr/100km) Combined 37.5mpg (7.5ltr/100km)

DEVELOPMENT OF THE ELISE 111R AND THE FEDERAL ELISE

For clarification, the 111R is the Euro car and the Federal Elise is the North American market model. The 2004 Series 2 Elise was powered by the all-aluminium, 189bhp 1.8-litre Toyota engine with its Yamaha-designed twin-cam head and variable valve timing on intake and exhaust valve gear, driving through a six-speed manual Toyota gearbox. The best version of the Elise to date, road tests produced acceleration figures of 0–60mph in 4.9 seconds, or 4.7 seconds with the Sport Package. The engine management computer was a Lotus-programmed unit, and a cam-timing shift at 6,200rpm gave a radical power boost.

Back in 1957, North America was Lotus's first overseas market, and the marque has always retained a dedicated following across the pond. Stymied by complicated vehicle legislation and public liability issues, however, the 2005 Elise was the first model year to go on sale in the United States, with deliveries starting in the summer of 2004. Type approval required the intervention of the National Highway Traffic Safety Administration (NHTSA), who provided a three-year exemption for the car as it had yet to meet US bumper and headlight height regulations.

This model was followed by the 2006 Elise 111R and Sport Racer models, and Lotus made a limited edition (fifty in the USA) version called the Elise Sport. The 2006 models also differed from the 2005 models in that they were equipped with LED tail lights, an updated ECU, improved economy and more comfortable ProBax seats. All Elises manufactured after 1 January 2007 included the new sealed headlamp units and 2.5mph (4km/h) front bumpers required by US federal

Press shot of the 2004 Federal-spec Elise 111R on the promenade at Nice, now fitted with the 189bhp 1798cc 4-cylinder Toyota driveline.
WILLIAM TAYLOR

Both 2004 Elise models, the Federal Elise and rest-of-world 111R, were powered by the all-aluminium, 189bhp 1.8-litre Toyota VVTL-i engine with its Yamaha-designed twin-cam head and variable valve timing on intake and exhaust valve gear, driving through a six-speed manual Toyota gearbox.
WILLIAM TAYLOR

The 2004 model year Elise 111R was capable of reaching 60mph in 4.9 seconds, or 4.7 seconds with the Sport package.
WILLIAM TAYLOR

standards, although they were effectively concealed in the panel work. For the 2007 model year, the LOTUS name on the rear of the vehicle, which previously consisted of flat stickers, was changed to raised lettering. In order to comply with US federal bumper restrictions, the frontal crash structure was slightly changed and embryonic rear bumpers were added next to the number plate mount, although around 100 units of the 2007 model year cars were shipped from Hethel to the USA without these bumper changes. Also in 2007, the Elise S was released and the 111R renamed the Elise R.

ELISE SC

For 2008, Lotus built a second version of the Elise, the Elise SC, to run alongside a new normally aspirated model, with the same easy-riding cockpit and a non-intercooled Rootes-type Eaton supercharger producing 218bhp (163kW), developed in house by Lotus Engineering. With no intercooler to weigh it down, the Elise SC lost 8kg (18lb) compared with its supercharged Exige S stablemate, and as far as horsepower and torque were concerned, the Elise SC gave much the same sort of figures as its coupé cousin. The Elise SC was distinguishable from its normally aspirated sibling by its rear spoiler, borrowed from the Type 72 edition, together with new wheels – plus it had the knock-on bonus of decent visibility through the rear windscreen.

Black beauty: the 2012 model year Elise S was fitted with a new 1.8-litre Toyota 2ZR-FE engine and Eaton-type Magnuson R900 supercharger, developing 217bhp, coupled to the EC60 six-speed gearbox.

WILLIAM TAYLOR

The Eaton supercharger cut the Elise SC's 0–60mph to an impressive 4.3 seconds, from the base model's 4.9 seconds, or 4.7 seconds for the Elise plus Sport package. Weight remained a claimed 901kg (1,987lb); just 1.5kg (3lb) more than the previous model. The SC finally ran out of speed at 150mph (240km/h). I can personally verify this cracking pace, having had the dubious pleasure of maxing out on an unrestricted German autobahn in one. I say dubious, because although safe enough, it isn't what these cars are built for: put them rather on writhing two-lane blacktop for the most blistering fun. Or better still, the Nürburgring Nordschleife.

WHEELS AND TYRES

Wheels

Over the years Lotus hasn't offered that many wheel options on Elises. The original standard issue alloy was a five-spoke star pattern with slashes along each arm towards the wheel rim, four bolt holes and Lotus logo hub cap at centre. A new six-spoke design replaced this in May 1999, which was similar to the 340R without the split-rim sophistication. The original wheel was painted gold on the fiftieth anniversary edition, and the 111S went to a plainer six-spoke wheel. In February 2000, the Sport 160 model was equipped with a smart, unfussy five-spoke wheel, spokes tapering slightly towards the rim.

Wheels were originally produced by Alloy Wheels International, 5.5J × 15 and 7J × 16, and shod with Pirelli P-Zero tyres, unique to Lotus, measuring 185/55 R15 and 205/50 R16. Early Series 1 cars were equipped with Brembo silicon

This five-spoke wheel was standard fitment on the original Elise of 1996.

TOM WOOD

This five-spoke alloy wheel adorning the 1999 Elise Type 49 is shod with a Yokohama Advan tyre.
WIM TE RIET

carbide metal matrix brake discs, but these were replaced by cast iron discs. Magnesium alloy calipers reduced unsprung weight. Series 1 Elises had two wheel options, the forged one being lighter than the cast option, which gave the choice of forged alloys as part of the Sport pack. For 2011, a set of new Lotus Elise forged wheels weighed 29.26kg (64.4lb) per set, 2.14kg (4.7lb) lighter than a set of lightweight cast versions.

Once you move into the zone of different-sized aftermarket wheels, you are in murky waters and could upset the work that Lotus have done to get the car right in the first place. An upgrade like Sport 160 Dymag or 111S wheels on a standard car is acceptable, but a standard S1 wheel weighs 7kg (15lb) and, ironically, a Motorsport wheel is a few pounds heavier. Magnesium Dymag, OZ or Speedline weigh roughly 4kg (9lb) each so it's clear that fitting aftermarket wheels is a simple way of reducing weight. Expect to pay between £1,000 and £1,500 a set and include a hub fitting kit too. Another make of aftermarket wheel available for the Series 1 Elise, Rota, is much cheaper (at £500 a set), with five spokes, finished in gunmetal or matt black. Nothing short of a stripe over the top of the car affects its look more than a set of wheels, and a set of black alloys gives any Elise a more racy image.

Tyres

Tyres have moved on a long way in fifteen years, and the original Pirelli P-Zeros (front 185/55 R15, rear 205/50 R16) used on the Series 1 are no longer available, so most owners fit the factory-approved Yokohama Advan Neova LTS equivalent. Out in clubland there are differing views on what gives the best possible results; Michelin Pilot SXs, Dunlop D98s and Toyo Proxes are workable options, though they go off quickly. The company-approved Yokohama C-Drive (185/55 front, 205/50 rear) have more conventional tread and are thus more suitable for S1 winter use. Series 2s used to be fitted with Bridgestone Potenza RE040s, 175/55R16 front and 225/45R17 rear, and they suited the car very well. In 2010, the Elise tyre of choice was the Yokohama Advan Neova AD07 LTS, 175/50 R16 front and 225/45 R17 rear.

A road trip to Geneva, Morzine, Chamonix and the ice-racing stadium at Serre Chevalier a few years ago demonstrated to me how well winter tyres serve you in the snow. The Lotuses were shod with Yokohama W*Drive winter tyres and Pirelli Sottozero studded tyres for the labyrinth of the Andros Trophy's ice rink and were sure-footed and utterly unshakable. Everyone should have spare set of wheels shod with winter tyres, ready for snow.

Dr Mike Van Dingenen checks tyre pressures on Johan Dirickx' Elise 2-Eleven during a track day at Abbeville Circuit in northern France.
ANTONY FRASER

GOING TOPLESS

Removing and replacing an Elise soft-top is a one-person job, accomplished in a leisurely couple of minutes – or quicker if it starts raining!

So, you're buying a sports car? That's wind-in-the-hair motoring you're after, then? Well, on a hot day in St Tropez, topless is matchless, but the crucial convertible conundrum is not how good it feels with the top down, but how well it works with the top on, when it's raining, and your passenger is, shall we say, keener on comfort than carbs.

The fundamental cause of water coming in is seldom the hood itself; it's more likely to be a problem with the fine adjustment of its fitting, though a water-repellent coating on the soft-top will improve the hood's resistance to leaks. Even if you get the fitting perfectly correct, you can still expect a few drips on the sill when you open the door after it's been standing out on a rainy night.

The Elise soft-top is not a quick bit of kit to erect, however. To do it at a leisurely pace can take maybe five minutes, so there's none of that 'up and down at the traffic lights' stuff. It's easier to describe how to assemble the hood than how to take it down. So here goes: assuming you've started with the top off, to put it up you first need to locate the cant rails that pass down either side, between roll-hoop and A-pillar, just above the side windows. These cant rails are tapered towards the front and have a ball fitting that pops into the windscreen header rail, while the back end has a neat little clip.

You hold the cant rail and apply a little bit of pressure by leaning into the windscreen, and the clip at the rear fits into its housing on the door shut. The cant rails are braced by two virtually flat hoops that pass from side to side across the car, and they spring-fit into place.

Then you take the hood itself and cast it over the lattice frame you've just created. A plastic fillet runs along the leading edge of the hood, and you slide that under the ridge along the length of the windscreen header rail. It's best to start with the corner sections, which are separated from the major part of it.

When you're satisfied that the front is flush, you can pop the chrome spikes at the rear into the receptacles provided in the flying buttresses. At the sides, poppers press on to fixings in the cant rails inside the cockpit. Finally, return to the rear and tension the whole canopy by means of a pair of Allen bolts set in the spikes using the Allen key provided. This little tool has a home in the rear bulkhead just behind the driver's seat.

If you plan to use the car all year round, or if you prefer the coupé shape or security of a firm lid, you can fit a works GRP hard-top, transforming the Elise into a coupé. When I visit him in Porto, my Portuguese acquaintance António Queirós suggests that whether this is worthwhile depends on the circumstances:

continued overleaf

GOING TOPLESS *continued*

FAR LEFT: The sprung support bars are direction-marked and slot into the roll-over hoop and windscreen header rail.

LEFT: Having released the pins securing the side sections of the soft-top, both sides of the top are rolled up, wrapping the two support rods in the process. It all gets unwrapped in the opposite way before it's put back on.

Elise owner António Queirós points to the pale grey pin that locates the side section of the hood canopy into the slot on the windscreen header rail. Both front and rear pins are released with thumbs, by levers just visible, tucked into the side sections.

> If it's for better weather protection, don't bother, because the soft-top is fine, especially on modern cars, and if it's about noise reduction, a top doesn't make any difference. But if you need it for everyday railway parking or on street parking every day, then the security case makes it worth it.

All Elise hard-tops are removable, so if you go to view a prospective car with the roof on, bear in mind that the standard car has a soft-top anyway, ready to go on if you need it.

LIMITED EDITIONS

The Series 2 Elise was available as the 111S model with VVC engine technology, though this was discontinued for the 2005 model year when the K-series engine was abandoned in favour of the 1.8-litre Toyota powerplant.

Two more track-focused versions of the Series 2 were available, the 135R and Sport 190, delivering 135bhp and 192bhp respectively. These also came with handling upgrades, including Lotus sport suspension and wider wheels with Yokohama Advan A048 tyres. In certain markets, the 135R was replaced by the Sport 111, which was similar, apart from deploying the 156bhp VVC engine in place of the 135bhp K-series.

Like the Series 1's Type 49 Gold Leaf special edition, the Series 2 spawned a few limited editions commemorating famous Lotus F1 racing cars: the Type 23 (white with two green stripes over the top), Type 25 (British Racing Green with paired yellow stripes), Type 72 (JPS black and gold livery), Type 99T (Camel yellow), Elise Club Racer (pale blue) and Exige Club Racer (white with green stripes). They were made in batches of between twenty-five and a hundred units each, identified by a little plaque on the dashboard for authentication.

Released in 2003, the S2 Elise was also offered in Gold Leaf Team Lotus colours, celebrating the Type 49 Formula 1 car driven by Jim Clark and Graham Hill, with which Hill won the 1968 world title.
ANTONY FRASER

ABOVE **The special edition Elise Type 25 channelled the ground-breaking monocoque chassis Lotus Type 25 Formula 1 car from 1962, with which Jim Clark won the F1 World Championship for the first time in 1963.**
WILLIAM TAYLOR

Four decades separate these two special editions: the 2007 Exige Sprint mimics the yellow-over-cream colour scheme of the S4 Elan Sprint Coupé from 1971.
WILLIAM TAYLOR

NEIL THOMAS INTERVIEW

Now Evora platform manager, Neil spent eight years overseeing the Elise platform models.

JT: You joined Lotus Cars in December 2011; what was your previous background?

NT: Prior to joining Lotus Engineering in 2011, I was at Land Rover, in concept engineering as launch manager for Freelander and Evoque. We were doing lightweight concept vehicles based on the same technology as the Elise, so the chassis that we designed and put under the vehicle was largely based on a bonded, extruded chassis frame with composite body panels, a 1,250kg (2,750lb) lightweight Defender, and examples of it now reside in the museum at Gaydon. So I'd already been indoctrinated in lightweight thinking before coming to Lotus. The reason I came here was on the back of the Dany Bahar era. The line-up of cars he was proposing to build was a little bit ambitious, but at least if one of them came through, it seemed like it would be a great place to go: the Esprit in particular was a beautiful concept.

I began in the engineering division, working on the Hydrogen Taxi, which we re-engineered and then manufactured five vehicles for the London Olympics in 2012. Next I joined Richard Rackham as the platform manager and then launch manager to put the Evora 400 into production. Even during that period, the instability was apparent; especially lack of investment, but that's definitely different now. It was a transition period, from Dany Bahar on his way down,

ABOVE LEFT: **Neil Thomas has worked at Lotus Cars since 2011, and spent eight years overseeing models built on the Elise platform.**
LOTUS CARS

ABOVE RIGHT: **The 2011 model year facelift gave the Elise a cleaner frontal aspect, enclosing the new LED headlights and turn indicators in almond-shaped nacelles, creased to harmoniously match the bodyshell swage-line. Marketing man Johnny Lamb is at the wheel.**
ANTONY FRASER

the new ownership by DRB-HICOM, the consolidation through the Jean-Marc Gales period, on to the present Geely years.

JT: Once that stability was reliably in place you could then start thinking about another new model.

NT: We're already starting to see the fruits of that, and at least one new model was conceived at the onset of the Geely ownership. That would never have happened without investment and stability, so in the next year or so you'll start to see the replacements for the current cars beginning to be developed.

JT: Elise and Evora?

NT: All our current production vehicles, absolutely. We've a succession plan and we're looking at a five- to ten-year horizon rather than the former two years.

JT: To recap then, were you behind the Elise Series 2 facelift, which some people refer to as the Series 3?

NT: We did do a facelift of the Elise. It was relatively light, because obviously we were consolidating losses and trying to get the company back into profitability, so we didn't have huge amounts of money to spend. That said, perhaps one of the largest sums of money that we did spend was on the Elise facelift, which was code-named '1 ½ model year', which would have been the end of 2016, early 2017 before its introduction.

That consisted of a refreshing of the front, a light touch on the interior and some quality improvements. It was a relatively small project, nine or ten months, just to keep the product fresh, keep it in the market place, keep it in front of the journalists just so we could keep new stories going and maintain general interest. That's one thing that Jean-Marc was extremely good at – creating little sound bites that kept Lotus in the mainstream and sustained the press interest. So that was one of the biggest revisions we undertook on the Elise. All the philosophy was about making it lighter and coming back to the original concept, which was a huge power-to-weight ratio in a very light package, and trying to improve the quality all the time. That was fundamentally the essence behind that project, and that is the car that's in current production today.

ABOVE **This Elise Sprint 220 from 2017 is finished with several gloss-finish carbon-fibre panels, including the engine cover, the roll-hoop cover and vented bonnet panel.**
WILLIAM TAYLOR

The 2017 Elise Sprint is all about weight-saving: swing open the door, and there's the open linkage for the gearshift, and a blanking plate where a radio head unit should be. The sill tops are clad in carbon-fibre, with the bare chassis beneath.
WILLIAM TAYLOR

Subtle graphics identify the Elise 220 Sprint; power unit is the supercharged 1.8-litre Toyota in-line four, which produces 217bhp and does 0–60mph in 4.1 seconds.
WILLIAM TAYLOR

Final inspection, post assembly, featuring a couple of S2 Elises, and – in the mirror – a VX220 receiving a once-over in the engine bay.
WILLIAM TAYLOR

EXIGE SERIES 2

In 2004, the Series 2 Exige was announced, powered by the 1.8-litre Toyota engine, and the following year output rose from 190bhp to 243bhp with the small-run (fifty units, in either yellow or black only) supercharged Exige 240R, harbinger of the supercharged Exige S that debuted in February 2006. It deployed the frontal design cues of the Series 2 Elise, revved up with a front splitter, rear wing and air-scooped beetle-back coupé shape to give it an added sense of purpose. It was always the plan that the Exige would have a small power advantage over the Elise, which, combined with the aerodynamics package, racetrack appearance and feel should give it an edge. In fact, as the Elise SC moved onto 240bhp, it could match the Exige's performance. Values are more straightforward than for the S1 Exige, apart from one-offs, like the Red Bull GT3 Exige, built and raced by Lanzante Motorsport, with input by Adrian Newey, in Britcar and other endurance series. Priced at £130,000, that 345bhp beast could even be used on the road.

Exige S

The Exige S was first produced in 2006, and has been described as absolutely bulletproof and fairly vice-free. The engine was not overly stressed and the supercharger was not over-powerful, given that Lotus raced with it in excess of 300bhp. On the 2009 Dutch Spring Run across the Netherlands and into Germany, I found the Exige 260 S quite thirsty, though, without trying hard, and of course even more with the blower on full thrust on the autobahn. It proved a good, comfortable companion going down to Abbeville for some track-day action, even on the autoroute.

The Series 2 Exige, launched in 2004, was not only a hard-top version of the Elise, with which it now shared its 1.8-litre 4-cylinder Toyota power unit, but its racetrack credentials and purposeful demeanour were clearly evident.

PAUL HARMER

An Exige S with its engine lid open – pictured here at Abbeville Circuit in France – is a curious sight, because the rear wing is projected even further into space. Its 1796cc Toyota engine is topped by the Eaton M62 supercharger apparatus.

Unveiled at the Geneva Show in February 2006, the Exige S had an enlarged roof duct and was powered by the supercharged Toyota 2ZZ-GE 4-cylinder 1.8-litre engine coupled with the Toyota C64 six-speed gearbox; 3,306 units were built up to 2011.

The Exige S Roadster of 2013 took the track-oriented model into pastures new, having a removable soft-top roof canopy like its Elise siblings. The Roadster was built on the expanded extruded aluminium chassis, and, like its Exige S sister, was powered by the 3456cc supercharged Toyota V6 engine.
WILLIAM TAYLOR

RUSSELL CARR INTERVIEW

Russell Carr joined the company in 1990 as a member of Julian Thomson's design team, and took over as chief designer in 1998.
LOTUS CARS

Head of design at Lotus Cars, Russell Carr joined the company in 1990 as a member of Julian Thomson's design team, and took over as chief designer in 1998. As well as contributing to the final evolutions of the Esprit, Russell was closely involved in the styling of the S1 and S2 Elise, as well as the 340R and the Exige, and all derivatives. He's seen the design department expand from five to thirty members.

JT: Let's pitch in with the Series 2 Elise, Russell. At what point did you get involved with redesigning the Elise, following on from the S1?

RC: It was right at the start. Julian left when we started the 340R programme, and after that came the first Exige, which was based on the S1 model, and then we started the S2 after that. We'd already got a long way down the line with the M250 [the Evora prototype] and we'd got the seeds of the 340R, and those are what prompted the design language of the second-generation Elise. It was good that we had some reference – it was quite a daunting task because at that point the S1 was still hugely popular, and some of us were questioning whether we needed to redesign this at that moment. It was a very successful vehicle, and we could have been doing another car all together. But we were also working on the VX220 Speedster for Vauxhall, so it was in our interests to move the Elise on because we knew this car was coming. We were developing the surfaces of the VX220 in the studio here, and that's what gave us the impetus to do it.

JT: What were your criteria then? You didn't have a totally free hand in what you could do?

RC: Aesthetically, we wanted to give the Elise a fresh twist. I wouldn't say 'make it modern', because I don't think the S1 looked 'not modern' at the time. The first Elise was very soft and organic; we wanted to keep some of that softness and still keep the muscularity of the car, but introduce some crisper lines. And then of course there were some functional changes to the car; the sill went lower to make ingress easier, and we wanted to make the roof on the car easier to use, because when Richard and Julian designed the S1, it really was supposed to be a very short-run car – we were only going to make 750 a year for three years. It was seen as a sort of Lotus Seven replacement, so the roof is a bonus on that car. But once we realized we were selling 2,000 or 3,000 of those a year, and people were using them every day, aspects like keeping the water on the outside of the car became much more important. There was a desire to make the roof much simpler to erect and much more durable, and that had an effect on the design.

To make the exterior more bespoke, we concentrated on its technical detail, giving it a bit more precision in crucial areas. So, on the second-generation S2 car, we could do bespoke lights – insect eye shapes with separate indicators – and they were unique to that car. The rear lights were made by a company we were working with, and they were bespoke to Lotus, rather than being off the shelf like they had been on the first-generation S1 Elise. And we had some nice injection-moulded grilles with fins on the side. Details like that lifted the styling, and then we were able to up-size the wheel diameters from 15/16s on the first generation to 16/17s on the second generation. The widths changed as well, but for a designer the bigger the diameter of the wheel, the more modern it looks and the better it sits for the ride, so that was really important to us.

JT: But there's still a balance between stance and ride quality with lower-profile tyres.

RC: Very much so, yes. Working with Richard [Rackham] and Gavan [Kershaw] over the years, we feel very close to the technical aspect of the products, and form and function is really important on a Lotus. So we respect those requirements: unsprung mass, aerodynamic efficiency, ride performance – all those things that are seemingly less sexy until you experience the car but that do contribute to the entity of the car. A Lotus is the sum of all its parts, and working on the Evija recently it reinforced the importance of that to me. It causes you to look back at Lotus history, and of course Chapman was just brilliant – the Type 25 is purely a functional machine to win races, but achingly beautiful, and I grew up with that. So, for me, bringing the technical and the aesthetics together is really important. Motorcycles are a great example of that, because they're very functional structures; you can often see the mechanics of them, and that's the pleasure of it – seeing the function as well as the form.

JT: So who were the leading stylists?

RC: Steve Crijns and Barney Hatt, who worked on the car, had a lot of experience, and I could trust them and we respected each other's judgement. We had an understanding, and things started to happen much more naturally. You can achieve more because of that collective experience: you've done it before, so you know what works and you know what doesn't work. It was an interesting time, because we were still doing the M250 [Evora prototype] when we started the S2 Elise. We were doing the development of that in Coventry at the facility that's now HPE, and we were doing the VX220 Speedster and S2 Elise back here at Hethel, so I was going to and fro. Steve was looking after the Elise and Barney was working with me on the M250. Steve did both the exterior and the interior on the first generation of the S2, and then Barney did the Federal interior when we put air bags in the car. And then, ironically, Barney did the most recent facelift on the car. So those two guys, together with me, have seen the car through from the second generation to present day.

The important thing is, there's always been the team spirit in the studio and getting on together, and that's something that Julian initiated. You need that when you're sometimes working silly hours; we're usually here to 8 o'clock at night, most nights, and when the push is on we're here sometimes weekends too.

JT: In practical terms, how does the design evolve from renderings to wind-tunnel clay?

RC: Going back to the S2, the process from the first movement on a clay model to fixing the clay is probably about six months, and the first two or three months you're actually still moving things. Quite big moves, with less intervention, but you're still thinking about engineering criteria. And then we start focusing down. From the S2 to today, the digital modelling side has become more and more important, and that was the first car where the physical model and

Rendering by Steve Crijns of the Series 2 Exige, done in 2003.
WILLIAM TAYLOR

The clay model of the Elise S2 centre stage in the Lotus design studio, pictured in November 2000 – though the Series 2 had already been announced at the NEC in October.

WILLIAM TAYLOR

the digital car model were done side by side. We led with the clay for more of the process, but there was a team of digital modellers who were capturing the surface of the clay, turning it into a digital surface that engineering could then use, whereas in the old days it would have been hand-drawn – engineers drawing surfaces by hand. These days, it really is a personal choice as to which side leads, but there is always a huge digital design content, and once we've got a digital surface we can machine models as well as manually model them. We can do animations, and we can use the surface as it allows for more understanding of what the design looks like. We can go into the VR [virtual reality] world as well – put the headsets on – which not that long ago you wouldn't have believed could happen at Lotus.

JT: So you're saying that the S2 was created by both clay and digital modelling?

RC: Yes, all that's become normal now. During the S2 gestation period, we had a clay model that we would scan and take data points off, and then the digital modellers would turn it into a digital surface. In those days, maybe once or twice in a process, we might take the data they'd got and machine it back into the clay as a kind of insurance to make sure it was aligned. The reality is that a good clay modeller can take digital data, point it into the surface, and then manually model it really closely. But at that point we would always correlate it a couple of times to make sure it was accurate. Then it gets to the point where the clay model is frozen, and we would paint it so it looks like a real car. That's when you do the final surface release. Back then, say twenty years ago, we would have spent six or eight weeks on it, which is really quick compared with our current process, which is more like six months on that phase.

JT: So, is there any room for alterations after that?

RC: As designers, we will be reviewing the digital models, and we would probably pull the surfaces a little bit to just make sure highlights run correctly, and maybe tweak things for manufacturing or engineering reasons that we didn't know about earlier. We would also be looking at how the panels come together, making sure the gaps are all equal. We are interested in how big the gaps are, and also where the panels stick together; sometimes you don't want the panels to be continuous and flush, you might actually want one to be over-flush so that from certain angles you can't look inside the gap. Different parts of the car will have slightly different tolerances in manufacture, with regard to where the panel sits, and so you want the data to take that into account; the best way of doing that is digitally, once you've got the main form of the car. We've become obsessive about that, and about the finesse of the highlight – how the light falls on the surface and whether it does it progressively or is there the whole time. We have to remind ourselves sometimes to be happy about things, because we always see the problems in what we're doing, not the successes.

JT: Is the Exige a different story to the S2 Elise, or is it a developing parallel?

RC: No, the S2 Exige came after the S2 Elise. Quite early on, when I took over, we started the Sport 160 and the 190 Motorsport Elise. In December 1999 it was decided that we would do a car for Geneva, and that meant we had twelve weeks to do the S1 Exige. We rapidly did that first shape for the car that went to Geneva, and it was actually a different designer, John [S]. It was basically an overpowered Elise – see the muscular arches, the roof scoop, the wings – and then the decision was taken to make it into a road car that became the first Exige. When we did the S2 Elise, I don't think there was an appetite to do an Exige as well. The budgets probably just didn't allow it, but we also made about 900 S1 Exiges a week anyway. So, I think the view was, there wasn't a business case to spend the money on it, particularly as the S2 Elise used different body-manufacturing processes that required more complex, more expensive tooling that gave better quality panels and quicker turnaround. It's one of those questions we always ask in design, because we like to think of the big picture first of all. We always ask, is there going to be a motorsport version, is there going to be a convertible and, over the years, is there a Federal version, because these factors all have effects on the design. I'm pretty sure at the time there was no appetite to do a second Exige, and it was three or four years before the S2 Exige came out in 2004.

JT: And how did you rationalize the styling of the S2 Exige with the S1 version?

RC: I remember the first proposition for doing an Exige on the S2 Elise came from outside the design studio, and that was to do it economically – basically do it as cladding panels, so the wheelarch extensions were stick-on ones, rather like the Esprit had in later life or the pop-riveted ones of the 993 GT2 Evos from the mid-1990s, and they thought it was fantastic because bonded-on arches, bonded-on roof scoop looked like a race car should, with visible fixings and stuck-on bits. Of course, we as designers thought it looked like a dog's dinner! Anyway, it became a real programme, but there was slightly more limitation on the second-generation Exige than on the first, because obviously the steering wheel position was changed, and while we could do the roof scoop, we could put wings on the car and we could change face of the car, but we couldn't pull the wheelarches down.

After we'd finished the Exige we were doing other variants with different wings, and in that era we were also doing Elise and Evora evolutions, and we were still really heavily doing third-party consultancy work, which is still really important to the business. Between 1992 and 2010, we did a huge amount of third-party work, with Korean companies, American companies, European and, latterly, Chinese; obviously with Proton, who were our owners for a long time, so there were always those programmes on the go. About the same time as we were doing S2 we were working on the Opel Speedster and the Tesla Roadster as well.

The Exige Cup 260 came out in 2008, with 300 cars made over two years. Seen here in action at Abbeville Circuit in France, it was fitted with a comprehensive array of track-oriented components including LTS compound Yokohama A048R tyres, four-pot AP calipers, adjustable Öhlins dampers and Eibach anti-roll bar. Its aero embellishments produced 40kg (88lb) downforce at 100mph (160km/h).

The cockpit ambience of the Exige S Roadster with its quilted upholstery is far removed from the dynamic austerity of the Exige's trackable concept. It is, nevertheless, 68kg (150lb) lighter than the coupé.
WILLIAM TAYLOR

The Toyota 3.5-litre V6, topped with supercharger and intercooler, is a tight but extremely neat fit in the Exige's extended chassis. Like all Elise and Exige models, luggage space is at a premium.
WILLIAM TAYLOR

The Exige S Roadster was deprived of a front splitter as a matter of aerodynamic prudence in order to balance the aero front to rear, because it wasn't provided with a rear wing, just a modest flip-up tail.
WILLIAM TAYLOR

JT: And the long-wheelbase Exige S from 2011 that spawned the Roadster and V6 Cup? How difficult was that to rationalize from the regular Exige, when you've got to put a bigger engine in it?

RC: It was a brilliant job to do, because if you think back, the first Exige S1 was really an Elise S1 on steroids, with wider wheels and wider arches, roof air intake and significantly more prominent aero. I think the S2 Exige is a brilliant car – I'd love to own one myself, and actually two of our digital modellers have owned them. But I think it missed an opportunity; we had done a one-off car for racing in Malaysia, where we took an Exige and stretched and pulled it out, and put a longitudinal engine in it. We'd seen already what Hennessey had done with the car (the Texas-based Hennessey Venom, thirteen cars built) so we just knew that if you pull an Elise lengthways and widthways, you're going to get a pretty cool-looking car – a real sports prototype-looking car along the lines of the original Type 115 GT1. So, it's a fantastic design opportunity; you get brilliant proportions, and when you look at the ratio of width to height and wheel to height, you're in real supercar territory but at a fraction of the price, so you're off to a winner to start with.

We had two bites of the cherry, because we started the car before the Dany Bahar era, and working with Roger Becker – he was sort of 'Mr Product' at the time – we got as far as a full-size model, and it was looking pretty good. Then the new management came in, and they didn't want to pursue that because they wanted to just do brand-new cars, and so it got parked. But then, when they realized that a new product would take longer to come through than expected, and we still needed something new to complete the range, they went back to it and we picked up where we left off. We matured the car so it was a bit more racy than the original; it's perhaps hard to believe that, but it was racier than the one we were doing before. We gave the car more sophisticated surfaces – and that's the car you now know in production. As with everything, we would love to have gone further; we would like to have changed more of the Elise parts when we were doing that car, but carrying things over is an economic necessity. I think it's a brilliant car. I was lucky enough last year to have an Exige Sport 410 (0–60mph in 3.3sec, 174mph/280km/h max), which I drove from February through to November and I loved it. My wife is not a car obsessive: her background is being a banker, but she absolutely loved that car and was really upset when we had to hand it back! So, yes, the third generation, the V6 Exige, is fantastic.

JT: And it's available as a roadster and coupé too – best of both worlds?

RC: Hah! True, but the only thing I missed on it was not being able to take the roof off, because the one I got was the fixed-head. There's something nice about the Elise that it can be this really serious driver's car when you want it to be, and then when the weather is right you take the roof off and you can potter around in it and it's still fun to drive. It's fun in all aspects: if you're Gavan [Kershaw], it's fun to drive on the track, if you're a 'normal' person it's fun on a summer's day on a wandering road. There's a fantastic sense of connection with the road that even a non-driver – a non-professional driver – can just feel. It flatters you that you're better than you are, because the connection between input and sensation is so direct. It's a brilliant car, which is why it's still selling pretty healthily, twenty years since the second-generation car came out. It was endorsed as 'the people's choice' in *Autocar*, icon of icons!

Lotus designer Russell Carr in an Elise R lined up on Snetterton's start/finish straight during the parade of Lotuses at the Lotus Festival in September 2009.

CHAPTER THREE

SPECIAL DERIVATIVES

THE GENERAL MOTORS VX220

The base model VX220 was launched in 2000, having been developed alongside the Series 2 Lotus Elise. Badged as an Opel or Vauxhall in deference to its GM ownership – even a Daewoo – it came with a 2.2-litre normally aspirated engine, which produced 144bhp and 149lb ft torque, enough to achieve a 135mph (217km/h) top speed, and a 0–60mph time of 5.6sec.

Always destined to be a short-run product – with 7,000 units built – it got the attention it deserved in 2003 when the VX220 Turbo arrived, powered by the turbocharged 2.0-litre 4-cylinder engine that developed 197bhp and 184lb ft torque. It could now do 151mph (243km/h) and hit 100km/h (62mph) in 4.7sec. The VX-R220 launched in 2004 was a special edition version with sixty-five built, based on the turbo engine, tweaked to give 216bhp and 221lb ft, with top speed increasing by 4mph (6.5km/h) and taking 0.5sec off its 0–60 time. It was fitted with Öhlins suspension and 16in rather than 17in wheels for sharper handling.

EUROPA S AND SE

Introduced at Geneva in 2005 and in the showrooms for 2006, the Europa S was conceived as a sports car for Proton,

The powertrain of the VX220, the 2.0-litre turbocharged GM Ecotec Z20LER 4-cylinder engine, also fitted in the Type 121 Europa S and SE.

Lotus Type 121 Europa S 2007–9

Layout and Chassis
Lotus-designed lightweight structure of epoxy-bonded and riveted aluminium alloy extrusions with integral steel seatbelt support structure and lightweight steel rear subframe

Engine	
Type	Turbocharged General Motors Ecotec 2 Z20LER, transverse mid-engine
Block material	Cast iron
Head material	Aluminium
Cylinders	4 cylinders in line
Cooling	Water
Bore and stroke	86mm × 86mm
Capacity	1998cc
Valves	DOHC, 16 valves, 4 valves per cylinder
Fuelling	Multipoint sequential fuel injection, electronic ignition, GM turbocharger
Max. power	197bhp (147kW) at 5,400rpm
Max. torque	201lb ft (272Nm) at 5,000rpm
Emission control	Three-way catalytic converter
Transmission	
Gearbox	Getrag M32 close-ratio 6-speed transaxle driving rear wheels
Clutch	Hydraulic
Ratios	1st 3.818 2nd 2.158 3rd 1.475 4th 1.067 5th 0.875 6th 0.744 Reverse 3.25
Final drive	3.94
Suspension and Steering	
Front and rear	Unequal-length double wishbones, Eibach coil springs over Bilstein gas-pressured monotube dampers and front anti-roll bar
Steering	Rigidly mounted rack and pinion; 2.8 turns lock to lock
Wheels	Cast alloy 15-spoke, 17in front and rear
Tyres	Front: Goodyear Eagle F1 GS-D3 175/50 R17 Rear: Goodyear Eagle F1 GS-D3 225/45 R17
Brakes	
Type	Servo-assisted track-tuned 4-channel ABS with Lotus/AP Racing twin-piston fixed aluminium alloy front brake calipers, Brembo single-piston sliding rear calipers. Cast iron ventilated and cross-drilled discs, Ferodo DS25HP pads
Size	308mm diameter front, 288mm rear, 26mm thick
Dimensions	
Track	1,457mm (57.4in) front, 1,490mm (58.7in) rear
Wheelbase	2,330mm (91.7in)
Overall length	3,900mm (153.5in)
Overall width	1,714mm (67.5in) excluding door mirrors
Overall height	1,120mm (44.1in)
Dry weight	995kg (2,194lb)
Performance	
Max. speed	143mph (230km/h)
0–100km/h (62mph)	5.8sec
0–100mph (160km/h)	13.8sec
Fuel consumption	Urban 22.2mpg (7.9ltr/100km) Extra urban 38.7mpg (13.7ltr/100km) Combined 30.4mpg (10.8ltr/100km)

but was reabsorbed as an in-house project – a nod to precedents like the collaboration between Volkswagen and Porsche on the 914 and 924 models. Taking its name from the Renault- and Lotus-Ford Type 47 twin-cam-powered, mid-engined Lotus model of the late 1960s, the new generation base model Europa was powered by the 197bhp 2.0-litre GM turbocharged four. It could do 0–60mph in 5.6 seconds (0–100km/h in 5.8sec) with a maximum speed of

The Type 121 Europa S was styled largely by Barney Hatt, based on the Elise extruded aluminium chassis and powered by the turbocharged 2.0-litre GM Ecotec Z20LER 4-cylinder engine.
WILLIAM TAYLOR

143mph (230km/h). The justification for fitting the GM turbo 2.0-litre unit was that the Europa was intended for everyday use, and the unblown Toyota engine was thought to be a little bit frenetic: there's a big step-up in power at 6,000rpm, where it all comes alive on the second cam, but you've got to be prepared to drive it quite hard. The Europa, on the other hand, wasn't really designed as a hard-edged car, and the turbocharged engine gave more usable power lower down. Two years later, the Europa SE version was announced, its power uprated to 222bhp and its cabin more refined. When it first came out, and until the Exige S was introduced at 218bhp, the upgraded Europa with 225bhp was the most powerful car in the Elise line-up.

Combining the power of the Elise with something approaching the cabin comfort of the Evora, albeit in two-seater format, the Europa is, in that sense, the least raunchy of the Elise range. The Europa was announced at the same time as Audi relaunched its 4×4 3.2-litre V6 TT, yet it cost £1,000 more than the Audi, giving the press a useful stick with which to beat it. Also based on the same chassis, the Vauxhall/Opel VX220 Speedster employs the same normally aspirated and turbocharged 2.0 GM drivelines, and while it's less aesthetically refined than the Europa, it is much the same car – in convertible format.

Intended as a 'business class' incarnation of the Elise, the cockpit of the Type 121 Europa S was suitably refined and comfortably appointed.
WILLIAM TAYLOR

ANDY PLEAVIN INTERVIEW

JT: Andy, you are quality director of Lotus Cars. How long have you been in that role?

AP: Well, title-wise, relatively recently, but job-wise, for several years as the head of quality. It wasn't until we changed to Geely ownership that we started using director titles again. Under the Proton ownership you couldn't be a director because that's a very serious title! Now I report straight to (CEO) Phil Popham as quality director, and before then I reported in very much the same role to Jean-Marc Gales. But the job's changed a bit, because with Geely ownership we're now able to do all of the things that we really wanted to do, and put in all of those elements of quality – certainly the more preventative side of things – that we would have liked to have done in the past, had we had any money. So, for example we have a perceived quality group now that looks at touch, feel, smell – smell is very important in certain countries inside the car, particularly China. We consider how panels line up, how colours match with each other, how things interface, which, in the past was always left to the design studio. We have a quantitative way of scoring everything – rattles in panels, that type of thing – and we do all the preventative work, all the value mode analysis, and all the dimensional side of things. I've gone from roughly thirty staff to sixty, and we will be up to about 140 by mid-2021.

Andy Pleavin joined Lotus Cars in 1977, and is now director of quality.
LOTUS CARS

JT: Will this all be in the new factory building?

AP: Yes, this will be about bringing everything in far earlier, and then building it; we're going to be building more cars. The world's a different place from what it was; if you go back to the start of Elise, we did it on a wing and a prayer. This is probably the best period of true stability that we've had, in fact. We're now being able to do what we wanted to do.

JT: Give me an idea of what you and your sixty guys are actually up to.

AP: Okay, to give you some shape to it, I'm responsible for new product quality, and they're the guys who look after perceived quality – the dimensional engineering of the car, the reliability and the durability testing. There's a team that do all the engineering, and reporting to them are the supply quality side, to which there are two fundamental sections. One is working on new product to make sure we're choosing the right suppliers and we're getting the parts made in the correct way, that the submissions are there, legal and compliant, and they're everything that the design intent called for. The other leg to the supply quality side is looking after current car issues. Production quality is the people who oversee the cars as we produce them, people who are embedded in the system on the way through, so by the time we get to the end of the line it's a tick box, not car inspection exercise.

There's another leg that looks after quality management systems, so all the things about how we run our business, our quality standards and our business operating system, which says how you release an engineering part, how you send a part back to a supplier if it's not perfect. All that is documented, so anybody in the business can go on the internet and look up 'How do I do this, how do I do that.' There is another branch that looks after anything in the future that could be outside the UK, but down the side of that I have my vehicle line quality managers. They work on a matrix fashion [meaning, in this case, staff and resources being shared across different assembly and construction tasks], so for each new model that's coming through, I have a manager who looks after all the quality elements of that in the matrix fashion, and any new project will have that. So, we have someone with a complete overview of what's going on, on that particular model, from concept right through to the car going into the field.

JT: Phew! How are the responsibilities divided up?

ANDY PLEAVIN INTERVIEW *continued*

AP: For each project we have one vehicle line quality manager, and in the engineering section of that there may be twenty quality engineers working on it, and ten supply quality engineers, and they will report to their boss. The vehicle line quality manager will ensure that they're deployed in the right places and they're doing the right thing for the project, prioritizing supplies.

JT: I don't remember there being this degree of focus and emphasis on monitoring production and manufacture.

AP: No, there wasn't. It was fire-fighting. It was what we could afford to do. We've always been very good at looking after our customers, making sure we've got feedback from the customers and trying to act on it. At the moment, we 'build' cars while the higher-volume firms 'assemble' cars, but we're now making that transition – not on the Evija, which will be hand-built, but on the next model, where we will become far more of an assembler and less of a builder.

JT: Yes, I can see that there's more room for slight differences in tolerances in build methodology.

AP: The more automation you have, the more repeat ability that gives you. Toyota build a car in nineteen hours where we will take days. The Chapman thing about using other people's parts underneath is still a sensible thing to do: if you use a high-volume switch, maybe with a different cover on it, at least you know it's been through ten million cycles. If we start with the Series 1 Elise, Tony Shute would always quote how much it cost to put the Elise in production, and I used to say, 'Yes, it cost us twice that to actually make it suitable for customers.' It was a humorous thing, of course, and over the years we've turned it into about as bulletproof a product as you can get.

We've progressively engineered the cars to make them more robust. There's an argument that says that we may have increased the mass of it slightly, and there's no doubt that some of the more fragile elements of the car have been engineered and developed out of it, but that's all to the good. Interestingly, if we go back to the wind-up windows scenario, when we put a motor system in instead, everyone was dead against it – oh it's not a Lotus, you can't have electric windows, you'll increase the mass – but they were wrong: we fitted electric motors and it decreased the mass of the window mechanism by about 15 per cent, which was because motors got lighter and, of course, the hand-winding mechanism was somebody else's.

JT: So, the cars are better made now than when the Elise first came out?

Final check-over for Type 111S Elise S2s before leaving the production line.
WILLIAM TAYLOR

Elise chassis go down the assembly line; brake discs, calipers, hubs and suspension are fitted, along with wiring loom and fluid pipes.
WILLIAM TAYLOR

With clamshells fitted and drivelines installed, Series 2 Elises proceed through the assembly process.
WILLIAM TAYLOR

AP: There's a lot that we've done, and that's the difference of where we are with the Elise now. The warranty figures, and the incidence of claims is very low, and so it should be, as we've been building the cars for a lot of years. As a quality group, we commissioned a customer survey a few years ago, before Geely, and we sent all our customers in Europe a simple questionnaire that looked at the quality of the product, any issues they'd had and their dealer relationships. The return rate was about 35–40 per cent, and the figures were really good. All the models scored well, and the Elise scored the highest.

I drive an Evora every day, and it's a lot more complex car, whereas the Elise is relatively simple; it's a very analogue product, but very robust for a lightweight product. Most people buy it because they know what they're buying. I don't think there is much else that gives more smiles per mile, and the satisfaction level is high. But we have to continually improve it, and now, the product that started off as the very lightweight Chapman-esque car, doesn't have many issues and there isn't a great deal more to hone anymore. It's unusual to have an Elise with a problem, and if there is something it's very easily rectified. I use a Series 2 Elise, and the later ones are very cheap to run. Every bit of feedback gets reviewed at our weekly quality meeting, any issues they've had in plant together with any issues from customers or from warranty, and it's dealt with by supply quality or the engineering team. If the manufacturing guys need to change the process, a lot of that is about the philosophy of continuous improvement, and that's one thing we push for here.

JT: To what extent are you conscious of the marque's heritage when you're refining something – say something that stands for the marque's reputation, going back to the World Championship?

AP: So, over the years, we've got those really good bits, and then we've got the bad bits – things falling off and fragility, and that's what we've tried to eliminate. That's been one of my main goals, to eliminate the fragility without losing the core DNA of all the products, but particularly on the Lotus Elise, because those things really came when Chapman was here, so I definitely get the ethos.

JT: You go back to the 1970s, do you?

AP: I go back to 1977. I'm the third-longest serving employee here these days – not the oldest – but yes, it's about achieving that Lotus blend and still having those driving characteristics.

JT: You were also closely involved with the GM VX220, weren't you?

AP: Yes, I become a project manager on that product. I went to Tesla for a while, and that led to the Elise, and the Series 2 Elise followed that. The VX220 was engineered by Lotus, but that project paid for a lot of things to be done on the Elise. It was a big opportunity for us; we could redesign the chassis because it had a different powertrain in the back and the transmission was a bit heavy, so the centre of gravity went a bit too far back, and then we went onto the turbo version, which probably put the centre of gravity back to the centre. We learned a lot from GM, and we were able to use the investment and use a lot of their systems and processes without any pressure, so it brought us huge benefits. The Series 2 Elise was one of the things that came out of that.

Almost complete, S2 Elise 111R and Federal versions near the end of the production process; wheels and tyres, running gear and seats are installed.
WILLIAM TAYLOR

The complete range of Elise and Exige models is on show to attract buyers in the Lotus Cars enclave at the Silverstone Classic meeting, July 2007.

JT: So it was a symbiotic relationship?

AP: Yes, absolutely, but don't forget we were Lotus people working on a GM project, what we would now call a disrupter product; it was very much a disrupter, which was there to bring changes in to help make the GM organization become a bit more agile. Although it wasn't a Lotus product, it essentially *was* because it had an awful lot of Lotus in it, and we had a free hand.

JT: Who made the panels for that?

AP: All the RTM [resin transfer moulded] panelling, including the front and rear clams, rear panel and the closures – doors, bootlid and bonnet – were made by Sotira (Les Sociétés de Transformation Industrielle de Résines Armées) at Mayenne in the middle of Brittany.

JT: And whose design was that?

AP: The design was GM's. It was a combination of an Australian guy called Niels Loeb and his boss Martin Smith who did the design, but they were using our architecture, and some things they got wrong, some things they got right: it's not the most beautiful car in the world, but it's interesting. We did all the engineering, so I'd probably use the term styling and say they did the style, where our design studio people these days are true designers; they do far more, they take everything into account. The other guy who had a great deal of influence over it was Bob Hendry, the Opel chairman. The more traditional people thought it was going to be stillborn, but it went ahead, and I'd buy one now if you could get one.

We worked on the Tesla Roadster, the 111, 2-Eleven, 3-Eleven, and we basically underpinned them with the Elise chassis. Take the Tesla Roadster: it's an Elise with an electronic system and a battery, albeit a very good one. We had the opportunity to do that for ourselves and we didn't take it, so there you go.

JT: If you have an electric or even a hybrid version, how do you keep that Lotus DNA intact?

AP: The Elise is very analogue, so if the road conditions are different, the car is different; if the temperature is different, the car is different; you feel everything, you enjoy everything, it makes you smile. Keeping that driving enjoyment, that involvement, that sensation and level of connectivity where you can still feel the car – take it close to the limits so that if the car happens to step out you can just tweak it back – through a far more digital product is going to be a real challenge.

LOTUS ELISE CUP 260

Introduced in 2017, ahead of the company's celebration of its seventieth birthday, the Elise Cup 260 was a limited-edition version that manifested Lotus's motorsport heritage. The Cup 260 benefitted from design philosophies of its Exige Cup 380 and Evora GT430 stablemates and more specifically the competition-only Elise Race 250. Referencing Team Lotus's racing successes down the decades, the Cup 260 bore a laurel wreath decal on the left buttress, and a Union Jack on both rear wing end plates, with the option of having the entire car finished in Championship Gold. Apart from the black and gold John Player Specials, Team Lotus did run the Type 69 gas turbine car hued almost entirely in gold for the 1971 Italian Grand Prix, when Emerson Fittipaldi placed eighth. It was on the cusp of the transition from Player's red, gold and white Gold Leaf livery to JPS's black and gold, and because of the possible ramifications with the Italian authorities a year on from Jochen Rindt's death, the entry was pragmatically made under World Wide Racing.

Whilst it was also the lightest version Elise Cup, the 260 generated up to 180kg (400lb) of downforce at 151mph (243km/h), said to be due to its louvred front wheelarch vents, lightweight carbon-fibre front splitter and broad, high-mounted rear wing. This represented a 44 per cent gain on the already impressive Elise Cup 250, enabling greater grip levels and higher cornering speeds. Further features fitted as standard included the sill covers, roll-hoop cover, front access panel and engine cover, which were all in carbon, and the two-piece brake discs. Developed by Lotus Motorsport, adjustable Nitron high-performance dampers now equipped an Elise for the first time, plus wider road-legal motorsport tyres, polycarbonate backlight glass, and hand-trimmed interior with bespoke detailing.

The new aero was derived from the Evora GT 430, specifically the louvred front wheelarch vents that reduced lift, and a motorsport-derived rear wing developed from the Lotus 3-Eleven. The Cup 260 was also 15kg (33lb) lighter than the Cup 250, tipping the scales at 902kg (1,989lb) unladen and 862kg (1,900lb) dry weight.

The all-alloy, charge-cooled, supercharged 1.8-litre Toyota engine had new induction components and revised calibration and delivered 250bhp, enabling a lap of the Hethel test track in 1m 32s, a full 2.5 seconds faster than the Elise Cup 250. Acceleration meant 0–60mph could be dispatched in 3.8 seconds, with a power-to-weight ratio of 290bhp per tonne. Emissions figures were 175g/km CO_2.

The Cup 260's suspension consisted of double wishbones with an adjustable front anti-roll bar, Nitron coaxial coil springs and, for the first time on an Elise, adjustable Nitron

In 2016, the Elise Cup 260 cost around £60k. The 1.8-litre supercharged Toyota engine produced 250bhp, and the spec was improved by two-piece brake discs and two-way adjustable Nitron dampers and a T45 steel roll-over bar.
WILLIAM TAYLOR

The 2016 Elise Cup 260's aerodynamics provided 180kg (400lb) of downforce at 151mph (243km/h), generated by the large rear wing with its angled end plates and the elaborate rear diffuser.

WILLIAM TAYLOR

high-performance dampers. With twenty-four settings for rebound and compression, the dampers allowed owners to dial in the car's set-up precisely to their preference. The Elise Cup 260 was fitted with ultra-lightweight forged alloy wheels – 16in at the front and 17in at the rear – shod with Yokohama Advan Neova AD08R tyres, 205/45 R16 front and 235/40 R17 rear, measuring 10mm wider both front and rear than the tyres fitted to the Elise Cup 250. Braking was by AP Racing's twin-piston front calipers and Brembo at the rear, allied to the lightweight two-piece brake discs.

The Elise Cup 260's cockpit exemplified the car's hand-built character, displaying the manual gearbox's open-gate mechanism, which is technically and aesthetically arresting. Developed in house, it also enables quicker shifting. The Lotus carbon race seats were trimmed in black Alcantara with contrasting red or yellow stitching, echoed in the door panels and face-level vents. Bodywork-keyed colour inserts for the seats, transmission console, HVAC surround and window switches were complemented by the cabin's exposed aluminium and carbon-fibre elements, including carbon-fibre instrument binnacle cover. Interior options also included an Alcantara-trimmed steering wheel and sill covers, leather or tartan trim packs for seats or door panels and an in-car entertainment system including iPod connectivity and Bluetooth.

The Elise Cup 260 cockpit is kitted out with Alcantara-clad carbon-fibre bucket seats and door panels, highlighted with matching body-colour stitching, and the gearshift mechanism is exposed.

WILLIAM TAYLOR

Lotus Exige Sport 410 2018–20

Layout and Chassis

Lotus-designed anodized, lightweight aluminium, extruded, epoxy-bonded and riveted high-stiffness chassis and lightweight steel rear subframe. Lightweight front clam including drag-reducing air curtain and carbon-fibre splitter; carbon-fibre front access panel. Lightweight carbon-fibre tailgate with aerodynamically optimized rear wing in carbon fibre. Lightweight carbon-fibre side pods. Lightweight aluminium rear diffuser, polycarbonate backlight. Hard-top or soft-top

Engine

Type	Toyota 2GR-FE 3.5-litre V6, 24-valve, with Edelbrock supercharger and charge-cooler; mid-engined
Block material	Aluminium
Head material	Aluminium
Cylinders	V6
Cooling	Water
Bore and stroke	94mm × 83mm
Capacity	3456cc
Valves	DOHC, 24 valves, VVTL-i (variable valve timing and lift with intelligent) system, hydraulic tappets, 4 valves per cylinder
Fuelling	Multipoint sequential fuel injection, electronic ignition
Engine management	Lotus T4 engine control unit
Max. power	410bhp (416Ps) at 7,800rpm
Max. torque	310lb ft (420Nm) at 6,800rpm
Emission control	Three-way catalytic converters. Full on-board diagnostics (OBD)

Transmission

Gearbox	Toyota C64 6-speed manual transmission with gearbox cooler, coupled to Lotus's precision shift aluminium mechanism
Clutch	Lightweight, single-mass, low-inertia fly wheel and 240mm diameter clutch
Ratios:	1st 3.538
	2nd 1.913
	3rd 1.407
	4th 1.091
	5th 0.969
	6th 0.861
	Reverse 3.831
Final drive	3.238

Suspension and Steering

Front and rear	Unequal-length, lightweight steel double wishbones (front), unequal-length, lightweight forged aluminium, double wishbones (rear), adjustable Eibach tubular front and rear anti-roll bars. Lotus-tuned, Nitron three-way dampers, adjustable for rebound (24 click adjustment settings), low-speed compression (24 click adjustment settings) and high-speed compression (16 click adjustment settings) and Nitron springs. Driver-selectable ESP modes – Drive/Sport/Race/Off. Tyre pressure monitoring system
Steering	Rigidly mounted rack and pinion; 2.8 turns lock to lock
Wheels	Lotus-designed, ultra-lightweight, 10-spoke fully machined forged aluminium wheels, 17in front and 18in rear in silver or black
Tyres	Front: Michelin Pilot Sport Cup 2, 215/45 ZR17
	Rear: Michelin Pilot Sport Cup 2, 285/30 ZR18

Brakes

Type	Servo assisted, race-derived, lightweight two-piece J-hook ventilated brake discs and AP Racing four-piston calipers
Size	332mm × 32mm (front), 332mm × 26mm (rear)

Dimensions

Track	1,457mm (57.4in) front, 1,507mm (59.3in) rear
Wheelbase	2,300mm (90.6in)
Overall length	3,797mm (149.5in)
Overall width	1,727mm (68in) excluding door mirrors
Overall height	1,159mm (45.6in)
Dry weight	875kg (1,929lb)
Kerb weight	916kg (2,019lb) including full tank of fuel

Performance

Max. speed	147mph (237.6km/h)
0–100km/h (62mph)	4.9sec
0–100mph (160km/h)	13.2sec
Fuel consumption	Urban 23.3mpg (12.1ltr/100km)
	Extra urban 41.5mpg (6.8ltr/100km)
	Combined 32.1mpg (8.8ltr/100km)

THE LOTUS EXIGE TYPES 49 AND 79

A number of top-line manufacturers of sports cars, including Porsche, BMW and Mercedes-Benz, have in-house departments that specialize in building small runs of certain models, endowing them with enhanced performance and upgraded interiors and perhaps cosmetics too. In Lotus's case, it has Lotus Exclusive, which does just that, and its delicate touch can be applied to all Lotus cars, from the entry-level Elise to the range-topping Evora, implementing a full range of performance options.

Typical of their endeavours were the Exige Type 49 and Type 79 Celebration models intended to mark Lotus's fortieth, fiftieth and seventieth anniversaries at the Goodwood Festival of Speed in 2018. Hand-built by Lotus Exclusive, the Exige Type 49 marked the fifty years since Graham Hill clinched both the Drivers' and Constructors' F1 World Championships in the Gold Leaf Team Lotus Type 49, while the Exige Type 79 celebrated the forty years since Mario Andretti won the Drivers' World Title and Team Lotus the F1 Constructors' Championship with the John Player Special Types 78 and 79 in that melodramatic 1978 season. Obviously, anniversaries move on, dates come and go, and those specific anniversaries have been and gone. However, there's nothing wrong with maintaining an iconic livery, and both those striking colour schemes reference directly some of the team's finest hours in the era of big-time commercial sponsorship. Folk wishing to celebrate the pre-sponsorship era can go to the green-with-yellow-stripes of the 2003 Elise S2 Type 25.

As befits race-refs, they were quick. Both Gold Leaf and JPS anniversary models were based on the wildest-ever incarnation of the Exige: the Cup 430, and these Types 49 and 79 set the fastest lap time for a road car around the Hethel test track, covering the 2.2 miles (3.5km) in 1m 24.8sec. Employing a supercharger and charge-cooler designed specifically for their potent engines, both Exige Type 49 and 79 developed 430bhp at 7,000rpm and 325lb ft (440Nm) of torque from 4,000rpm. Acceleration? 0–60mph was reached in just 3.2sec (0–100 km/h in 3.3sec), cracking on to a top speed of 180mph (290km/h). As the eponymous Types 49 and 79 did, back in their day, encapsulating the very latest state-of-the-art technical and aerodynamic methodology, the two Exige special editions brought to bear the latest current technologies and advanced materials, weighing in at 1,056kg (2,328lb) in their lightest configuration, based on carbon-composite body panels, endowing them with a monstrous power-to-weight ratio of 407bhp per tonne. The high-gloss, visible-weave components included the front splitter, front clam air blades, unique bargeboards, roof panel, rear tailgate, straight-cut wing and diffuser surround.

Pictured outside Classic Team Lotus's former premises, where back in the 1970s, Team Lotus also operated, the Exige Cup 430 Type 49 commemorates the Lotus Type 49 that won the F1 World Championship in 1968 in the hands of Graham Hill and, in 1970, Jochen Rindt.
WILLIAM TAYLOR

Resplendent in Team Lotus's Type 25 colour scheme from the mid-1960s, this Sport Exige 240R is testing at Snetterton in 2019. The model was developed by Lotus Sport in 2004.

STEPHANIE EWEN

In 1978, John Player Team Lotus's Type 79 F1 car followed in the tyre tracks of the preceding Types 77 and 78, which pioneered the aerodynamic phenomenon known as ground effect, by trapping air underneath the car's side pods and sucking it to the track surface – the more effective, the faster it went. The Exige Cup 430 Type 79 of 2018 celebrates its forebear's trouncing of the entire F1 circus in 1978, when driven by Mario Andretti and Ronnie Peterson.

WILLIAM TAYLOR

The car's aerodynamics deployed 220kg (485lb) of downforce by managing airflow underneath and over the upper body surfaces. Playing a contributory role, air-curtain elements and louvres in the front clam panel regulated turbulence and drag, and reduced pressure within the front wheelarches. The cutout sections behind the rear wheels also reduced wheelarch pressure, while the high-mounted straight-cut rear wing and rear diffuser optimized traction and stability at high speeds.

As for running gear, both cars ran Nitron three-way adjustable dampers – with options for tuning rebound as well as low-speed and high-speed compression – and Eibach springs and adjustable front and rear anti-roll bars as standard kit. Tyres were Michelin Pilot Sport Cup 2, 215/45 ZR17 front and 285/30 ZR18 rear, fitted on lightweight machine-forged aluminium wheels. Braking was by forged four-piston AP Racing calipers and race-derived, two-piece J-hook brake discs.

The Exige Types 49 and 79 also reprised similarly dedicated examples of the Elise – the Type 49, which was a Series 1 heritage edition offered in 1999, and the Series 2 Elise Type 72, liveried in black and gold and available in 2002. Then there was the 3.4-litre supercharged Toyota-powered Exige R-GT rally car of 2012, which also referenced the black and gold JPS theme. There's no doubt that iconic race-derived liveries can be repeatedly and justifiably applied to Lotus models – several Evoras have also been similarly hued – and we shall see more Gold Leaf and JPS special editions in the future.

Lotus's first take on the Gold Leaf Type 49 theme was the Elise Type 49, introduced in October 1999, with 134 cars thus liveried built over two years. Power unit was the 1796cc Rover K-series, producing 143bhp.
WIM TE RIET

For a brief period, between 2010 and 2012, Lotus Cars produced some ambitious new designs that might have eclipsed the Elise, Exige and Evora. One project that came to fruition was the Exige R-GT, a one-off 309bhp rally car, intended to celebrate the Talbot-Sunbeam Lotus victory in the 1981 World Rally Championship for Henri Toivonen and Guy Frequelin. After a promising start in the hands of Bernardo Sousa and Corrado Mancini, however, the Exige R-GT crashed on stage 2 of the 2012 Portuguese Rali Vinho do Madeira.
WILLIAM TAYLOR

EXIGE SPORT 410: 20th ANNIVERSARY SPECIAL

In June 2020, Lotus introduced a special edition 20th Anniversary model to celebrate two decades of Exige production. Essentially a cosmetic exercise, the Sport 410 is available in a range of striking hues, with exterior features commemorating the Exige Series I from 2000, including body-coloured roof, side air intake pods and rear wing, and black shark-fin stone-chip protectors ahead of the rear wheels. Cabin upholstery offers different-coloured Alcantara trims, with seats decorated with panelled stitching, echoing that of the original car. A black '20th Anniversary' silhouette logo featuring a profile image of the Series I Exige appears on the front wings (fenders) and the rear bumper panel, along with '20' logos on the rear wing end plates.

In June 2020, Lotus released the Exige 20th Anniversary, marking the model's two decades in production.
LOTUS CARS

BARNEY HATT INTERVIEW

Barney Hatt joined the Lotus design studio in 1995, and was responsible for the styling of several important models created on the Elise platform, including the Type 123 2-Eleven, 3-Eleven, Tesla Roadster and Type 121 Europa
S. LOTUS CARS

Stalwart of the Lotus design studio since 1995, Barney Hatt played a key role in the styling of several striking models, including the 2-Eleven, 3-Eleven, Tesla Roadster and the Type 121 Europa S.

BH: I started [at Lotus in 1995] on a week's contract: Russell [Carr] phoned me up and said, 'We've got a mad panic, can you come in and do some sketches?' and that was twenty-five years ago.

JT: What did you start off working on that was so urgent at the time?

BH: The first Lotus job was doing the proposal for what became the Series 2 Elise. The Series 1 had obviously been done at that point. So I did some proposals, Steve [Crijns] did some proposals, and Steve's was the one that was eventually chosen.

JT: You make it sound competitive.

BH: Yep, I came second in a competition of two! But then Steve and I worked closely for many years, and I guess we have similar interests, but we got on pretty well.

JT: That kind of smacks of how Lotus was, probably in the 1960s!

Styled by Barney Hatt, the Type 121 Europa SE was the enhanced evolution of the Europa S, with larger rear wheels and brakes, released in 2008 with just forty-seven units built. The power unit was the transverse-mounted turbocharged 4-cylinder GM Ecotec Z20LER 2.0-litre unit, using Lotus's own engine management system rather than Bosch and producing 225bhp. A one-off Diamond Anniversary Europa was crafted to celebrate the firm's sixtieth anniversary, finished in black, trimmed with diamond quilted leather and encrusted with £110k worth of diamonds.
WILLIAM TAYLOR

BH: I daresay it was! We quite often have that debate internally, about which is the best way to design something, because when you've got that urgency, that 'We need a sketch by tomorrow,' sometimes that instinctive trigger response is the purest; adrenaline is pumping, and it's like, 'What do I need to do,' and it elicits something a bit special. Obviously, the counter argument to that is you should think about it calmly and evolve it, not use the first thing that comes into your head. I suppose it depends on the outcome as to which way you think works best. But, yes, a lot of those projects were pretty instantaneous. I can't remember exactly how the Europa came about, but I'm pretty sure it would have been, 'We need something quick,' and it evolved from there.

JT: So you had to make it significantly different to the S2 Elise externally, as well as the way you dealt with the cabin?

BH: Yes. Obviously, being a fixed hard-top, effectively, we were keen to visually differentiate it from the open-top cars, so we deliberately made it more coupé-like, rather than a roadster or convertible. And the thinking was to move it upmarket, to be a bit more premium, and possibly a little bit less austere or motor sport-based. There's a lot of motor sport and club racer flavour about the Elise, and we deliberately try to steer away from that, because the Exige takes care of all that imagery, and that's where, with hindsight, some of those elements didn't come across quite as well as they might have done. I suppose the Europa is just one of the ones that didn't quite gel.

JT: How about the powertrain? Did you feel that it was saddled with the General Motors 2.0-litre turbo engine, and would you have preferred to have got a Toyota motor in there?

BH: No, I don't think so, because there was quite a lot of good press around the GM engine, certainly in turbo form in the VX220, and that's become a desirable car, hasn't it?

JT: Speaking of which, let's move onto the VX220. Did you design that as well?

BH: No, it was designed by a chap called Niels Loeb, who was a GM designer. He designed it under the direction of Martin Smith, who was GM design director but got lured pretty quickly to Ford after that. They did the sketches and a scale model, but the full-size design was actually done on site here at Hethel. Niels would fly in on a Monday morning and stay for the week, and when he wasn't around and the modellers needed a line or something, I would oblige, but I didn't design that car. Time-wise, it would have been before 2000, because it was in the old studio, over on what is now the production line, so it would have been around 1998–9.

JT: But did you feel that you were refining it?

BH: No, I don't think there was any conscious connection between the two cars. I always felt that the VX220 was more closely related to the Elise than the Europa, really. Maybe not visually, but in character and aspiration. I would say that the two are close in terms of their driving characteristics. It was very much a conscious decision from Opel to separate the two models – Elise and VX220 – so we had our more sculptured language, and they went for their form of language, which was much more Teutonic at that time. Roll on twenty years, and they're much more organic now. They'll probably be going back to faceted sheer design again soon (like the Lamborghini Diamante concept); all these things go round and around.

JT: Tell me some of the other cars you've worked on.

Variation on a theme: Lotus Engineering was commissioned to fine-tune and set up a number of General Motors products over the years and, in 1998, GM enlisted Lotus to create the VX220 Roadster, based on the Elise Series 2 chassis and running gear.

Styled by GM's Niels Loeb, the VX220 was created at Hethel and in production between 2000 and 2005. It was available with 2.0-litre turbocharged engine or 2.2-litre normally aspirated engine, allied to a Getrag F23 five-speed gearbox.
SCOTT MATHESON

The cockpit of the GM VX220 is, unsurprisingly, very similar to that of the Elise rather than the more sumptuous Europa, despite being closer stylistically to the Type 121. The treatment of the central tunnel and sill covers are distinctive features on the Vauxhall model.
SCOTT MATHESON

BH: More recently, the 3-Eleven, which came out in 2015, and the Exige 360 Cup, which appeared in 2016. Going back in time, the Sport Exige GT3 concept from 2006, which never formally made it as a production car, although a handful of people raced it (five units built), and some of the bodywork evolved into Lotus Motorsport and the one-off GT2 Exige 300 RR. That had a V6 supercharged engine and raced in Malaysia when we were owned by Proton, and it was done through our motor sports division, which had Martin Donnelly giving it its first shakedown here on the track at Hethel. Even though it was a one-off, it was still a really enjoyable project in the sense that you start with the Exige, which was already a nice-looking car, and then you take a hacksaw to it and you add 100mm (2.5in) to the wheelbase and 100mm on each side and it turns into a monster.

JT: Anything less exotic?

BH: Yes, I was responsible for the Federal Elise interior. Before we went to the States with the Elise, the S2 already had a new interior, relative to the S1, but it didn't have a passenger airbag at that point.

The Exige GT3 was based on the 2006/2007 Exige GT3 that ran in the British Manufacturers' GT Championship, with rounds at Donington Park, Oulton Park, Snetterton, Silverstone, Brands Hatch, Rockingham, Mondello Park in Ireland, and Pau and Magny-Cours in France. It was raced successfully in GT3 by Gavan Kershaw, Barrie Whight, Alistair Mackinnon, George Mackintosh and Sam Blogg.
WILLIAM TAYLOR

That was the crucial thing, and an awful lot of time and brain power went into designing, producing and installing something that no one will ever see! We had to work out how to make the whole IP [instrument panel] symmetrical, so that you can have left- and right-hand-drive cockpits without needing any new tooling. Obviously, cost was often at the forefront of our minds, so the binnacle area and the switchgear can be swapped from one side to the other. And that paved the way for us getting the Elise into the States in 2004.

JT: What about the bare-bones entry-level Elise from 2011?

BH: Yes, the Club Racer was eventually a spin off from that. It was visually stripped out, and it had the 1.6 Toyota engine and lower horsepower – really minimal, a nice car. When we were working on that in the studio, we were playing around with the seats, and one night there was a car in the workshop – a really ratty old car that we had this seat in, and I was trying to work out whether it was any good or not, and I thought I'll just go for a quick spin on the road in this thing. As soon as you got to a corner there were washers and nuts and bolts flying around the inside, and the screen was covered in grease, but the car itself – even in that kind of state – produced

Despite the exposed aluminium of the chassis, the cockpit of the 2014 Exige S 'Lotus F1 Team' limited edition offers a modicum of civilization – for a track-oriented car – including 'Premium Pack' gold stitched upholstery. The plaque identifies it as #05 out of #81 cars, celebrating Innes Ireland's victory for Team Lotus in the Type 21/Climax at Watkins Glen in 1961.
WILLIAM TAYLOR

STYLING THE TESLA ROADSTER

The Tesla came out in 2008, and I was working on that before the 2-Eleven. It was designed here [at Hethel], and it was obviously a fairly sizeable project for Lotus, and certainly for me personally. It was an interesting one to work on, because the thing that struck me at the time was the kind of mindset these real entrepreneurial guys from California had. It was the cultural thing too – everything was an opportunity. They loved talking a lot about disruptive technology, and they loved nothing more than finding an angle and thinking, yes, we know we can upset the establishment; we can do things differently, we're more intellectually agile – and they were in many cases. So it was a nice mixture. Tesla's co-founder, Martin Eberhard, especially was passionate and enthusiastic, so you couldn't help talking to him, just drawing on his vision. He was a very down-to-earth guy as well, really charming and self-effacing, good fun to work with.

He and Marc Tarpenning, the other co-founder along with Elon Musk, were already talking to Lotus, because they had the technology, and they had the confidence in their ability to deliver the technology in terms of the batteries and motor, but they didn't necessarily want to engineer a whole new car. So, they picked up on the Elise as being a good potential donor chassis, and there were a lot of discussions with Malcolm Powell, who was project programme leader for the Series 2 Elise. Martin set out various design criteria, drawn up by Bill Moggridge from IDEO, matrices between aggressive and friendly, or classic and futuristic, to help fine-tune what they were trying to get to. He came over a few times, and we did some sketches, and they then got all the sketches together at Martin's home and invited all their people around, and this was the design that was chosen. And then we developed a clay model in the studio here, first a scale model and then a full-size model, and they came over periodically to check out how it was going.

There's a hint of Ferrari 250LM, especially in the flying buttresses going from the roof to the tail. And there was a reference to the Pontiac Firebird from the 1960s that gave the car a kind of pointed nose. Cut and flow, that was their terminology, which Bill Moggridge came up with, and gave us something to latch onto. What I had in mind was something shark-like, and you can see the gills idea in the front three-quarters. To look at, they're rather beautiful – muscular, elegant, but kind of dangerous as well, so giving a good mixture of messages. Many people have been inspired by the same things.

So that was a fun one to work on, and I'd be pushing it through with input from the Tesla people. That went from first sketches and clay models right through to production. That's the case on most projects, that we're involved in every part of it. Being part of a small team, it's almost inevitable really.

Elon Musk launched his own Tesla Roadster into space in February 2018, and that was the ultimate experience for one of my designs! Elon sent his own personal cherry-red Roadster into an Earth/Mars orbit, primarily to promote the payload capability of his Falcon rocket. This was the first Tesla production car, and they launched it via a Falcon heavy rocket from the Cape Canaveral Space Center in Florida. They predicted it would stay orbiting the sun for a billion years, travelling at something like 300,000mph (500,000km/h).

It's a juxtaposition of completely opposite power sources: sending the ultimate eco automobile into space using the most ginormously powerful space rocket. It's quite surreal and worth a look on YouTube. The space-suited 'driver' at the wheel was known as Star Man, and there's a great image of the car floating around in space with the earth moving behind it. I remember us sticking tin foil on the clay model to check the highlights on the side of the car in the studio, and now you're witnessing exactly the same flow of light over a surface, but it's the earth reflected in a car – which is in space. So, to go from a sketch, a model, maybe seeing one on the road around here – which is always satisfying in itself – to actually seeing your car in space is pretty fantastic.

It won't return to earth, like the space shuttle; it's still up there. It will never come back; the car being in space wasn't anything to do with me or Lotus, but it's flattering that he elected this to be the payload – or maybe he just didn't want to see it again!

The 3-Eleven 430 is Lotus's lightest roofless car, powered by its most ferocious engine, the 430bhp supercharged V6 from the Exige Cup 430. In 2015, it was the fastest car around the Hethel test circuit, lapping in 1min 24sec, 0.8sec ahead of the Exige. The 3-Eleven does 0–60mph in 3.1sec and hits a 180mph (290km/h) top speed.
WILLIAM TAYLOR

one of those moments where driving just gels into quite a magical thing, and I thought, 'This is actually rather nice to drive!' So I went back, cleaned the windscreen, took all the crap out of it and went out again; it was a late summer evening, nice and warm, and driving that quite modest car was so pleasant that it sticks in my mind as one of those moments where it all clicks, the whole Elise experience.

JT: But you know, for it to be a user-friendly road car, it's got to have all the cabin installed.

BH: Exactly, and that's a puzzle we increasingly have to solve. People like the idea of a stripped-out race car for the road, but the reality of buying that car is often different. So we have to find ways to include sat-nav and cup holders and all of that stuff without making it look then like a mainstream car and losing the raw essence.

JT: OK, then, take me back to some of the other cars.

BH: Well, for instance, there's the Exige Cup 260, which is obviously the 260hp version of the Exige, where it was a case of trying to differentiate it visually from the current car. It had various carbon elements, including the roof and the engine cover. In fact, one thing we did – which was a nightmare to do – was where the stripes went down the roof, the carbon element was exposed so you could see the structure of the car emerging through the paint; this was quite nice, but obviously to line up the carbon weave and the stripe and getting it going across all the panels was extremely tricky – and I'm not in the production line.

JT: So that was the main stylistic difference?

BH: Yes, everything else about the bodywork was very similar. We just liked the idea of doing a matt and gloss combination. It looked amazing when we did that on the 2-Eleven GT4 as well. There were a few done that were matt black with gloss, and they looked really good. That would have been around 2007–8.

JT: Turning the 2-Eleven into the 3-Eleven, what did the brief involve?

BH: The 3-Eleven was a good, fun project. The brief for that was in the Jean-Marc [Gales] era, and he primarily wanted to push what we had to the maximum to get maximum exposure, but on a very tight budget. That was all too familiar territory for us, though obviously the 2-Eleven had been quite successful. Its designer was John Statham, who's also been here for quite a long time, and it was really to take that a step further, because that was a 4-cylinder engine. But we were now in the era of the Exige and the V6, so that was again run with a very small group of people, headed up by Gavan Kershaw, Louis Kerr – who was senior motorsport engineer, because at that point in time it was the motorsports division – plus a few other characters. The idea was to see how far can we push the envelope, so it was quite aero-led.

They wanted sizeable downforce, but it was important that the car was visually attractive as well, and I guess that is a design ethos, a kind of mantra within the studio: that combination of form and function is always at the forefront of our minds. Ultimately, cars have to be beautiful, but combine that with functionality in a very efficient way. We're talking 2017 by now, and part of the face of the car has been adopted in varying degrees on the current line-up, so it's become a familiar aspect of their construction – you see it in the shape of the outer intake, like when we did the facelift on the Elise and the GT430 Evora. It's the same kind of language, but taken to a new level with these aero features.

JT: You've got the air blade idea on the leading ends of the front wings (fenders); can you explain the purpose of those?

BH: Their function is to blast a jet of air out of the side of the bumper to stop the air getting drawn into the wheelarches, so it creates an air curtain, pushing it outside the car. Basically, the air that's coming around the front of the car normally gets ingested into the wheelarch, and then loads of turbulence comes out from behind the actual wheel; to counteract that, you have this little draught of high-speed air created by the air blades, which diverts the air around the wheel and then reconnects on the body side, so you reduce the drag. Again, it's this thing of combining form and function: it's nice when you find a technical solution that leads you in a direction which is visually intriguing and sculptural, captivating in some way. We often joke with our chief aerodynamicist, Richard Hill, who's been heavily involved in all of our cars over the years, about his 'ugly stick', which he keeps in a wooden box. He brings it out occasionally to prod our cars, when we've spent all our time designing something we think is beautiful and it's totally hopeless aerodynamically. We then have to have a rethink.

Air flow around the front of the Exige Sport 360 is controlled by air blades that direct the airstream around the outside of the wheelarch instead of inside.
WILLIAM TAYLOR

Stylist Steve Crijns makes a point in the Lotus design studio. Having joined Lotus in 1994, he was responsible for styling the Series 2 Elise, with input into the 2-Eleven and Evora, and since 2014 has been senior design manager at McLaren Cars.
WILLIAM TAYLOR

JT: Which you obviously did, quite fundamentally, with the Series 2. Tell me how that transition came about. The most obvious design language in the Series 1 Elise is the rotund Ferrari 330 P4 from 1966–7 – starring in the Le Mans 66 movie, Ford versus Ferrari.

BH: You probably know when Julian [Thomson] designed that car he had the P3/4 and the 286 Dino very much in mind. He owns a Dino, so I'm sure that was very much a deliberate thing. Steve Crijns designed the Series 2 iteration, which went for sharper edges than the curvaceous S1. That was done to inject a bit more modernity into that S1 shape. And it is inherently a classic shape because it's still fundamentally highlighting the haunches of the car and that feeling of muscularity: a wheel at each corner, with the cabin very much planted in between the wheel housing: a classic 1960s race car layout, really. So we still have the same fundamental recipe but with the addition of a few crisp lines in among the softer forms.

Steve was nervous because the S1 had already gained a cult following, but over time I think he was vindicated. Relatively speaking, the Series 2 has lasted three times as long as the Series 1, although there have been minor updates through its lifetime. The first one was because the original S2 had the separate indicators. It had the main headlight and then another lamp that was the indicator, but then a few years later we combined everything in one unit.

JT: And presumably now everything is LED?

BH: The indicator and the daytime running lamp are LED, but the main units aren't. That fundamental design has stood the test of time very well. I suppose when something is inherently right, it has that timeless quality, and the Elise has always had that.

JT: How often do you change wheel designs? Do you draw a wheel and think, 'This will look good on that model,' and then have it made up?

BH: We've done countless wheels over the years: I can't remember how many I've done! But, definitely, getting a wheel to match the shape of a car is not always a given. In fact, you often go through twenty designs and subtle permutations to find one that looks like it actually belongs on the car. Sometimes what's chosen is a compromise. Typically, all our wheels are as light as they can be, but a lot of road wheels that you see on cars in general are not the optimum lightweight solution, but are designed for a certain look. We are very much focused on making a wheel as light as possible in the quest for minimum unsprung weight and all that, and that does drive the design and perhaps limits it in some respects. For a five-bolt pattern, having five, ten or fifteen spokes is generally a good place to start, because then, in multiples of five, the stresses are equal around the number of bolts, and that helps keep it lighter. We have a combination of cast and forged alloy wheels; obviously forged wheels are more expensive, but you can make them stronger and lighter. The properties of the forging process make the metal stronger. A ten-spoke wheel is generally considered to be the most weight-efficient solution, certainly with a five-bolt pattern.

By 2004 and the launch of the Series 2 Exige, Lotus wheel design had evolved to include this five-spoke version with each spoke divided into two prongs where they join the rim.
WILLIAM TAYLOR

With five spokes, each spoke has to be that bit thicker and heavier to resolve all the forces, so ten spokes is generally the lightest solution.

JT: And there's no role for split rims and multi-piece wheels?

BH: No, unless you're employing a different technology. There are a few carbon wheels out there, which have a carbon rim and an aluminium or magnesium centre, or vice versa; they can be used for what is most applicable for that technical solution, which may drive you to a mix of materials, but it's not something that we've employed. The most recent wheels we've done for the Elise and the Evora are probably the lightest wheels we've ever done. This is actually becoming increasingly difficult because our cars are generally getting more downforce, so you have to factor that in as well. There's more stress going through the wheel, because at high speed you've got more downforce working on the whole car, and it's those stresses that ultimately dictate how thin the spokes can be.

JT: How will you know when a vehicle has reached its limit? Is it down to trial and error?

BH: Working with whichever wheel supplier it is – in recent times it's been Rimstock, but any wheel supplier will do the same thing – they run the wheel for computer stress analysis. There's a margin of safety built in, and they have a figure in mind for maximum acceptable stress. Usually, the first time we submit a design it fails hopelessly because we've made the spokes far too thin. Then we incrementally increase the spoke section until we just pass the test – when the analysis comes back we want to see +1 per cent, because that means you have passed the test.

JT: This is real Colin Chapman territory!

BH: Absolutely! We don't want any superfluous material. Also, spokes that have sudden changes of angle or direction, or very sharp features, will introduce more stress. There are certain things which, by design, you need to avoid.

The Elise Sport and Sprint models were available with normally aspirated 1.6-litre Toyota engine or supercharged 1.8, which gained the 220 suffix on account of its 217bhp. The Sport 220 was voted *Evo* magazine's Sports Car of the Year in 2017.
WILLIAM TAYLOR

Lotus 3-Eleven 430 2018–20

Layout and Chassis

Lotus-designed anodized, lightweight aluminium, extruded, epoxy bonded and riveted high-stiffness chassis. Lightweight carbon-composite roadster body, sculpted part-exposed carbon side panels and carbon interior panels and flat floor. MSA-approved roll-cage as standard for national use. Optimized straight-cut rear wing with profiled end plates, long front splitter, lip spoiler and rear diffuser. Carbon-fibre driver's seat with 4-point harness.

Engine

Type	Toyota 2GR-FE 3.5-litre V6, with Edelbrock supercharger and charge-cooler; mid-engined; Motorsport baffled sump
Block material	Aluminium
Head material	Aluminium
Cylinders	V6
Cooling	Water
Bore and stroke	94mm × 83mm
Capacity	3456cc
Valves	DOHC, 24 valves, VVTL-i (variable valve timing and lift with intelligent system), hydraulic tappets, 4 valves per cylinder
Fuelling	Multipoint sequential fuel injection, electronic ignition
Fuel capacity	48 litres (10.6gal)
Engine management	Lotus engine control unit
Max. power	430bhp (436Ps) at 7,000rpm
Max. torque	325lb ft (440Nm) at 4,500rpm
Power-to-weight ratio	467bhp per tonne
Aerodynamic downforce	265kg at max. speed (100kg front, 165kg rear)

Transmission

Gearbox	Toyota C646-speed manual transmission, with gearbox cooler, coupled to Lotus's precision shift aluminium mechanism. Adjustable traction control, Torsen limited-slip differential
Clutch	Lightweight, single-mass, low inertia flywheel and 240mm diameter clutch
Ratios	1st 3.538 2nd 1.913 3rd 1.407 4th 1.091 5th 0.969 6th 0.861 Reverse 3.831
Final drive	3.238

Suspension and Steering

Front and rear	Unequal-length, fully independent double wishbones with Eibach tubular front and rear anti-roll bars, Öhlins DFV one-way adjustable coil-over dampers
Steering	Rigidly mounted rack and pinion; 2.8 turns lock to lock
Wheels	Lotus designed, ultra-lightweight, 10-spoke fully machined, forged aluminium wheels, 18in front and 19in rear in satin black finish
Tyres	Front: Michelin Pilot Sport Cup 2, 225/40 R18 Rear: Michelin Pilot Sport Cup 2, 275/30 R19

Brakes

Type	Lotus-tuned ABS, servo-assisted, race-derived, lightweight two-piece J-hook ventilated brake discs and AP Racing 4-piston calipers
Size	332mm × 32 mm front, 332mm × 26mm rear

Dimensions

Track	1,457mm (57.4in) front, 1,507mm (59.3in) rear
Wheelbase	2,300mm (90.5in)
Overall length	3,797mm (149.5in)
Overall width	1,727mm (68in) excluding door mirrors
Overall height	1,159mm (45.6in)
Dry weight	875kg (1,929lb)
Kerb weight	916kg (2,019lb) including full tank of fuel

Performance

Max. speed	180mph (290km/h)
0–60mph (110km/h)	3.1sec
0–100mph (160km/h)	13.2sec
Fuel consumption	Urban 23.3mpg (12.1ltr/100km) Extra urban 41.5mpg (6.8ltr/100km) Combined 32.1mpg (8.8ltr/100km)

GREEN MACHINE: THE EXIGE 270E

The Tri-fuel Exige 270E was launched at the 2008 Geneva Show and was hailed as a quantum leap forward in alternative fuelling, hitting the headlines with its unique capability to run on petrol, ethanol or methanol. Given the green light, the 270E's performance is fantastic, taking a mere 3.8sec to reach 60mph, warping on to a shade under 160mph (257km/h) before howling 'enough'. At the time, it was the fastest Exige in the range, and the fastest road-legal bio-ethanol car ever built – coupled with the fabulous responsiveness and secure handling of that well-honed Exige chassis.

The 270E designation affirms that power output is up 50bhp over the standard car, and the fact that it runs on E-for-ethanol. That's a hybrid alcohol fuel with motor racing applications, made from fermentation of crops and mixed with petrol, resulting in a 70 per cent reduction in carbon-dioxide emissions. Ethanol is a clear, colourless liquid, the essential ingredient of all alcoholic drinks produced from any fermentable source of sugar. Additional oxygen atoms attached to the ethanol alcohol molecules make the combustion process much more effective, taking place at a higher temperature than petrol, giving an octane rating approaching 110 and so releasing more power. That's why it's so quick. Lotus Engineering re-engineered the supercharged Toyota engine to run on wheat-derived

At the time, the Tri-fuel Exige 270E was quickest in the line-up, with 270bhp available from its supercharged Toyota 1.8-litre engine, using ethanol and methanol bio-fuels. It certainly took off along the straights linking the east coast and Broadland.

JASON PARNELL

fuel. The aluminium-block Toyota four is standard, but the supercharger and intercooler have been adjusted to cope with the power hike, while the ECU is remapped to handle the new fuel. The inlet manifold's quartet of injectors is bigger, and an additional pair of injectors is installed at the supercharger inlet to augment the fuel entering the engine at higher speeds; they also help cool the air charge ahead of combustion. Leaving nothing to chance, the brakes are upgraded to AP Racing four-pot calipers containing sports brake-pads, and 310mm drilled and vented discs at the front allied to Brembo single-pot sliding calipers with 282mm diameter discs at the back.

The major obstacle to running any bio-fuel car is accessing the vital fluids. In the whole of East Anglia, it's available at five Morrison's supermarket filling stations. I took the Exige 270E for a drink at their Riverside Road site in Norwich, where E85 bio-ethanol (85 per cent ethanol, 15 per cent petrol) was 2p a litre cheaper than petrol. The next hurdle is timing your fill-ups so you're in the vicinity of a bio-fuel outlet, otherwise you have to ensure your Exige tank is virtually empty before pumping in enough regular petrol to get you to the bio-fuel station. This problem is compounded because your mpg won't be as good running on bio-ethanol, simply because it uses more energy and burns faster.

Bio-ethanol has the potential to be carbon-neutral, because all the carbon dioxide emitted during use is balanced by absorption from the atmosphere during the fuel crop's growth. In Brazil, sugar cane is the favourite crop, due to its high sugar content and fuel yield. In North America, over fifty production plants produce fuel ethanol from starch crops such as maize, while most European ethanol is produced from sugar-beet, wheat and barley. For bio-fuels to take off, the government needs to commit, and encourage the establishment of a bio-ethanol fuel station network. Sweden has some 200 outlets, and there's a sketchy network of filling stations in France and Germany. At the moment, the main sources in the UK for bio-fuel are a handful of supermarkets in Norfolk and Somerset.

The Tri-Fuel Exige 270E consumed sustainable alcohol such as synthetic methanol, reducing its CO_2 footprint.
JASON PARNELL

CHAPTER FOUR

ROAD TRIPS AND DRIVING EXPERIENCES

THE ELISE S1: FIRST DRIVE

Going back to the beginning, here are my initial impressions from behind the wheel of the Series 1, back in 1997.

The S1 Elise is fingertip-sensitive on the steering wheel, more so than almost any other car I'd driven at that point, so that only the smallest input is needed to make a change of direction, and any apex can be clipped with spot-on precision. I address the steering wheel with elbows bent and hands at ten to two, and that means a reasonably straight-legged seating position, pushing me back into the seat, with

I spent a week with one of the S1 Elise press cars in 1997; steering is fingertip-sensitive, and apexes can be clipped with absolute precision.
TOM WOOD

the right knee nestling comfortably against the side of the chassis. The driver's seat is biased towards the centreline of the car, and the passenger seat is immovably fixed further back.

I feel it in my fingers, I feel it in my toes – throttle response is instantaneous, and the car rips away from traffic lights in second and third gear. The 1.8-litre K-series performance is athletic at low speed, scintillating on bendy country roads, and more than adequate on fast A-roads. It's a gutsy engine, and quite adequate for the car in standard trim, although a rasping exhaust note might make the heart race that little bit faster. The Elise can idle along at just under 1,000rpm, and at low revs it feels like any small car. Except of course you'll

Setting out from Ketteringham Hall yard in the Series 1 Elise press car, 1997.
TOM WOOD

always feel special, even in traffic, because you're in this little gem of a sports car.

As you increase speed, it really beefs up, all the way to 100mph (160km/h). The ride is taut, yet far from uncomfortable, but the rear end does respond with a bonk if you encounter a pothole or similar abrupt depression. The suspension is quite noisy on undulating rural back roads, but there's no hint of the scuttle-shake that, even now, still bedevils some wannabe sports cars and cabriolets. The brakes are fiercely efficient and confidence-inspiring. You can be certain that the car is going to anchor up safely when approaching imminent challenges, and that encourages you to negotiate them with proper vigour.

The spartan cockpit focuses your concentration on the matter at hand. There's a purity about the bare, uncarpeted aluminium chassis defining the body of the interior, but its intimacy is reassuringly womb-like. Getting in and out requires traditional sports car contortionism. Assuming it's a right-hooker, support your body weight by clutching the side of the chair and the sill, then get your backside and left leg in first before swinging your right leg in. To manoeuvre yourself out, push yourself up using the side of the passenger seat to obtain leverage; extract your right leg, holding onto the steering wheel with your left hand while your right hand supports your weight on the sill; when your right foot is on the ground, bring your left leg over so you're sitting on the sill, and lift yourself out. It's not really the pantomime this description might suggest, but hardly a quick getaway.

Once ensconced though, the controls are well laid out and accessible, with about 75mm (3in) between the steering wheel and the gear lever – the width of outstretched thumb to little finger. The light-control stalk (this is the Series 1, remember) and two-speed wiper switches are right where you need them, and the window winder is just 150mm (6in) from the wheel. The light buttons are activated by a single push. There's an integrated electronic speedo and tachometer system by Stack with multifunction LCD display, and the dials are appropriately minimalist. The speedo is on the right, calibrated in mph and km/h, and the rev-counter on the left. There are warning lights under the speedometer, and fuel and temperature symbols are below the rev-counter. The digital petrol gauge reads 75 litres (16 gallons) when the tank is full. Air-con? I believe it does sap engine power slightly, though the compressor is relatively small so it doesn't compromise the car's light weight. So, it's a mixed blessing, and even then not that efficient in hot climate running. The milometer and trip recorder are in a little space to the left, and all are housed in the single binnacle clearly visible through the top half of the steering wheel. The radio aerial is mounted behind the rear window, and in case you have a

Lotus's former press officer Prunelia Stuart takes the controls of an Elise Series 1 press car in 1997.
TOM WOOD

stereo fitted by your dealer, Lotus supply a couple of trim sections to go either side of it on the dash panel.

To hold the S1 engine cover up, you simply prop it open with the luggage compartment cover. Luggage space is better than you might expect, and there's room for a holdall or smallish suitcase, but this is compromised if you need to accommodate the soft-top. The cant rails and cross-bars stow away neatly enough behind the seats, and if you're pushed for space, the hood could probably be tucked away there too. There's also a net behind the seats to enclose other small personal effects so they don't fly around when you're on the move.

Though I was lent two Elise S1 press cars and received on-track tuition at Hethel with Dave Minter and Alastair Stewart, my motoring experience with the S1s never got me out of my home county, Norfolk. However, during the first decade of the twenty-first century, I wrote extensively for the in-house *Lotus Club International* magazine, edited by Caroline Parker. She and I, together with Lotus's resident photographer, Jason Parnell, would identify a picturesque location, racetrack or driving route, either with an amenable Lotus dealer close by who would lend us a car, or I would drive one from the factory press fleet to the designated venue. That enabled me to drive thousands of miles in a variety of Series 2 Elise models, as well as Exiges and left-field models like the Type 121 Europa and the 2-Eleven Type 123. It was a fantastically exciting era, and I recount several road trips here.

ABOVE: **There's a purity about the bare, uncarpeted aluminium chassis defining the body of the interior, but its intimacy is reassuringly womb-like.**
TOM WOOD

Lotus's erstwhile handling maestro Alistair Stewart shows us the ropes on Hethel's handling circuit, effectively a vast roundabout at this point on the circuit, which could be driven with the car virtually sideways all the way round – that is, until its tyres cry enough, and it pirouettes.
TOM WOOD

RIVER DEEP, MOUNTAIN HIGH

Leaving no cliché unturned, I motored from Las Vegas to the Grand Canyon in an Elise on an American road trip.

Nothing wrong with a good cliché, though, and that's what the Mojave mecca of Vegas is about: gambling and entertainment and home to every fantasy you ever had. The architectural icons crowd in: Luxor's pyramid, New York New York's Manhattan skyline, Excalibur's Camelot, the Bellagio's fountains, and Romanesque Caesar's Palace muscle for attention along the palm-lined Strip. We are billeted at the Treasure Island, and the cacophony of the slot machines and gaming tables is deafening. Night and day, herds of small-time gamblers, hen-nighters, show-boaters and newly-weds drift from one attraction to another in search of the new high. Celine Dion is playing Caesar's, with Davy Jones from the Monkees just out and Elton's next in. We are hedonists in bed with Mammon for the weekend.

I've picked up the Lotus from Vegas main dealer Norm Baker. An Esprit V8 vies with Cobra and GT40 replicas in his showroom while all manner of American muscle cars stand head to head with Porsches and Lotuses on the suburban forecourt. I'm driving out of Las Vegas in a white-hot Elise S2 in 43° sunshine (110°F), and the radio's playing homegrown band The Killers' 'When You Were Young': '...we're burning down that highway skyline...!' Wherever we stop there's a buzz around the Elise – 'That's a real pretty car you got there. A Lotus? From England? What'll it do?' Incredulity's matched with respect, and inevitably people want to know not just how fast it'll go, but how fast I've actually been in it. The answer never disappoints.

Lake Mead and the Hoover Dam

The anticipated four-hour run to our Grand Canyon destination takes a hit when we arrive at the Hoover Dam, the man-made wonder 30 miles (50km) southeast of Vegas. Although the water level's depleted, Lake Mead is still a vast body of water, stretching 110 erratic miles (177km) behind the dam, and massive speedboats abound: Clive Chapman (national junior powerboat champ in 1981) would be right at home. The Colorado River that emerges at the base of the dam is minuscule by comparison, but another 50 miles (80km) and it will be further dwarfed into insignificance by the enormity of the Grand Canyon.

Now terracotta cliffs meet grey concrete, and vertigo sufferers had best avoid glancing over the edge. The gigantic bowl of the Hoover (also known as Boulder) Dam and its art deco hydroelectric buildings is 220m (720ft) high, a monument to the navvies who built it (114 died on the job) between 1931 and 1934. Imagine dangling on a rope, inserting dynamite into the rock, and swinging clear while it explodes. Still, they only poured the concrete a few inches at a time so probably no one got buried alive. Allegedly, there's sufficient material (2,480,000cu m/3,250,000cu yd) to pave a two-lane highway from San Francisco to New York, and it is still curing even now.

Signs in the Lake Mead recreational area warn of rampant deer, a 65mph (105km/h) speed limit, and that littering the roadside will cost you $500. As before, it's straight-as-an-arrow dual carriageway across rocky desert, with cacti and sagebrush and far-distant mountains. There are occasional truck stops, ranches, shanties and scrapyards, some by the roadside, and some deep in the desert. The sky grows ominously dark. Visibility plummets, and the anticipation of the oncoming meteorological phenomenon carries a frisson. It's a sandstorm. Grains rattle on the windscreen and the lightweight car rocks with the turbulence. The dust clears after a few minutes but forked lightning splits the livid purple sky ahead, silhouetting the hills, and we enter a sudden squall. Best drop to the proscribed maximum to preclude aquaplaning. By coincidence, there's a crossroad sign saying 'Big Wash Road'. It sure is.

Kingman to Flagstaff

The sun's shining again, and as the speed signs reduce in quick succession to 35mph (56km/h), we arrive at Kingman, and make a left onto White Cliff Road – the I-40 – towards Flagstaff and Phoenix. There's still 166 miles (267km) to the Grand Canyon.

Is the Elise a fun car in this landscape? You bet! It may not be tasked to deliver of its best, but a Lotus is a Lotus, and hang the comfort; you'd rather be in this gem than a soulless MPV. There's always its fluent handling to appreciate, though all we're really doing is changing lanes. Whenever I hit a poor road surface with lots of joins in the blacktop there's a pronounced bonk, but I can live with that. Welcome as it is, the air-con saps the power, so even revving to 6,000rpm it's not giving brilliant acceleration up a long hill. But the car's progressively loosening up now we're cruising closer to the ton. Some welcome curves come up through a gorge, boulders heaped like potatoes and mind-the-elk signs at the edge. The oncoming carriageway is perhaps a mile away to the left, and I'm hardly aware of it. Arizona is more verdant than Nevada, though the comparison's relative. Scattered trees now become a virtual forest, though they're stunted by heat. A plain stretches ahead to mountains. Signs say 99 miles (159km) to Flagstaff, and I peel off for gas.

Abruptly, the I-40 becomes the old Route 66, and the action comes alive with small settlements that haven't changed since the halcyon days of the 1950s, filled with mostly single-storey, timber-clad shops, garages, diners and motels that saw better days between the 1930s and the 1950s, though hardly prosperous. Average vehicle age and quality drops a couple of notches out here too. I dimly recollect Monte Hellman's *Two-Lane Blacktop*, a celluloid paean to this legendary highway. The equally symbolic Santa Fe railroad is just behind Seligman's main street; long freight trains frequently run by. We buy some munchies at the general store and take a coffee at the Roadkill Café. The products are modern, but they're displayed in time-honoured fashion, stacked on old shelving and hanging from beams. Next door, there's the jailhouse gun shop and livery stables. At the gas station – pay before you fill – the proprietor tells us, 'They buried most of Route 66 under Interstate 40.' Arizona, he reckons, has more stretches left of the original road than any other state. Travelling them entails detours, so for now we decide we'll stick with the more direct I-40 and make as much of the return run as we can on the 66.

Fifty miles (80km) of winding dual carriageway from the Canyon, the vegetation changes to dense pine forest. A sign proclaims 'Altitude 1 mile above sea level'. As dusk falls, we turn off the I-40 just short of Flagstaff, onto the US-64 at Williams: unswerving two-lane blacktop in a vast wilderness dotted with blob trees. 'On a dark desert highway,' sing the Eagles: 'cool wind in my hair…'. The only cool wind I can perceive is coming from the air-con, as outside it's still a searing 35° (96°F). Still, live the dream!

I'm cruising at a steady 80 (129km/h), but a sixth sense tells me to slow as a pair of headlights is catching up in the mirror. I drop to the mandatory 45 (72km/h) as I go through a settlement, and spot the red, white and blue lights atop the SUV that's now close behind. Oh no, I'm in for a citation, for sure. But, praise be, come the de-restriction, the county sheriff's past me and on his way at well over the limit.

The Grand Canyon

Tall conifers and scrub oaks greet the approach to the Canyon, and signs proclaim entry to the Kaibab National Forest. We've reached our Tusayan stopover, and it's a ten-minute ride to the Holiday Inn. A bunch of quasi-ethnic restaurants beckon, and we opt for the busy, log-cabin-style Yipee-Ay-Yay steakhouse. Yep, literally! Sombrero'd Mexicans serve up Sol beers and margaritas and, as a dare, Jason and I choose rattlesnake for starters. The batter's nice, but it's more texture than taste, and the gigantic slabs of beef that follow are a distinct improvement in flavour. 'Eat an 85oz steak in an hour, and get dinner for free,' challenges the menu. I'll take the quarter-pounder and pay as normal, thanks.

Next morning, we pass the Tusayan ranger station, and two wooden sheds with columns the size of telegraph poles form the entrance to the Grand Canyon National Park. Each car pays a toll to go along essentially the same road as they've arrived on, two-lane asphalt with robust vegetation, including aloe, agave and prickly pear beyond. In some places, the road surfaces are warped due to climatic conditions. It's only 7.30am, but already busy with sightseers. Nothing prepares you for the sheer scale and spectacle of the Canyon: the red, orange and grey-blue strata, innumerable erratic zigzags, buttes and pinnacles close by and stretching as far as the eye can see: it's vast, majestic, unfathomable, making us tourists perching on the perimeter seem utterly insignificant. However long you gaze in bewilderment, there's too much to take in. Perhaps as an antidote, almost as many people take pictures of the Lotus (and of themselves beside it) as they do of the natural wonder they've turned their back on.

I'm on the south rim, which is around 300m (1,000ft) lower than the northern one because of the tilt of the plateau, but still a mile above the Colorado River snaking way below, and mostly out of sight. Averaging 15m (50ft) deep as it passes through the Canyon, the Colorado River carried out most of its erosion between 5 million and 1.5 million years ago. It's along here, ironically, in view of the major topographical distraction over to the left, that I have the most fun with the Elise. The trail follows the rocky defiles, swooping up and down, and it's good asphalt. I drop a cog and boot it, instantly whizzing down into a sharpish left-hander that winds back into an uphill right. The Yokohamas stick like glue and, without lifting off, I place the car exactly where it needs to go for maximum thrill. There are a few of these entertaining rollercoasters, but I can't behave like this for very long: too many rangers about.

The Elise parked on the south rim of the Grand Canyon, a mile or so above the Colorado River.

There are several designated viewing places, attended by small car parks and a handful of villages. Angel Lodge is a Wild West 'Center Parcs', with log cabins, railhead, and mule farm for intrepid souls who want to take the Bright Angel trail. We pause at Moran Point and Grand View, where Canyon tourism started in the late nineteenth century, with pioneers making the eleven-hour stagecoach ride up from Flagstaff. That, and the Last Chance mine, were quickly seen off by the railroad that opened up the Pacific coast. Centrepiece is a crudely built watchtower, close to the general store and trading post, with souvenirs and the ubiquitous restrooms.

Having covered 25 miles (40km) of the Canyon's 270-mile (435km) length, there's nothing but the welcome sign facing oncoming traffic to tell us we've emerged from the park. We aim for Cameron on the US-89, which will take us south to Flagstaff. We're in the Navajo Indian reservation, and Lotus and Jeep mothership stop at a roadside stall to look at their craftwork trinkets and irresistible jewellery. It's high limestone country, dotted with blob trees. I scan a vast plain stretching out to my left. It looks deceptively flat but it's bisected by an abrupt chasm – the Little Colorado River Gorge. Passing straggling Indian settlements, tin shacks and ad-hoc trailer parks, there's blue sky and cotton-wool clouds, but rain sheets are draped over the mountains – right where we're headed. Soon enough, we're in the cloudburst, rain cascading off the shale in rivulets. A pair of dishevelled Harley riders have no option but to pitch into the downpour.

Back on Route 66

Pretty soon, it's sunny again, and I'm among pines in Cocanino National Forest and the San Francisco peaks, and driving fast dual carriageway, entering Flagstaff, Arizona. Soon, I'm motoring west on Route 66, 'the highway that's the best,' as the song goes. The motels, drive-ins, car and bike dealerships on the outskirts of Flagstaff are redolent of how it was fifty or sixty years ago, although the road must be twice the width it was back then. Route 66 wasn't fully paved along its entire length until 1938, but from inauguration in 1926 to 1985, when it was decommissioned, the configuration was frequently altered according to local traffic priorities, bypassing more and more towns. Traversing 2,448 miles (3,940km) from Chicago to Los Angeles, the 66 provided migrating settlers with a route west to California during the Dust Bowl years of the 1930s, and since much of it was over flat terrain it became popular with trucks. John Steinbeck's *Grapes of Wrath* catches the flavour of the blacktop dream on the 'Mother Road' in the Depression. Family-run businesses sprang up along the route, and the 66 quickly became a sinuous microcosm of American society, and eventually a national emblem. The downturn came in 1956 with the inauguration of the Interstate Highway Act, pushed through by President Eisenhower, who was keen to replicate the German autobahn system he'd seen in action during World War II. Despite the 66's demise, by 1990, route associations had sprung up to preserve and promote surviving sections such as those on which the Elise and I are now getting our kicks.

Just out of Flagstaff, brief snatches of 66 recur at Bellemont, almost a ghost town and, at 2,100m (7,000ft), allegedly the highest point on the 66; the Pine Breeze Inn was a location in *Easy Rider*. We turn off to Crooktown to follow the longest stretch of the 66, a down-to-earth two-laner, up hill and down dale as the crow flies across fenced moorland, with mountains in the distance. Homespun homilies sponsored by Burmah Shave sprout periodically from the verge: 'It would be more fun to go by air if we could put these signs up there,' split up into four or five separate hoardings (as seen in *Three Billboards Outside Ebbing, Missouri*). Or how about: 'The one who drives when he's been drinking depends on you to do his thinking.' Other, more official commemorative plaques proclaim 'This stretch of Highway is Sponsored by the Family of Cyrus B. Hornblower' or whoever. At Ash Fork, the DeSoto Beauty-and-Barber shop is unmissable, mainly due to the DeSoto sedan parked on the roof. Kerbside at the Rusty Bolt café in Seligman, there's an immaculate Edsel, and amongst the banners and bunting there are plenty of motels too. At 65mph (105km/h), the rate of progress is good enough on patched surfaces. If time's not of the essence, it's more relaxed than the Interstate, and you can revel in the detail: little ranches straight out of *The Waltons*, cattle grazing on sparse pasture, roadside flowers, rock formations, and the omnipresent Santa Fe railroad.

Between Seligman and Peach Springs there's a broad plain, and the highway goes direct to the horizon, calling for a rethink of the velocity. Now I'm on a mission. For a moment out there in the desert, I am Raoul Duke in *Fear and Loathing in Las Vegas*, Dean Moriarty in *On the Road* – maybe not Thelma and Louise, but definitely Jimmy Kowalski in *Vanishing Point*. I switch off the air-con and go for it, scanning any side roads for blundering trucks.

A comfort stop for the Elise S along Route 66 at Seligman, Arizona, still an important staging post on the Santa Fe railroad.
JASON PARNELL

OPPOSITE BOTTOM:
American diners are unfailingly romantic, and a godsend on a road trip. The Elise S is parked outside Rosie's Den café in White Hills, Arizona, 25 miles (40km) southeast of Boulder City on highway US 93.
JASON PARNELL

Our US Federal-spec Elise S stops for gas at Hackberry General Store near Kingman, Arizona, Sadly, there is no gas, and it's now a souvenir shop, but we got our kicks on Route 66 anyway.

I'm running at 120mph (193km/h) with a bit more to go, and still the road disappears unwavering into perspective. Eventually, small-town Peach Springs approaches and I lift off. The Grand Canyon's still visible over to the right, and the only access to the valley floor is from here, 19 miles (31km) down Diamond Creek Road. It's also the site of the Skywalk, a glass-bottomed viewing platform that juts dauntingly 20m (65ft) into thin air, 1,200m (4,000ft) above the Canyon, with nothing but fresh air between you and the Colorado River.

At Truxton, we have another comfort stop, a refill in a scenario from the 1950s, at a stores and garage plucked from the haze of the childhood memory bank. The Elise gets through four tanks' worth on this circular tour. Each one costs around $25 for 91 octane – the highest unleaded rating you can get. The milometer read 2,376 miles (3,824km) when I picked it up, and it'll be 800 (1,290km) more when I drop it off. For a mile or so, I pass through another rain shower at abated speed. There's more majestic mountain scenery between Truxton and Hackberry (where the gas station and general store brims with mementos), giving way to prairie plants like Joshua Tree yuccas that look like crazy people frozen in time.

After Kingman, I'm back on the Interstate, though the only tangible difference from the 66 is that it's dualled. As the sun goes down, the hills seem to slump and take on a deeper colour, contours revealed in sharper focus by the shadows. The Elise rolls into a lonely truck stop. The big rigs outside the diner – Kenworth, Freightliner and Peterbilt semi-trucks – have conventional bonnets; I don't see a single cab-over model, except an International in a junkyard. No escaping the icons though. I play Little Feat's trucking anthem 'Willin' on the juke box: '…driven every kind of rig that's ever been made, driven the backroads so I wouldn't get weighed…'. It requires a different mindset, a stoicism and not a few stimulants, according to the song, to do these kinds of distances.

The run from Hoover Dam to Vegas on the I-93 is wearisome because of the high-set beams of following SUVs dazzling in the Elise's mirrors, but it's swiftly done with. As I crest the rise above the city that never sleeps, the plain below is an electric carpet of shimmering light. I wouldn't mind betting we'll get some interest on the Strip tonight, me and the Elise. On the radio, America play 'Horse with No Name': 'in the desert you can't remember your name…'. How apt.

Great image of a 2006 Elise, painted in acrylics by Vancouver-based artist Taralee Guild. She will paint your Lotus to commission.

TARALEE GUILD

GEARING UP

TV's *Top Gear* and *Fifth Gear* presenter Vicki Butler-Henderson obviously has a fierce passion for all things automotive, and sought to share her expertise behind the wheel as extrovertly as possible with her sister, Lottie. The venue was Rockingham Motor Speedway while filming for *Fifth Gear* in 2007. I contacted Vicki to get a quote for the book, and she explained:

> I was trying to teach Lottie how to perfect a racing line in what was then the new Elise S, so I gave her a demonstration of how it should be done, then set her a challenge to get within 30 seconds of my own lap time. The Elise is small and simple, so you feel well connected to the controls, and it's got a nimble chassis that darts through corners. The 1.8 Toyota engine only produces 134bhp, but that doesn't matter because it's light, and because it's light, it's agile and you can brake really late! It is one of the best cars for driving quickly, and just about the perfect driver's car, because it can turn anyone – even my sister – into a track-day hero!

Our paths crossed briefly at Emap Publishing at Peterborough in the mid-1990s: Vicki was working on *Max Power*, I was, ahem, features editor on *Land Rover Owner*. Different sides of the coin, perhaps, but we both love the Elise. Vicki continues:

> I was working for *Top Gear* when the Elise first came out, and I fell for its charms as soon as I drove it because of its fantastic handling. Its design still looks cutting-edge today. Later on, in 2012, I drove an Exige S for *Fifth Gear* at Cadwell Park circuit, and I also wrote about it for a column I had in *Country and Town House* magazine. I wrote glowingly, as well as practically! I said: 'Lotus has created yet another top-notch driver's car. It is not a car you can relax in, even at a less frantic pace out on the open road. It's cumbersome to get into and out of too, being low to the ground, so best treat it as a second car or a track-day weapon. Albeit an expensive one.'

That's the Exige for you, spoken by someone at the very top of the arm-twirling game. But a lovely endorsement for the Elise, too.

Vicki Butler-Henderson drove this Exige S for a *Fifth Gear* review at Cadwell Park in 2012, and declared it is not a car to relax in, even out on the open road.

VICKI BUTLER-HENDERSON

A filming session at Rockingham Motor Speedway gave *Fifth Gear* presenter Vicki Butler-Henderson the opportunity to give her sister Lottie some lessons in circuit driving – in a 2007 Elise S.

VICKI BUTLER-HENDERSON

ELISE SC – YOUR FLEXIBLE FRIEND

It's hot, raunchy, yet subtle and refined: that's the supercharged Elise SC I drove at its 2008 Barcelona launch.

'We're here to have fun,' proclaims Lotus PR supremo Alastair Florance, and that we most certainly do, at the January 2008 Barcelona launch of one of the company's most pioneering models yet – the Elise SC. The event is a perfect mixture of serious and frivolous pleasures, party time in the splendour of the Florida Hotel on the heights above the city, matched by the hard graft of making a rigorous assessment of the new car. My kind of fun, indeed. So, here's the programme: on arrival we journos attend Alastair's informal presentation, followed by buffet lunch and the test drive in the new cars.

As if you couldn't guess, SC stands for supercharger, suggestive of the massive boost that historic racing cars received when forced induction was de rigueur from the 1920s to the early 1950s. Whether this power surge advantage is true is the test of the new Elise. Supercharging was commonplace in competition cars during the 1930s, exemplified at its most extreme in the Silver Arrows, the Auto Union and Mercedes-Benz Grand Prix teams that reigned supreme in the latter part of that decade. Use of supercharging declined in the 1950s in favour of normally aspirated engines.

The difference between the two types of forced induction units, supercharger and turbocharger, is that the supercharger derives its power from the crankshaft, whence it's driven by a belt (in the same way as the water pump and alternator), whereas the turbo draws power from the engine's exhaust gases. Superchargers spin at up to 50,000rpm, while the turbocharger can spin much faster. Emissions-wise, the supercharger doesn't have a wastegate, whereas turbos have catalytic converters to lower carbon emissions. Turbochargers run extremely hot and need to be well insulated. Superchargers deliver boost at lower revs then a turbocharger, whereas the turbo works best at high engine speeds. In practical terms, the supercharger is easier to install, though it takes a small portion of the engine's power in its operation. Turbochargers are quieter in operation, and fuel economy is affected less adversely with a turbo'd engine, while super-

The Elise SC – sporting the Magnuson-Eaton supercharger on its 1796cc Toyota engine – was released to the international press corps in March 2008 in Barcelona. Accompanied by Lotus ride and handling guru Dave Minter, I drove a press car on the Catalonian mountain roads north of the city.
JASON PARNELL

chargers are more reliable and easier to maintain than the more complex turbocharger.

Costing a basic £32,550, the 2008 model year Elise SC was unveiled in October 2007 at the Tokyo Motor Show, and the bare bones are these: it's fitted with the Magnuson-produced Eaton M45 supercharger with no intercooler, producing 217bhp, more than enough to propel the 903kg (1,991lb) sportster to 60mph in 4.4sec and on to 100mph in 10.7sec, topping out at an autobahn-storming 150mph (241km/h). We'll have the chance to see how that all stacks up after the presentation.

It's instructive how Lotus's PR team handles a launch. It takes two weeks for Alastair and his team – John Lamb, Andreas Maenner and Tracey Parnell – to ease the international press, a few at a time, through the learning process, with engineers Chris Kemp and James Webdale present as technical back-up, and photographer Jason Parnell on hand to provide pics for individual journalists. I'm here with half a dozen Dutch pressmen and Adam Towler representing *Pistonheads*. Alastair briefs us, showing where the new model is located in the marketing firmament, using a graph to position Lotus products relative to other sports cars. While the Exige SC and track-oriented 2-Eleven are up with the Ferrari F50 and Ducati 997 motorcycle, and the Elise S and Elise R occupy the middle ground, the Europa, being more relaxed, is closer to the Porsche Boxster and Audi TT. The Elise SC tops the upper middle segment.

The Technical Specs

Next, it's the turn of Lotus senior engineer Dave Minter (development engineer on the original S1 Elise project) to provide a technical overview of the revised specification. He explains that the all-new Eaton supercharger package was developed in house by Lotus Engineering, and the absence of the intercooler gives an 8kg (18lb) reduction in engine weight compared with the Exige SC. Apart from the forced induction version of the Toyota engine already powering the Elise R, connoisseurs of the model will notice some subtle external changes. There's a single exhaust outlet, a new alloy wheel design, and a low-set rear spoiler said to enhance stability when approaching top speed.

There are innovations in the cockpit, too. Like all other Lotus models there are now driver and passenger airbags, and superb ProBax seats support the skeleton, making the driver sit up straight whilst also providing side support. They are claimed to enhance blood flow, which benefits the body's tactile abilities and suppresses tiredness. When I drove the Exige SC in Italy, I was amazed how comfortable it was, and the same is true of the Elise SC. These seats are a quantum leap forward in padding the posterior.

The dashboard is coated in a material called SensaSoft, which gives a sleek finish without resorting to the leather look. There's a starter button, and a new instrument cluster in which the previous black figures on a white background

On our drive, development engineer Dave Minter explained that absence of an intercooler in the Eaton supercharger package gives an 8kg (18lb) reduction in engine weight, compared with its sibling, the Exige SC. No intercooler also means that Elise SC drivers can see out of the rear screen.
JASON PARNELL

have been replaced with white on black. Another innovation is the use of intelligent, progressive, shift warning lights. Previous Elises had an LED that flashed when the rev-counter needle approached the redline, but now there's a sequence of three warnings as the 8,500rpm redline looms. The computer recognizes how quickly the needle is swooping around the dial, so to avoid hitting the redline the flashes come earlier down the rev range. The driver can thus concentrate more on the road ahead without perpetually scanning the information on the dials.

The analogue mph speedo carries a digital read-out in km/h, and vice versa. There's an unfastened seatbelt warning light, and the key fob has been redesigned in an almond shape. It features lock, unlock and a panic button, should you feel threatened getting into the car. The sound system has an iPod connection, so gone are the days of CDs cluttering up the cockpit. We hear about other attributes. Paint options extend from the standard range through metallics and contemporary 'lifestyle' colours, which include the enigmatic hues that alter according to the light and the angle at which you see the car.

Although it's not intercooled, as far as horsepower and torque are concerned, the Elise SC gives roughly the same sort of figures as its coupé cousin. There is more capability in the intercooled Exige SC, whereas the Elise SC is breathing the ambient air temperature outside the car. The absence of an intercooler means that Elise SC drivers can see out of the rear screen, which begs the question, why not install the Elise supercharger on the Exige with the same result? Dave Minter believes that there is nothing to be gained in putting the Elise blower on an Exige just so you can see out of the back window. 'Exige SC customers like to make a point of saying, "You can't see out of the back: the engine's there, that's the intercooler," and they like all that. Elise customers are much more road-orientated and they do like to see out of the back.'

The Elise SC doesn't need a limited-slip differential, according to Dave, though that is useful in auto tests where first gear traction is paramount. So it is offered as an option in conjunction with traction control, which is also a stand-alone facility that runs off the ignition; if the car loses traction at the rear as a result of over-exuberance, it is applied unobtrusively.

Test Drive

Time to get down to the serious business of driving. I ease into the familiar cockpit and slide my seat forward for the bent-arms posture, adjusting the mirrors manually. Dave clambers in beside me for the ride – I am in the presence of a motoring god! I press the plipper to release the security system and push the starter. Like the family dog asking for its walk, there's that enthusiastic and agreeable bark. The tickover is more staccato than the unsupercharged car, and as I tap the throttle, there's a more guttural exhaust note because of the single exhaust pipe.

Dave Minter's instruction was, 'You just squeeze the throttle, because it is so light and delicate,' and the power and torque provided instantaneously by the supercharger was something of a revelation.
JASON PARNELL

Our 80-mile (130km) test route begins with some sweeping bends heading out to challenging back roads in remote Catalonian mountain country, northwest of the city. Here, on the wriggling mountain lanes, the Elise SC really shines, winding along the cliffside, offering intimate contact with the scenery in the event of a mistake. We turn off onto the remote pass that Jason has designated for the car-to-car photography. It means going from lock to lock around the hairpins, blasting through rocky woodland and over a summit before twisting back downhill to open country, where the top-end performance can be exploited. Some of the hairpins cry out to be driven time and time again, though there's no shortage of them. I love these photo sessions because I can do just that, till Jason signals he's got the shot he wants.

Seen here on the terrace of Barcelona's Florida Hotel, the 2008 model year Elise SC was unveiled in October 2007 at the Tokyo Motor Show. It's fitted with the Magnuson-Eaton M45 supercharger, and the 1796cc Toyota engine produces 217bhp, whizzing the 870kg (1,918lb) Lotus to 60mph in 4.4 seconds and on to 100mph in 10.7 seconds, topping out at 150mph (241km/h).

My 80-mile (130km) test route with the Elise SC was mostly on challenging mountain back roads northwest of Barcelona, as here, winding along the cliffside.
JASON PARNELL

As well as the rear visibility issue, I'm aware of another difference between the Elise SC and the Exige SC, and that's because Dave and I can hold a civilized conversation at normal road speeds without raising our voices. As we pause during the car-to-car photography session, I examine the new aluminium bottle holder. It's a minor work of art, matching the cool cockpit, and means no more scrabbling to find the water bottle tucked behind the seats. It's January, yet here we are, cruising with the top off – partly because we left it in the camera car. But fear not, Dave has cranked the heater up, and we're warm as toast.

Being familiar with other versions of the Elise, I'm immediately registering the new levels of torque, gelling with the flexibility that's always been a feature of the model's performance, even at a lowly 2,000rpm in fifth gear when negotiating narrow village streets. It pulls straightaway, without the need to find 6,000rpm for the second cam to come into play. It's such an able car. The power is accessible on demand, so you can be tooling along in fourth or fifth and, if you want to have a little squirt to get out of somebody's way or to overtake, it's right there; you don't have to screw it up to 4,000rpm to get a result. Dave aptly describes it as a squeezable car: 'You just squeeze the throttle, you hardly push the throttle, you actually squeeze it.'

Uncompromising speed freaks have been applying forced induction to Elises for some time, though the results are perhaps a bit harsh. A lot of aftermarket kits concentrate on providing a big push in the back, just to show how hard they are, but that destroys the balance of the car. 'It's all to do with being smooth and progressive,' says Dave, 'and if you've got an engine which is giving those sorts of characteristics you feel so much more confident in the car, because you're not going to suddenly get another 30bhp with half a millimetre of throttle.' That's when all Elises deliver their best.

In every other respect it's equally subtle. The six-speed gearbox is a joy to use, and its slickness never disappoints. We know how well it turns in, and that hasn't changed. Neither have those fabulous brakes, slowing the car imperceptibly, yet unerringly, from very high velocities, and peeling off speed with a mere dab between corners. 'There was no need to upgrade them, as they were always so capable,' says Dave. 'When we originally designed the car we packaged as big a brake as possible within the 15in wheel, because we wanted to disperse heat as much as we could, given a threshold temperature of about 350 degrees, and because of that they haven't needed uprating.'

We're some way up into the hills on our tortuous, miraculously traffic-free run, though I'm erring on the side of caution in case some great *camion* lumbers around the corner. That's partly why I'm double-declutching down to second (old habits die hard) for most of the turns, and not just the tight ones. 'Why don't you give it a try in third?' suggests Dave. It's like I'm suddenly transported into a different car. Not only will it run just as swiftly through these corners, both my hands are now on the wheel instead of working the shift. And I can still drive it round on the throttle with no delay powering out of the exit. Bit of a revelation there. 'That's what I mean about the squeezeability; you didn't need to accelerate much, you just squeezed it round.'

It goes exactly where you want it to, and it's so forgiving. I make a couple of misjudgements in corners and, thanks to lift-off understeer, it just tucks back in. Dave cites the Lotus analogy: 'Glove on the hand: you've got your glove on, and whatever you do with your hand, the glove mimics it totally, and that's the relationship between the driver and the car.' After scuttling through the hairpins, there's the feeling that, with the SC, you have to re-learn how to drive an Elise. It's a good lesson, trying to be in a gear higher than you would expect to be in an S or an R. In either of those, you want to keep the revs up to stay in their high power band.

This ability to deliver performance at lower revs doesn't make it more economical than an S or an R. In your drive cycle, you'll do plenty of different sorts of driving, and with more power and torque you'll naturally use more fuel, though not that much. Back to Dave: 'The point is, it's very much a lightweight car – it's got great emissions and good fuel economy, which demonstrates how green these cars are.'

This is a classic example of a car that invites you to drive it. 'If it doesn't do that then you are in the wrong car,' says Dave. 'In a track-day context, when you've done a few laps in one of these and come back into the pits, you are smiling because you've enjoyed the drive so much;

The Elise SC is a classic example of a car that's inviting you to drive it, and according to Dave Minter, 'If the Elise doesn't make you smile, you're in the wrong car!' Me? I am beaming from ear to ear.
JASON PARNELL

OPPOSITE: **A troupe of Elises and Exiges prowl the hallowed Indianapolis oval during the LOG28 gathering.**
JASON PARNELL

in other cars, you are sometimes smiling because you've actually survived it!' Once off the mountains and back on the A-road, we roll along with the flow of traffic in an easy third gear. I compare the relative power bands, taking the SC to about 6,200rpm, which is where the second cam comes in on the R. We are really flying in fifth by now, and it's the supercharger that's done the hard work. It's a nice, linear progression, without having to work the gears, which you'd need to do in an R.

Our route goes onto a section of fast, shallow bends where the cambers are all over the place, yet the car tracks really well and sticks tight to the road. There's no kickback from the steering wheel, and the asphalt surface – unblemished by frosts, despite our remoteness – is not influencing the position of the car. Despite the extra oomph, the Elise has lost none of its agility, nor its controllability on the throttle. What it has gained is flexibility of power delivery. Through most of the 12-mile (20km) section of hairpins, it was such fun that my face wore a solid grin. You can be so relaxed with it as well, establishing a rhythm and flowing through the turns, even though each one is subtly different.

There's an interesting nugget still in store. As the trip draws to an end, we're on an undulating motorway, doing 80mph (130km/h). 'Notice how good the SC's primary ride is,' comments Dave. I ask him to explain.

> So, the front and rear can go up and down at the same time. In a poor primary ride, it would be bucking and you'd start to feel sick if the frequency was wrong. It's about the ability of the car's suspension to come up in rebound and settle in rebound, so there is no overshoot back down again. Secondary ride is the ability to go over broken surfaces.

We wind back up the crag side to the extraordinary Vegas-style collection of playground architecture, a switchback and an Eiffel tower, dominated by the fabulous Florida hotel. In the party suite, someone's twenty-first birthday is gathering pace, and I reflect how apt that is: the SC can represent the Elise's coming of age too, and we raise a glass in the Florida bar.

THE BIG CHILL

The prospect of a caper at the Brickyard ensured US Lotus owners flocked to Indianapolis for the annual gathering of the clans – LOG28 – where an action-packed programme awaited.

In 2008, it's the turn of CHILL (Club House for Indianapolis Lotus Lovers) to host North American Lotus owners' LOG28 convention, with a few laps of the legendary Indianapolis Motor Speedway the icing on the cake. No fewer than 360 members of US clubs have descended on the state capital's Hilton Hotel, in an impressive variety of Lotuses, totalling 225 cars.

Top CHILLers include event organizer Terry Beasley, president Young Kim, and communications manager Jessica Mullendore. Also attending from US fraternity Lotus Ltd are president Peter Blackford, vice president Dominic Munofo and secretary Dean Giacopassi, to name but a few movers

and shakers. Other clubs and organizations present include LEO (Lotus Enthusiasts' Organization), Lotus Car Club of Southern Nevada, Spring Mountain Race School Nevada, Alabama Lotus Car Club, Barber Motorsports Museum and – winning the prize for best acronym – LOONY (Lotus Owners of New York). This congenial cross-section of Lotus fans is augmented by guest stars Roger Becker from Lotus Engineering, with Clive Chapman and Bob Dance representing Classic Team Lotus.

There's always a strong element of Lotus history at LOG events, and here, memories are revived of Team Lotus's assault on the lucrative Indy 500, which started with its first foray to the Brickyard in 1963. At a stroke, Lotus changed the face of single-seater racing in the USA, when Jim Clark placed second in the Type 29 with its rear-engined F1 technology. But for a tyre blow-out and subsequent suspension collapse, he probably would have won in 1964 as well, though his 1965 victory in the Type 38 was ample vindication. By then, the gargantuan front-engined roadsters were history. So, forty-five years on, this mission was all the more poignant, given that 2008 was the fortieth anniversary of Clark's death at Hockenheim – marked by the Jim Clark Revival meeting, which we also attend.

The Lotus entourage form up in readiness, nose-out around the circus at the heart of the city, surrounding its towering war monument. Motorcycle police have given up their free day to ride shotgun, so the retinue of Hethel and Cheshunt's finest cruised unchecked through intersection after intersection, waved on by swaggering biker cops. The leader actually climbs onto the saddle of his Harley-Davidson whilst in motion, arms outstretched in a Christ-like posture. Stuntman, or what!

There is no great palaver accessing the circuit, despite its illustrious reputation. We process through the tunnel under the stands opposite the pit lane, and into the museum car park for a preliminary form-up. I climb in beside Jessica Mullendore, one of the front-runners, for a ride in her Elise. Then we were let out onto the hallowed 2.5-mile (4km) oval, and it is a spine-tingling thrill to be actually driving on the Brickyard. Those mile-long straights are swiftly swallowed up, though the banking turns out to be less daunting than I'd expected.

As the parade of Lotuses forms up and before our speed increases, I lean out the back of Jessica's Elise and photograph Roger Becker and Jason Parnell in the car behind – the snapper snapped. I suppose we do three or four laps – maybe more, but I lose count, taking in the Oval's topography, and imagining how it would be driving a racing car and turning into the banking, draughting other cars and slipstreaming past.

There is an opportunity to see some genuine race cars circulating in earnest: later on, we watch the Richard Petty race school NASCAR stockers hammering round, and the asphalt dish takes on a different dimension as the nose-to-tail draughters steamed into the dip like surfers hanging in a breaking wave, their monster V8s howling on full song down

The LOG28 entourage was shepherded from Indianapolis city centre to the racetrack by a posse of motorcycle cops, one of whom was especially up for a prank.
JASON PARNELL

OPPOSITE BOTTOM LEFT: **The snapper snapped: Lotus photographer Jason Parnell and Lotus Engineering boss Roger Becker lapping Indianapolis in a 2-Eleven, an image secured at great personal peril from the passenger seat of Jessica Mullendore's Elise SC.**

CHILL communications manager Jessica Mullendore watches the NASCAR brigade whilst waiting to head out onto The Brickyard for some laps in her Elise.

the straightaways. That is an awesome spectacle, evoking memories of Tom Cruise's underrated *Days of Thunder*. To catch a glimpse of these titans in the metal, I work my way the length of the main straight at second-floor level, skirting the winner's rostrum below the famed Pagoda control tower along the way, heading for the pit lane via stairs next to Gasoline Alley. Close up, these monster Ford Fusions, Chevy Impalas and Toyota Camrys are only distinguishable by their respective lurid sponsor liveries, their body contours otherwise identical apart from specific manufacturer badging and stick-on headlights.

The Lotus lappery done, the cars fan out in starburst within the paddock area, model by model. It was time for the concours judging and group photo, with Types 34 and 38 IndyCars as exalted centrepieces. Speedway historian Donald Davidson treats us to an entertaining resumé of Lotus's Indy record, calling on his thirty-one years' experience of the track. He tells us that Dan Gurney was determined to get Colin Chapman to take on the circuit, even buying Chapman's plane ticket so he could see for himself how an F1 configuration could win at the Brickyard, by dint of better power-to-weight ratio and only a single pit stop (using gasoline) instead of the conventional three (using ethanol). Allied to Ford V8 engines, Lotus built the Type 29, and it was game on, culminating in Jim Clark's 1965 triumph.

The Hall of Fame museum beckons, and we are easy prey at the gift shops that snare visitors either side the entrance. The museum features many past winners of the 500, and we home in on Clark's Team Lotus-liveried Lotus 29 that ran in 1963 (Gurney's car was white), plus the Ferrari 250LM that Jochen Rindt and Masten Gregory won Le Mans with in

Exiges and Elises fan out in the Indianapolis circuit paddock for the concours judging.

The Hyper Sport Engineering Exige S in SCCA race trim lined up amongst a variety of Lotuses in the Indianapolis paddock.

BELOW: **After the on-track action and concours parades, the LOG28 participants made their way back into Indianapolis city centre for the soiree and dinner.**

1965. There's a 1955 Mercedes-Benz 196 streamliner and a 1979 Porsche 935 IMSA race car, plus the works Corvette that was meant to take GM into international sports car racing in the 1950s.

After soaking up the memorabilia, Loggers make their way back downtown. Along with dog walkers, joggers and lovers in gondolas, we stroll along the towpath of Central Canal that leads off the White River to Indiana State Museum, where a musical steam clock toots a tune on the quarter-hour. Like New York, the heart of Indianapolis is heated by steam, accounting for those mysterious clouds that seep from manholes in the street. The Lotus fraternity relax in the haven of the Hilton's convivial McCormick & Schmitt's brown bar, and between watching the NASCAR and baseball, we admire the dexterity of the shake-it-up cocktail bar staff.

Table decorations at Saturday night's banquet centre on what appears incongruously to be nothing more exotic than plastic bottles, but closer scrutiny reveals to be milk bottles – and the dime drops! Of course! The Indy 500 winner gets to drink the milk (rather than champers, a tradition started by three-time victor Louis Meyer in 1936) and, by association, we are all winners this evening. Adding a gloss to the proceedings, we are entertained by Classic Team Lotus mechanics Bob Dance and Sid Carr, who both worked on Team's Lotus Cortinas and Formula 2 cars in the 1960s.

We have plans to leave early on the Tuesday morning on a road trip from Indianapolis to that other fabled US racetrack, Daytona, down south in Florida and the best part of 1,000 miles (1,600km) away, across four different states. In an Elise.

CARS AND COFFEE

Lotus enthusiasts Stateside don't necessarily manage to make the annual LOG gatherings, due to distance and commitments, and there are plenty of smaller groups who fly the flag. In spring 2020 I hooked up with Oklahoma-based artist Stephanie Arnwine, and she revealed that she and her husband owned a couple of Elises, and met up with other Lotus-owning friends in Florida and Texas. Stephanie, who paints under the name of Grahound (an anagram of her family name, Draughon, in tribute to her artist father), told me:

> Our Lotus group used to meet up the first Saturday of every month at Cars and Coffee. You would see cars ranging from classics to exotics gathering from all over, and that was always a blast. I used to autocross with the two Elises I owned – Chrome Orange and Red. I personally liked the orange over the red, but if I really had my way, I would take Krypton Green or Chili Red over either. When we owned the orange Elise, we lived in Florida. My husband and I started a Lotus group there, as well as a group in Oklahoma, where we owned the red Elise. Our meet-ups in Florida were always a much bigger turnout than the ones in Oklahoma. But it was all fun: for instance, our group in Florida tried to pack as many Lotuses as we could into a driveway – and that was quite comical. These cars are an absolute blast to drive and open up on the track, though, and we have plans to purchase another one soon!

Stephanie happily takes commissions. Her painting of the Elise shown here is a 60cm × 122cm (24in × 48in) acrylic on canvas.

Oklahoma-based artist Stephanie Arnwine loves to autocross her Elise at multi-marque club events; this one is in Austin, Texas.
STEPHANIE ARNWINE

continued overleaf

CARS AND COFFEE *continued*

Stephanie Arnwine's Elise heads a drive-out of Florida-based Lotus petrolheads.
STEPHANIE ARNWINE

Stephanie Arnwine paints under the name of Grahound and this is her artwork of an Elise finished in Krypton Green, the colour she'd most prefer herself.
STEPHANIE ARNWINE

MOROCCAN ROLLER

A long day's run from Tangier, the Atlas Mountains provide amazing Lotus driving roads. My Marrakech Express is a Type 121 Europa SE.

I never imagined schoolboy French would come in so handy, but I found out that it did in Morocco. Hauled over by a couple of speed cops at night on an innocuous 60km/h (37mph) road on the outskirts of Marrakech, words like '*désolé!*' suddenly bubbled up, and in fluent Franglais I explained truthfully that I'd lost my way to my hotel. Graciously, they gave me directions and sent me on my way.

You soon realize you're in a different continent. Morocco is the first rung on the ladder south through Africa, and Marrakech is like the idealized French colonial city of Célésteville in the children's *Baba the Elephant* stories. Exotic it may be, but there are few bargains – haggling only realizes a fair market price; they just won't sell you that rug if your best offer doesn't match up. And, crucially for the sporting driver, one thing you cannot do in Morocco is speed. Up in the Atlas Mountains, you can exercise your Lotus's handling to a degree, but down on the main highway, forget it, or your wallet's toast.

Doors of perception: after its run to the Atlas Mountains, our Europa SE waits by the gates of the magnificent Ksar Char-Bagh hotel, Marrakech.
JASON PARNELL

Having collected the Type 121 Europa SE from Lotus Cars' European HQ at Stuttgart, I drove it through France and Spain, crossing to Morocco and motoring down into the Atlas Mountains for our photoshoot.

From Germany to Morocco

My mission was to bring the Europa SE to Marrakech, but because the bulk of Lotus's continental press fleet was billeted in Stuttgart, that's where my journey started. I collected the car from Lotus's European PR manager, Andreas Maenner, and gunned the zesty 220bhp missile out of Germany and down through France and Spain, overnighting at Orange in Provence, and Valencia, close to the GP circuit on the Spanish coast. On the unrestricted autobahn I saw 130mph (210km/h) in the left-hooker, and it felt very stable, though the fuel gauge told a more cautionary tale. Notwithstanding the Europa's appetite for the amber nectar, I decided that whilst these sorts of speeds were legal I might as well go for it.

The 2.0 turbo GM engine (from the VX220 Roadster) makes the Europa nearly as quick as the Elise SC. There's a deeper, less urgent engine note to the Europa than the blown 1.8 Toyota unit in the Elise, but the turbo kicks in with no lag whatsoever. Acceleration is blistering, from 0 to 60mph in 5.5 seconds and whistling up to 145mph (233km/h), working slickly through its close ratio six-speed gearbox. Short-shifting out of the toll booths on the *péage*, there's that funny little whistle every time you lift off the accelerator, like water gurgling down the sink. As a measure of limit-abiding fuel economy, an autoroute tankful got me from Orange to Barcelona, 267 miles (430km) in four hours – averaging 66mph (106km/h), which, bearing in mind *péage* halts and a comfort stop, wasn't bad at all.

The car was shod with winter tyres (Pirelli Snow Sport, 195/55-16 front, 215/40-17 rear) in case of snow in the Eifel, Vosges and Ardèche regions – and maybe even the Pyrenees and Sierra Nevada – not to mention the indifferent surfaces in Morocco. According to Andreas, I was the first person to drive the Europa with that set-up, and it was absolutely fine – perhaps a tad more squirm in high-speed turns, but no less grip than standard Yokohamas. Though snow-capped mountains were a frequent backdrop, I came closer to the white stuff in the Atlas Mountains than anywhere in Europe, and, as it turned out, a Moroccan thunderstorm provided the worst of the weather.

Such a lightweight is inevitably susceptible to crosswinds, and at 100mph (160km/h) on the Spanish autovia on that magnificent high-altitude stretch between Murcia and Grenada I was buffeted to the point where the weaving Europa needed a firm grip on the tiller. In an exhilarating climb over a small mountain pass, winding tightly to the summit, the Europa steamed ahead. These are wonderful roads for a Lotus, switching this way and that. I glimpsed 110mph (177km/h) tracking through the turns, it's that taut and poised.

Just after Algeciras and the Rock of Gibraltar, which you see from some distance, I reached Tarifa, an old fishing and ferry port with an ancient fortress and the inevitable modern sprawl. From the water, its Moroccan counterpart of Tangier doesn't look much different, only bigger.

Just 14 miles (23km) separate Spain from Africa across the Straits of Gibraltar, though the sleek FRS *Tarifa Jet* catamaran ferry takes the long way round, tallying 50 miles (80km) to Tangier. By now, I'd met up with editor Caroline and photographer Jason aboard the giant speedboat, doing 25 knots to make the crossing in thirty-five minutes, a passage that takes a normal ferry three hours. If it's too rough, the catamaran simply doesn't sail, though the conventional freighter still runs. FRS also operates a route from Algeciras to Ceuta, but Tangier has the better autoroute access going south.

Quayside at Tangier, disembarking was chaos because everything had been packed on board like sardines. I couldn't extricate myself from the Lotus without levering myself out on the door handles of the Mercedes jammed alongside, and to get back in I simply waited till there was nothing left parked next to me.

Now the fun starts. On the wharf you wait in line to go through the customs shed. You wait, and you wait. The posturing Tangier port authorities know how to take their time, lording it over the assembled voyagers while acolytes scuttle about to no good effect. Someone goes off with my documents – passport and car papers. Half an hour later he returns. They have been stamped, but they are proffered with one hand while the other is an outstretched palm. Then I have to take the passport to two more police officials, one in a pokey office, the other in a sentry box, for verification of the stamp. Along with the vehicle's paperwork is a new slip of green paper and this, I discover, is to be treasured. By the time I drive out of the port, I'm 150 dirham (roughly £14) poorer from 'gratuities', but the pompous official at the port gate demands to see *le papier vert* yet again. Luckily I find it buried under maps and jacket.

Tangier to Rabat

At last I'm on the road south to Rabat, with about 300 miles (500km) to go to Marrakech. Jason and Caroline follow in a freshly rented Citroën hatchback. Thank goodness I've already had ample opportunity to explore the Europa's performance potential, from unrestricted autobahn to arcing autovia, given the preponderance of Moroccan speed traps and traffic cops. I may be on state-of-the-art, newly finished autoroute (tolls gobble £17 between Tangier and Marrakech) but I stick diligently to the speed limit, with glowering policemen swaggering like gangsters in the central reservation, cameras pointing up and down the highway. I count four speed traps in the first hour, which begs the question, if everyone knows the cops are always going to be out and about, how come people get caught?

Instead, I contemplate the scenery. To the right is the Atlantic Ocean, and on either side of the road it's marshland, and with eucalyptus and poplar plantations by the roadside. It's like Holland with cacti. Agriculture in these parts is a mixture of strip farming in very small fields with lots of cattle, donkeys, sheep, goats and the odd camel, and in some places the land is cultivated though it's too early in the season to tell what the crops are. Occasionally there's an intensive poly-tunnel farm. Dwellings are mud-baked with flat roofs, and people pop up from everywhere, walking along the side of the autoroute, running across it, or picking herbs among the profusion of roadside flowers. Herds of goats roam the hard shoulder and I can't see what would keep them from coming down onto the road, though there are some barriers. Among the subsistence farming, brightly coloured carpets hang out to air on fences or off adobe roofs.

We stop for fuel and barbecued chicken at one of the frequent service areas – Afriquia, Mobil and Shell are the most common petrol brands – and discover for the first time that nobody takes credit cards: just cash, dirham preferably, or euros. Portions are generous but prices are high.

Rabat is roughly half-way. Policemen skulk at every crossroads and intersection but now there's a new phenomenon: every half mile or so, for perhaps 50 miles (80km), a smartly uniformed soldier stands guard, with a pair of colleagues watching out from every flyover. Though the limit is 120km/h (75mph), I keep below 100km/h (62mph), figuring that if there's Moroccan royalty due to pass this way we don't want some trigger-happy squaddie taking a pot shot. The king's palace is at Rabat, and the roadside guards peter out at Mohammedia, a port-resort just short of Casablanca.

Road signs are in Arabic and French. Drivers on the autoroute behave no differently from in Europe, except they tend to flash lights before overtaking and indicators aren't used to the same obsessive extent as in Spain. There's a whole gamut of cars of different makes and ages on the road, with the Clio-sized Dacia Logan most ubiquitous, many much the worse for wear. Trucks are 1950s American Fords and 1960s Japanese commercials, while the few big artics are invariably Spanish. In Morocco, the older the lorry the less good its lane discipline tends to be, and there's a certain amount of wandering; I was lucky when a heavily laden flatbed pulled out and I just managed to squeeze past him. The older lorries are inclined to go for height rather than length, elevated loads being more common than long ones. Punctures are commonplace.

Harmonious Drive

At this leisurely pace, I have plenty of time to contemplate the Europa cockpit. It's what used to be called a fixed-head coupé, since the roof doesn't come off. The roofline is higher than on its Elise siblings, and the sill of the extruded aluminium chassis is cutaway to allow easier access. The Europa is also more civilized in terms of its cabin upholstery and boot space, with enough capacity for a decent-sized suitcase, which you couldn't get in an Exige. The car's documentation and handbook are stashed here in leather holsters. Despite long days at the wheel, I get out each evening without any aches or discomfort – my drive will eventually wind up at Barcelona, by which time I'll have clocked up 2,850 miles (4,787km).

It has a more fully upholstered cabin than the Elise or Exige, clad in black leather with three white stripes down each door panel, and there's neat stitching on the dashboard and atop the main instruments. These gauges are set in their own twin binnacle, cowled like medieval monks, as are the facia air vents. The levers and switchgear are from the GM parts bin, as seen in Elise and Exige, and are plain but functional. It's austere rather than luxurious, but all harmonious. The seats are adequately padded and covered in leather, the white lines matching the door liners. As well as the parcel tray, there are several useful pockets for oddments, even in the roof headlining, plus those minimal sun visors, four huge speakers, an infuriatingly hard-to-access cup-holder between the seats, and the cigarette lighter socket, where I plug in the sat-nav. It's a nice place to be, even without the power-sapping air-con turned on.

South of Casablanca the road turns away from the ocean, and suddenly my expectations are fulfilled. Over to my left is the railway and, yes, there it is in all its pantograph-powered glory: the Marrakech Express. I'd deliberately downloaded the song onto my iPod and it's a matter of moments to shuffle it to Crosby, Stills and Nash's hippy paean: '…sweeping cobwebs from the edges of my mind, had to get away to see what we could find….' As if inspiration was necessary! The song is locked in my head for the rest of the week.

Marrakech – a Feast for the Senses

It's dark now, and the first glimpse of Marrakech is through a series of conical hills flanking the motorway, with the city laid out on the plains below, bathing the sky in orange. Night-time traffic around the 7-mile-long (11km) walled Medina is insane, a buzzing mass of mopeds, taxis and pickups mixing it with donkey carts and ambling mules. Rows of little shops and workshops spill out onto the street and are a hive of

The cockpit of the Europa SE – a left-hooker, being from the German press fleet – is much more sumptuous than that of the Elise, let alone the Exige, and was seen as an upmarket business-class cabin to its siblings' more austere version. It certainly made for a more relaxed journey, no matter what the speed.
JASON PARNELL

Broadside shot of the Europa reveals a more linear, less curvaceous aspect, quite different to its siblings.
JASON PARNELL

activity. We pull into a garage for directions, and a young guy offers to ride with us to locate our hotel, the Ksar Char-Bagh. Without him we would surely not have found it, though the hotel did offer to bring us in – if only we knew where we were.

Late evening, we arrive, and rarely does the sanctuary of a hotel feel more welcome; a couple of miles out of town, the fortress-like Ksar Char-Bagh with its Alhambra-like courtyard enables a total unwind. Next morning, we head for the Medina in one of the hotel's London taxis, where a barrage of unfamiliar sights, sounds and smells assail the senses. In the Djemaa El Fna main square there's a freak show of snake charmers, hedgehog handlers, monkey minders, donkeys and carts, mules, horses and carriages, feral cats: the complete menagerie. Metalwork, pottery, carpets, leather, an abundance of spices, pastries, fruit and nut stalls create a riotous, dazzling palette.

Spurning the touts who jump you the instant you appear in the marketplace, we've engaged Azedine, an official guide who speaks excellent and witty English. The souk is an absolute maze of narrow streets and mysterious alleyways, dark doorways leading to *riads*, or inner courtyards. The *moukef* is a rabbit warren where innumerable artisans are hard at work in tiny cells, crafting leather goods – from bags and hats to sandals and slippers – while hides cure on the ad hoc roofs covering the alleyways. Around the corner, metal workers solder and stamp candelabra, lanterns and birdcages, and as you move along, there are woodturners, carvers and marquetry inlayers. We don't see any potters, but the intricately patterned ceramics in the *foundouk* shops are fabulous. Weavers tailor *djellabas* – traditional full-length hooded robes – and it costs well over £100 for a good one; locals buy them on HP, says Azedine. Part and parcel of the action is the incessant traffic of mopeds and scooters, ridden at breakneck speed despite the narrowness of the alleys, usually two-up. Horns blare and fumes linger. One rips the button off my shirt cuff with his brake lever; he stops to make sure I'm not injured and, without further ado, winds on the throttle.

All the while, people are exhorting you to enter the confines of their shops; of course you inevitably succumb, and then the bartering starts. Which is why Jason and I come away with a Berber Kelim rug each. Over sweet mint tea the vendor leisurely unravels a selection of wonderful carpets woven by different Moroccan tribes, and smartly whittles them down to the one that most appeals. It will cost me £1,200, he says. I don't want to insult him, I say, but I was thinking more like £50. Eventually we shake on £250. It seems a bargain, but you're never quite sure.

Back in the open square, a charmer hangs a serpent around Jason's neck, uninvited, and, to his credit, he doesn't flinch. Felt cold, he says. Azedine explains how the snake's venom is milked first thing in the morning. The creature is relatively placid because it's used to its circumstances in the square and doesn't feel threatened. Most of the time the cobra lies limp like an old hosepipe, responding to the motion of the charmer's pipe rather than the sound, and if it gets a bit hot and edgy they just put it in cold water and it calms down.

The brightly clad water sellers are a splash of glamour, and soothsayers abound, from tarot readers to the guy who scatters fifty human teeth to predict the future (a trip to the dentist maybe?). Then there are the contortionists, the belly dancers, the cacophony of Gnaoua buskers – pipe band, drumming band, ethnic stringed instruments – plucked *ouds*, *lotars*, *buzuks* and the bowed *rabab* fiddle, plus haunting flutes and *doumbec* and *djembe* drums.

Prevalent aromas depend on what spices are in the wind – turmeric, cumin and dried roses, to name but a few – and what meats are being barbecued. A blast of strange perfumes draws us into an apothecary's shop, where we sniff a galaxy of concoctions said to cure all known ailments, though we leave empty-handed.

We end up on the terrace of the Café Argana, where marketplace meets souk, to watch the world go by. Jazz-fusion performed by Moroccan power trio Zahar belts out, catching the mood exactly. As dusk falls, we move to the enclave of tarpaulin-roofed outdoor cafés, where you sit at a trestle table while they cook delicious tagines, couscous and vegetables to order, plus the inevitable mint tea, and watch the callers vie with each other to lure passing tourists to choose them. Daylight quickly fades and, as the illuminations come on, the atmosphere becomes totally magical, with a sense of excited anticipation at this most evocative moment of the day.

Next day, in deference to generous support from the Mobil fuel company on this jaunt, we apply their decals, giving pause to contemplate the contours of the Europa body. They are quite different to those of the Elise and Exige, but no less pleasing. Styled as a Grand Tourer and designed in house at Hethel by Barney Hatt, the frontal aspect has more in common with Evora than Elise. The roofline is higher than its siblings' – just as the sills are cutaway for ease of access, and the rear clams have less rounded, more angled wheelarches than the junior Hethel line-up. Look in the side mirrors, and you can see the rear spoiler as well, so it's easy to judge the size of the car in parking situations.

In any context, the Europa is a brilliant car. It has much of the raw sportiness of the Elise in terms of handling and performance, yet it's a civilized version, clad in a more sophisticated – less raunchy – body. Accelerate hard through the gears, and that raw edge is immediately apparent. There's still the hard, uncompromising sports-car ride, so that whilst it rides the bumps and doesn't necessarily transmit them to your backside, it certainly does go bonk over drains, potholes and gullies. Mostly though, you can avoid these hazards, as the Europa is hyper-responsive to steering inputs. It's so beautifully manoeuvrable that you can place it anywhere you like on the road, which is especially useful in sweeping mountain passes where you can be fairly sure no velocity vigilantes are lurking.

Into the Mountains

We move to the expansive Amanjena hotel on the opposite side of Marrakech, out on the road to Ouazarzate and the Atlas foothills. We fuel up in Marrakech, though we do pass one or two filling stations later, negotiate the burgeoning suburbs and head southeast to Asni, a small town 47 miles (75km) distant, within sight of snowy Jbel Toubkal, North Africa's highest mountain at 4,167m (13,671ft). Domestic architecture consists mainly of mud-walled buildings in varying degrees of decrepitude, terracotta-coloured, and flanked by olive groves, eucalyptus and palms, inhabited by people living cheek by jowl with their cattle. Donkey carts are laden with herbs and logs, while herds of sheep and flocks of goats,

The Europa SE is beautifully manoeuvrable on sweeping mountain passes and can be placed anywhere you like on the road, while every little input has an effect on the car's direction of travel.
JASON PARNELL

sometimes indistinguishable, stray onto the road. Every village has a mosque, and at certain times the landscape echoes to the sound of a dozen or so chanting muezzin calling the people to prayer from their lofty minarets.

By and large, the main roads are smooth asphalt, randomly fenced by giant prickly pear cacti, and olive groves beyond with sheep grazing in them. White milestones with yellow caps regularly divulge distances between towns. Every now and then, the surface degenerates into massive potholes and trenches. There's been a lot of rain, and water coming off the mountains cascades into churning pink torrents beside the road. Red mud has washed off the hills, creating sandbanks across the road, while dwellings in the middle distance are the same colour as the outlying ground, making them pretty hard to spot. Three miles (5km) winding up out of Tahanaout, there are serious rock falls, narrowing the slim thoroughfare to single track, with some recently installed Armco and old red-and-white painted wall to stop vehicles falling into the precipice. This is a major pass in the grand scheme of things but it is in pretty poor shape. They'll need major plant to shift some of those boulders: eat your heart out, Charles Atlas.

Past the watershed at Taroudannt village, the road is newly surfaced and winds down along the valley before climbing again towards the Tzi-n-Tichka pass (2,300m/7,500ft), final conduit from the snowy mountains into the desert. The sun is out under clear skies and it's hot, though at Kasbah Toubkal, just beyond Asni, off the main drag at Imlil the snow is still a metre or so deep. Winter tyres or not, we stick to the main highway, which is a proper Lotus driving road with a taxing variety of cambered bends and differing apexes. Every little input has an effect on the car's direction, but I can also control the turn-in by lift-off oversteer: off the throttle, it tucks in, back on the throttle the nose comes out again.

Time for lunch, and our chosen café has just opened for the summer season. Apart from mint tea, all the proprietor can offer is cheese omelette, but it's possibly the best I've ever had. Soaking up sunshine in the Atlas Mountains may have something to do with it.

The valley floor broadens out, revealing villages in amongst the olives and conifers, pink flat-roofed buildings protruding from the greenery. In spite of the remoteness, there are plenty of cafés, restaurants, B&Bs and auberges. For a short while, the road becomes single track with enough run-off either side to get two wheels on the rough when something comes the other way. A Peugeot hatchback overtakes with all four wheels in the dirt. Its occupants can hardly see out for their cargo of cannabis plants.

At one location, I spend half an hour driving the car repeatedly to and fro through a series of bends for lensman Jason's benefit, and a shepherd's family comes down to the roadside to see what's going on. Two beautiful children sit on the bank. They grin and wave, and Jason gives them a few dirham each. They thank him politely, and they and their flock drift off. It's much the same reception everywhere. In Asni the college students hail us enthusiastically, and everybody loves the Lotus; young or old, in local or European garb, they all wave and give the thumbs up as I pass by, and if they are within earshot it is, '*Comment ça va?*' or sometimes, from an older person or the hotel staff, the greeting is a more formal '*Salaam aleykum*,' peace be with you.

On the way back to Marrakech, we pause at the Adrar Tinmel café with its adjacent 'I saw you coming' gift shop. It's poised high on a ridge, with staggering views overlooking a big lake. We're surrounded by mountains with powder snow on the tops and covered in scrub, which the goats are tucking into. Locals squat on the hillsides chatting in the late afternoon sun. There's quite a drop-off on the side of the road down to the lake, and the road is peppered with rock falls and potholes.

Back to Tangier

Heading into Marrakech in the dark, the traffic build-up becomes increasingly chaotic, to the point of total anarchy at the Medina. This is not a good place for a brand-new car, though the Lotus's manoeuvrability doubtless helps keep us out of scrapes. There are many heart-stopping moments in a generally nerve-wracking experience; call it filtering, but the two-wheeled and four-legged brigades simply just do not look. This is in complete contrast to our accommodation. We've contrived a loop, necessitating the foray into the city before reaching our Amanjena hotel, which is actually 2 miles (3km) out of Marrakech. It's a splendid complex, vast in area, built with geometric precision around a carp pond the size of a rugby pitch, contriving to be both oasis and Saharan palace. The spaciousness of the site indulges monumental architecture, characterized by colonnades and an amalgam of 1930s art deco, Egyptian and Moroccan styles.

The Atlas Mountains foothill roads are perfect for a Lotus, with a taxing variety of cambered bends and differing apexes, allowing me to make good use of the Europa's 2.0-litre turbocharged VX220 powerplant.
JASON PARNELL

Rear three-quarter shot of the Type 121 Europa SE in the foothills of the Atlas Mountains, showing the hatchback, spoiler and distinctive light clusters.

GOING DUTCH

The Dutch Spring Run was an excellent opportunity to run an Exige Cup 260 over to the Netherlands for a cross-country drive trip.
ALBERT MENSINGA

One May bank holiday, I hooked up with the Netherlands Lotus fraternity for its three-day Dutch Spring Run, helming a 2009 Exige Cup 260 press car.

The Dutch road trip takes participants on a tour of Holland's northern and eastern Overijssel, Gelderland and Enschede provinces, and on across the blink-and-you-miss-it Schengen-style border into Saxony, Germany. Organized by Albert Mensinga, one of my regular comrades-in-arms at the Spa Six Hours, the route meanders through gorgeous landscapes, bookmarked by windmills and canals aplenty along the way.

Setting off from bourgeois Amersfoort in central Holland, a succession of charming vistas unfolds as the entourage of twenty-five sports cars passed through woods, heath, pasture, polder and marshland. What looked like only a short distance on the map takes all day to cover, as the retinue squirms this way and that down country lanes, where two vehicles can pass only by using the demarcated cycle tracks on either side. No question, whether it's family groups, lone riders, or athletic Tour de France packs out training, bicycles rule the roost in the Netherlands.

Small farms, with orchards and chestnuts in blossom, are grazed by horses, cattle, sheep and goats in a pastoral good-life idyll; everything is beautifully manicured in this manifestly prosperous country. Reapers and binders crop new-mown hay, and dandelions and cow parsley deck the roadside avenues of poplar running alongside the canals. Maypoles and bunting decorate villages, and locals, young and old, point excitedly as the red Exige 260 passes by.

You can be as careful as you like to stick to speed limits, but waver a little over and Murphy's Law says that's where the trap will be. Sure enough, on the home run near Rabat we're summoned into a gap in the central reservation by a pair of jackbooted cops for going a tad over the 120km/h (75mph) maximum. '*Vous alliez trop vite, toutes les deux*,' says one. I explain we're hurrying to Tangier to catch the ferry. They suggest €450 might be an appropriate forfeit, but after chatting about the Lotus – where it's made, how much it costs (but not how fast it'll go) – they think better of it, and with a cordial handshake wave us on.

On the outskirts of Tangier, kids run up to the car at red lights begging for goodies. By chance, I pick up Hassan, an amiable *djellaba*-clad official guide who bought me a pot of mint tea at the port a long week ago, and he breezes us past the glowering harbour police. Leaving Morocco is still time-consuming, but less fraught than entering it. After an uneventful sea crossing, at Tarifa docks a customs Alsatian sniffs all vehicles for drugs, but I do a dog whisperer on him and when it's the Europa's turn for scrutiny, he licks me instead.

In Morocco, though, the Europa is just one more paradox in a country that has plenty of them, most obviously the new autoroute and the subsistence farming it bisects. On one hand, I feel uncomfortable because the car attracts the attention of the authorities, and on the other it's a delight to ordinary folk. The surprise is how friendly everybody is – I find even a wave to policemen is reciprocated – but it's no

On through water meadows, past lifting bridges and church spires silhouetted against big blue skies, we reach Kampen on the River IJssel, a handsome town like all the old Hanseatic ports, with barges lining the quay making a quaint backdrop to holiday boating. A fiendishly convoluted and devious route means it isn't long before the motoring line-up becomes dispersed. Sometimes 'lost' cars are encountered going in the opposite direction, but no one is astray for long, as GPSs faithfully plotted a course to lunchtime café and evening meeting points. The latter is the Sandton Resort Hotel at Bad Boekelo, where the entourage sample *oude ginevra* nightcaps on the terrace. The final day brings a blast of uncensored autobahn across the German border at Bad Bentheim, another medieval town with a substantial fortress at its heart. Then, after fond farewells, it is only 450 motorway miles (725km) back to Hethel.

Poised beside the Twentekanaal near Enschede, the Dutch Spring Run took a party of sports cars, including the Exige Cup 260, from Amersfoort across the Netherlands to Bad Bentheim, just over the German border.

bad thing to travel out of your comfort zone; it makes the adventure all the more rewarding.

A MAN FOR ALL SEASONS: AN ENCOUNTER WITH STEFANO D'ASTE

Proprietor of Bergamo-based Lotus dealership PB Racing, Exige and 2-Eleven racer Stefano D'Aste puts a wealth of competition experience on both two and four wheels to good use, running the Lotus Cup Italy.

You'd think running a Lotus dealership would be enough to keep one man pretty well occupied full time, but Stefano D'Aste has other ideas. He also runs the Lotus Cup Italy series, as well as servicing seven participants' cars in an arrive-and-drive package through his PB Racing facility. Appropriately, he drives a Lotus 2-Eleven. On top of all that, in his spare time he's a professional racing driver, competing in the World Touring Car Championship (WTCC). We caught up with him at Brescia's Autodromo di Castrezzato Franciacorta racetrack, where he and his right-hand-man Pino were fettling a trio of cars for the next Lotus Cup Italy round. Two were customer Exige 260 Cups – one to GT4 spec – and the third was his own 2-Eleven.

Stefano D'Aste is the proprietor of Bergamo-based Lotus dealership PB Racing, putting his reputation on the line with his 2-Eleven race car.
JASON PARNELL

BELOW: **Stefano D'Aste was at Brescia's Autodromo di Castrezzato Franciacorta racetrack for a round of the Lotus Cup Italy series, fettling a pair of customer Exige Cup 260s and his own 2-Eleven.**
JASON PARNELL

It's a hands-on affair, right down the line. 'We organize the championship,' he tells me, 'and there are eleven cars in total – seven that we look after, and another four from the Paragon Interdrive team, Pugliese Motorsport and Rosso Corsa.' PB Racing hardly modifies the cars at all.

> If you buy a Lotus Exige to do track days, you really need nothing extra, and, for racing, you just need slick tyres and four shocks, but nothing more, provided it's got the cage. The quality of the car is very high, and you can do 1,000km [600 miles] with no problems, and you can even have a lot of fun queuing in traffic, because all the girls will look at you!

Spoken like a true Italian!

Stefano's first Lotus was an Elise S1, bought in 1997 when the first one-make series for the Elise got under way in Italy under the auspices of Peroni Promotion. That led to him founding PB Racing in 1999 (at the same time that the Autobytel series was formulated in the UK).

> I could see a gap in the market for a tuning kit, because it is a very good road car, and it can be a very good race car with little modification. I started the race preparation business at PB Racing, and went into partnership with the Lotus dealer at Bergamo before buying him out in 2004. We have built a showroom close to the Seriate exit on the A4 Milan–Venice autostrada, which has everything you would expect of a serious dealership.

PB Racing's state-of-the-art workshops are located in Lallio, a stone's-throw from Bergamo airport. The seven resourceful

The Exige Cup 260 prepped by Stefano D'Aste's Bergamo-based PB Racing displays a few battle scars gained in the Lotus Cup Italy, reminding me that his workshop similarly repaired an Evora in which I was T-boned on a roundabout at Como en route to a shoot at Verona.
JASON PARNELL

technicians working there are augmented to fifteen on race weekends for admin and fettling cars. As well as preparing, maintaining and repairing the cars, PB Racing provide customers with racing kit, transport their cars to the track, and give them trackside assistance. They also handle the paddock hospitality over the race weekend, which includes catering and music on Saturday night.

Keeping on top of his busy schedule is tough for Stefano, but he loves every minute.

> As well as selling and servicing Lotuses and running the race shop, I race in the WTCC and Lotus Cup Italy. It can get hectic, but racing and cars and engines are my passions, and for me, there's nothing better than spending the weekend doing that with my friends and my best customers. Lotus Cup events are more fun – relaxing, even – because when I do the WTCC there's too much to do, to think about, and then there is the pressure, the press conference briefing, and so on. It's a big deal.

Nevertheless, he's a proven winner, having taken the Independents' division of the WTCC in 2007, driving a BMW, no mean feat given the stature of the opposition.

As far as he's concerned, one of the principal objectives of the Lotus Cup Italy is for devotees of the marque to realize their racing aspirations and have fun together in an atmosphere that lacks the aggressive rivalry of other championships, such as the Clio Cup. From his point of view, he says:

> You can see a lot of accidents in WTCC, but we know what we are doing – a professional driver has to go hard, and sometimes we crash. But some drivers jump straight into a championship at a high level, and think that they have to crash to push out the other drivers. That's not the right way to go racing. With Lotus Cup, we have a great weekend with racing, relaxing, and fun.

Although he doesn't participate in the Lotus Cup Europe at the moment, he predicts that the two series will probably combine to race all together in a one-off at Imola, south of Bologna. 'That's a very famous Italian circuit,' he reminds us, 'because it was an F1 track for a long time, and we are organizing the weekend in conjunction with the WTCC as a support race. We are looking to have a deal to drive about fifteen cars from Lotus Cup Europe and Lotus Cup Italy.'

Stefano was turned on to motor sport at an early age:

> When I was a child of two or three, a racing driver was like a god, and I was very impressed by fast road cars. Then, my father brought me to Monza to see the F1 GP in about 1980 or 1981, and when I heard the noise of the 12-cylinder Ferrari, something stirred inside me. My father was not very happy, because he thought it would damage my ears, and he tried to close my ears with his fingers, but I told him, 'No, I want to listen!'

Stefano came to car racing a bit late, having started off on motorcycles.

> I arrived, aged fifteen, in the Italian 125cc championship, when it was won by Valentino [Rossi]. I was his team mate, and he is my friend. I beat a lot of riders that you now see in MotoGP.

Stefano D'Aste riding the kerbs in his 2-Eleven at Autodromo di Castrezzato Franciacorta during a round of the Lotus Cup Italy championship.
JASON PARNELL

> I signed a contract with the Cagiva team, but we had some problems with an engineer, so I changed to Aprilia and came fifth in the Italian 250cc Championship. I tried Formula 3 cars during the winter – it was the first time I'd even sat in a racing car – and an engineer asked me if I was a kart driver, and I told him, 'No, I am a biker.' He was amazed. He said, 'You are a biker, and you are here to test for F3? You cannot do it, because you don't have the experience.' But the team owner was a friend of my father, and he said I could do it, and after forty laps I was second fastest of the day, 5/10 of a second off the pole. I did Formule Renault and Clio Cup 3000, where I was second in the European Championship, and then I went with the European Car Touring Car Championship (ETCC) and then WTCC.

Twenty years at the marque's cutting edge testify that Stefano is a diehard Lotus fan.

> I love the Lotus brand. One of my biggest idols is Colin Chapman. He was one of the best constructors and practitioners in Formula 1, and without him, even forty years on, Formula 1 couldn't be what it is today. His ideas were always advanced, and sometimes incredible – for example, if you think of the wing on the rear of the Exige, it is so simple, but Chapman was the first guy to fit wings on his racing cars, and it was very daring at the time. Also, the carbon-fibre chassis that he innovated for F1, with a flat undertray and skirts to create downforce through suction; he was a great man. So, for me Lotus cars are the best conjunction between a racing car and a road car – the best in the world, in fact, and I drive a lot of cars. I sometimes do testing with Porsche and Ferrari, but when I drive a Lotus there's no comparison, because you can have so much fun. They are simple to drive, and you understand all the time what the car can do for you.

For track work, his preference is for the 2-Eleven. 'Because it's lighter, you can be a little more aggressive, and in changing direction it is quicker, but the Exige is also a great car because the chassis is very similar, and the response is very good, and its low weight makes it very easy on the brakes.' He drove an Evora on a recent visit to Hethel, when he and Pino received their training on the new model. 'It's fantastic, the Evora, and it could be a great race car. In fact, one of my dreams is to race a Lotus Evora with my own team in the FIA GT Championship.'

Rugged and handsome, Stefano is also a media star, fronting an Italian motor sport TV programme every Thursday evening. 'I go on every Thursday, and speak about what's happening in motor sport – F1, touring cars, MotoGP, World Superbikes – and there are always a lot of very special guests.' His favourite Lotus? 'The Exige, because we won the 24-Hours of Dubai with one last January, but on the road my favourite is the 260 Cup. It is very quick – a fantastic car.' With such a dynamic ambassador, Lotus fortunes in Italy are in very good hands.

AMERICAN GRAFFITI

Two racetracks, the Big Apple and an awful lot of forest – the Exige 260S takes all in its stride. I drove one from Manhattan to Connecticut and back to check out its all-rounder credentials.

New Jersey Turnpike provided my first acquaintance with this particular Exige Cup 260, and we became better acquainted on the run to Lime Rock circuit in Connecticut.
JASON PARNELL

Leaving New York

We're going nowhere fast, though. It should be half-an-hour's run up the Van Wyck Expressway from New York's JFK airport to the Bronx, but we're bottlenecked in the Bronx rush hour. It soon opens up, though, and the George Washington Bridge across the Hudson River sat-navs me through suburbia.

I'm in the Dodge SUV mothership with LCI magazine editor Caroline and photographer Jason, on our way to Ralph Stechow's place in suburban Bergen County, New Jersey. Ralph has been into Lotuses since the 1960s, and his RS Motorsports business runs the oldest independent Lotus dealership in the USA. He's lending me the Burnt Orange Exige Cup 260 so I can go and join in the fun up at Lime Rock circuit, Connecticut, where the Skip Barber Race School has just taken delivery of four Exiges.

It's dark when I hit the road. Heading north in the Lotus, I live out Chuck Berry's motoring mantra, 'You Can't Catch Me': '…New Jersey turnpike in the wee-wee hours, I was rolling slowly 'cos of drizzling showers…'. The rain builds till I start to ponder the effectiveness of my Exige's Yokohama tyres. This I hadn't bargained for. I do get my answer on the tyre question, though; they twitch momentarily where rivers of water flow across the road, but it looks like I'm safe from aquaplaning. Spray from fast moving semi-trucks makes overtaking hazardous up the Taconic State Parkway, and soon I take refuge in the slow lane. This is unfamiliar territory for both me and the Exige.

The main issue a Lotus driver faces here is the dreadful state of the road surfaces through New York state. They are potholed, bumpy and bodged, purgatory in any sports car. On the main Interstate Highway 84, cracks and lines abound where it's broken up from frost-heave, hard going for the Lotus with its sports suspension constantly in clunk mode. Yet would I be in the spongy Dodge? No way José.

Rustic New England

At last we're heading out of New York state, on generous rolling dual carriageway passing into Connecticut at Danbury. The weather, and the fact I've been up almost twenty-four hours, makes the Waterbury Diner a perfect stopover for a late supper of pancakes and maple syrup – welcome to America!

Our target is the Winvian Farm Hotel resort at Morris, a township on Highway 63. By now it's close to midnight out in the boondocks, and when we arrive the Winvian turns out to be a collection of charming cottages scattered in the woods. Florianna, the night porter, escorts us along the dark forest tracks to our respective abodes. Set in its own little glade, each cottage is themed – Jason's is 'Maritime' and Caroline's 'Musician's', while mine is 'the Artist's'. Care to pop over and see my etchings? Unfortunately, nothing could be further from the realms of possibility as, exhausted, I'm instantly fathoms deep.

We stay at the Winvian Farm Hotel at Morris, Connecticut, and the Exige Cup 260 poses beside the Artist's cottage, which I call home for a few days.

It's next morning before I get to contemplate the scenery of our immediate environment, the Humaston Brook State Park Scenic Reserve, no less – confirmation of which I receive on opening my patio door to be greeted by a garter snake with its bright blue stripes; it's non-poisonous, I'm advised. There are also bears a plenty in them-there woods, plus deer, foxes, squirrels and various scurrying rodents.

So, this is Connecticut, New England. And oddly disorienting it is too, to find Bristol, Windsor and Glastonbury juxtaposed by state capital Hartford. Norwich is just down the road, along with neighbouring Preston, which definitely messes with my head in a geographical sense. With its extended coastline protected from the Atlantic by Long Island Sound, it is one of the USA's favoured states: rich and densely populated with insurance company executives, hedge fund managers and trees. It's a hugger's paradise, with every temperate species making a showing in vast tracts of forest. No surprise, then, that all the domestic architecture consists of timber, pastel-coloured clapboard houses with brick chimney stacks. All is neat and tidy. The residents are obviously proud of their state, and fervently patriotic, judging by the number of Union flags in front yards. Virtually every house is flying a large stars-and-stripes from pole, porch, mailbox, gatepost or tree.

I leave the delights of the Winvian for the splendours of the Litchfield Hills, on the hunt for the perfect stretch for some car-to-car photography. Bantam Lake, with woods right down to the water's edge, a few jetties and enclaves with speedboats and fishing craft is straight out of *On Golden Pond*, and a lakeside campsite reminds me of Camp Grenada – Allan Sherman's paean to adolescent holidays – '…wait a minute, it's stopped hailing, guys are swimming, guys are sailing…'. Old-fashioned telegraph poles line the verges, posts festooned with creeper. Buzzards circle overhead, casting their shadows on the tarmac. Somebody's fishing from a boat in Lake Waramaug, where they've got vineyards, stone garden walls and split-rail fences. The closest town to here is Washington Depot, and everywhere there are undulating, densely wooded hills, green pillows differing in colour according to species. The lanes that crisscross them are canopied by branches so the sun doesn't fully dry them, calling for caution in the Exige.

On main roads like the 202, most of the speed limits are 45mph (72km/h), so that's not so onerous. I've found a nice twisty lane over the hills between Roxbury and Woodbury, and I'm able to squirt the Exige around these corners with some exuberance, though I'm lucky to miss no less than three highway patrol officers in different locations on the way, observing traffic in that inscrutable Ray-Ban manner. The surface is smooth enough not to throw the car offline, and it laps it up, until I'm hauled into order by an inexplicable 35mph (56km/h) limit, no doubt designed to keep the local traffic – tractors and cattle – firmly under control. So, instead of itching with frustration, I concentrate on the Exige's other attributes, things that maybe you normally take for granted. Its handling ability means I can go around

The Exige Cup 260 complements the splendours of Litchfield Hills, Connecticut, with Bantam Lake down below.
JASON PARNELL

any corner at 35mph without lifting, revelling in the instant throttle response, the sharpness of the brakes, the turn-in, the notchiness of the gearshift.

That night, the TV is hugely agitated over a tornado that's passing by up the Housatonic valley, newscasters advising people living in its path to take shelter in their basements. In time-honoured wartime spirit, we find a refuge in the Winvian's restaurant, where we manage to sit it out without incident.

Up to Lime Rock

Another day, another dollar, and I'm heading north to Lime Rock. There's no evidence of storm damage, though raised eyebrows speak of hailstones big enough to dent cars. Instead I watch the water droplets accelerating back towards me along the Exige's front clamshell. Highway 63 is quite a quick road between Litchfield and Goshen, flanked by a muddle of woodland draped with ivy and creeper. The closer I get to Lime Rock, the more automotive gems I spot in garages and gardens – from a sharp Datsun 240Z to a Z28 Camaro, and other more obscure 1970s pony cars.

Most of these long hills have decent bends half-way up or down, and I have to stay sharp and get the speed down before the corner comes up because of last night's storm – it may be damp under the trees, and there's no barrier. At West Cornwall, there's one of the state's best-known landmarks – the Covered Bridge. Like one of Clint Eastwood's in *Bridges of Madison County*, the 75m-long (250ft) West Cornwall version spans the Housatonic River at a particularly turbulent point. The bridge itself is tunnel-like and dark inside, akin to driving into a very long garage. The Exige rumbles over the railway sleepers that constitute the single-track road.

Now I'm on Highway 7 in the Housatonic Meadows State Park, designated a scenic route, though why here more than almost anywhere else in Connecticut is not clear. Recently resurfaced, there are still cracks in the tarmac but it is relatively smooth, and the best I've seen for a while. Again, it's quite a quick road, winding through forest, and though the sun is filtering through the trees, it hasn't yet dried the road out. The river's across to the right, choppy as it churns over the rapids. It gets hillier, with the state's altitude-topping Bear Mountain (709m/2,326ft) a few miles north. The topography is reflected in the ups and downs of Lime Rock circuit, a bit

like Cadwell Park – then imagine a pack of full-blown ALMS cars or a Grand-AM grid storming round Cadwell, which is what they serve up at Lime Rock. I'm greeted by genial Walter Irvine of the Skip Barber Race School, who goes straight into a skidpan display in one of the school's four Exiges. I spend the day watching pupils circulate in single-seaters and sports cars, sampling the circuit and the autocross track myself in the Exiges. It's huge fun, especially lapping three and four abreast while we do the photoshoot. This is an awesome circuit, especially the uphill surge and downhill dash. The Exige is absolutely the right car to get the most out of it, and it's easy to see why they chose it as a school car.

The Skip Barber operation is headquartered in nearby Lakeville, home to the deepest lake in the State, and they serve a good dinner at the bargeboarded Boathouse Restaurant, appropriately decorated with aquatic themes, including canoes on the ceiling. I have a laugh with Walter, his colleague Jim Altemus and one of the race school pupils, Antonia Salm, who runs a BMW in the 24 Hours of Lemons series, a sort of real-life Wacky Racers where you pick a theme – hers is saving sharks – and decorate your $500 car accordingly; then you race it for 24 hours at a number of US venues over the season. It's a light-hearted thing, but the Lemons guys take it fairly seriously.

I check out of the Interlaken Motel and head down the road to Goshen to meet my friend, historic racer Murray

ABOVE LEFT: **The Exige Cup 260 rumbles through the covered bridge at West Cornwall, Connecticut, which carries the Sharon-Goshen Turnpike over the Housatonic River.**
JASON PARNELL

Splashing an Exige through Lime Rock's Skip Barber Racing School skidpan.
JASON PARNELL

Smith, who lives nearby and who's got several classic Lotus racing cars, including a Type 15 and Type 18. Murray also presents a Type 26R Elan and a Type 23 belonging to Roy Walzer, another local and well-known character on the historic scene. His mechanics are discussing a brown bear they've seen on the track that morning – it sounds enormous, and a common manifestation in these parts.

Time to sample the Big Apple, and I hustle the Exige Cup 260 southeast on Interstate 17, flow from Garden State Parkway onto the New Jersey Turnpike, and emerge into Manhattan through the Lincoln Tunnel. Stevie Wonder's song 'Livin' for the City' comes to mind – 'New York, just like I pictured it – skyscrapers, everything…'. Hubris lends a hand. There's no dialogue with the traffic cop. As we wait to see where the hotel's parking lot is, he books the Dodge mothership. We are soliciting, he says, 'importuning, blocking the pavement,' – you name it, we're guilty. Unlike Stevie Wonder's character who gets banged up, Officer Krupke finally relents, persuaded our intentions aren't quite so heinous, and we merely get a parking ticket.

There's nothing like being in New York. In Times Square the buzz is palpable. I spend the morning in MoMa – the Museum of Modern Art – which blows me away, and the afternoon in Abercrombie & Fitch, which does the same for my wallet. Downtown, I pass the Empire State Building, though the Flatiron and Woolworth skyscrapers are more impressive for their quirkiness. I shuffle by Wall Street – where once a wall stood to keep the English out of New Amsterdam – and fetch up at the East River quayside by Brooklyn Bridge. Lower East Side, where most of the immigrants arrived (and the punks pogo'd at CBGB's) is still the poorest bit of Manhattan, though at $3k a month to rent a one-bed apartment, it's far from cheap.

Here's the thing; can an Exige ever be a car for New York? Perhaps: it certainly wins hearts on the cute factor, though the ones that call it that have no idea what it's capable of. So, that'll be a no, basically. Where the implacable yellow cab rules, citations come for nothing, potholes predominate and traffic crawls, it's not home turf. Connecticut will do nicely, though.

The Exige Cup 260 motoring through the Housatonic Meadows State Park, designated a scenic route, and relatively smooth, winding through forests.
JASON PARNELL

Back in New York, dwarfed by skyscrapers such as the Flatiron building, the Exige is out of its natural environment.

A Slice of Lime

Budding racers learn the tricks of the trade in the tyre tracks of Grand-Am and American Le Mans Series hot-shoes, courtesy of the Skip Barber Race School, at Connecticut's picturesque Lime Rock race circuit.

It gets mighty crowded at Lime Rock when a big-time Grand-Am or ALMS event hits town. Set in the lee of a northern Connecticut hillside, the 1.53-mile (2.5km) circuit has seven corners and a very fast main straight, plus a winding section that climbs the hill and almost instantly plunges back down again. Owned by prominent 1960s US racing driver Skip Barber (no relation to George Barber of the eponymous Alabama museum), Lime Rock began running SCCA meetings in the late 1950s, growing into USAC and IMSA events during the ensuing decades. Today, it hosts a dozen major race meetings a year, including ALMS, Grand-Am Rolex GT and NASCAR Camping World East championship rounds. There is no down time.

The eponymous Skip Barber Race School (which he founded but no longer owns) has recently taken delivery of six Lotus Exiges to augment its training fleet. The LCI team – Caroline, Jason and I – are welcomed by genial business manager Walter Irvine. He's in charge of client and sponsor liaison for the race school, and tells us a little of the circuit's history:

> Lime Rock was built in 1957 by the local farmer. Back then, there weren't a lot of very fast cars, so it is relatively small, just under 1.6 miles, and until recently there weren't a tremendous amount of sanctioned events here, and there just wasn't enough revenue to realistically reconfigure the track so they would be able to attract that clientele. So, Skip Barber, who owns the track and began our race school in 1975, started selling memberships to Lime Rock Park Club, the concept being that, if I bring along my Ferrari or my Lotus or my Bentley, there is a quantifiable amount of track time available. The allure is incredible, because members have free rein of the race track, and that is a very difficult thing to do in this country, for somebody with a nice car just simply being allowed to come in and have some track time. We have a real club atmosphere here now, and it brings in revenue to make a lot of improvements.

There are around fifty road courses in the USA, and that's not counting banked ovals. The list includes Indianapolis and Daytona, Watkins Glen, Laguna Seca, Elkhart Lake, Homestead and Sebring, and Lime Rock is up there with the best of them. Vast improvements were made during 2008–9, including resurfacing and easing various bends in the interests of safety. Like the other 'Barber' circuit, George Barber's track at Birmingham, Alabama, Lime Rock eschews grandstands in favour of grass banks for public viewing, fostering a picnic scenario for families. Nowhere does this come into its own more than the Fall Festival, the Rolex-sponsored historic meeting they've hosted for the last twenty-six years

ABOVE: **A riot of Exiges – as in four go mad at Lime Rock. Big Bend, seen here, is actually two turns, two apexes, taken very fast, riding the kerbs on the inside.**
JASON PARNELL

Walter Irvine was business manager at Lime Rock Circuit, as well as handling client and sponsor liaison for the Skip Barber Race School.
JASON PARNELL

JT learning the way round Lime Rock Park – the easy way: now we know where we are!
LAURA DRYSDALE

on Labor Day weekend – the first weekend of September – attracting 300 entries, including a concours on the Sunday. It's a busy weekend for Murray Smith, who runs the racing, while Kent Bain looks after the concours. An injunction going back to 1959 rules out racing on Sundays, though it permits unsilenced race cars any other time. Murray describes the track changes wrought by last year's makeover:

> The transformation from the old circuit eased some of the corners, especially Big Bend at the end of the main straight, which means the new layout is much more flowing because you don't have that dramatic speed reduction there was previously. The Uphill is a dangerous corner because that is where you can fly if you are not careful, and the chicane after the Uphill is really not so much to slow the cars down there as it is to slow them for the Downhill because the right-hander onto the straight is absolutely flat so cars like the ALMS Audi R8s are doing 155mph (250km/h) down the hill. And that's still some spectacle as it's not a wide track and there's not much run-off.

It's time to have a crack at circuit myself. Walter's going to show me the lines in the silver Exige, and I nose the orange Cup 260 out onto the pit lane behind him. The main straight seems broad enough, but we haven't started yet. First corner is Big Bend, which is actually two turns: turn one has an apex, and I let the car breath and come out of that and make for the second apex, turn two of this complex. Following Walter's line, I'm right down against the kerbing as I track out. Very quickly I'm into the only left-hand turn on the circuit, and it is very fast. This is the Esses. Instead of apexing and going out to the outside, we compromise this corner because the next corner, turn four, a right-hander, is much more important because it leads onto No Name Straight. Braking reference markers 5, 4, 3, 2, 1 are displayed prominently. This takes us into the Uphill section, a short, sharp elevation, where there's an alternative configuration like a chicane (named after IMSA racer John Morton, who had a fiery barrel roll here in 1989) designed to slow the quicker cars down. Both bits are used during a race weekend. We take the original route, which is very fast and very exciting, riding the kerbs on the inside a little. There's barely time to think on Back Straight before we arrive at West Bend, which also has an opposing route to slow the big boys.

The old bend is one of the most harrowing in North America, according to Walter, as it tightens up on itself and the car is in compression; it sits down, right up against the apex. Then, as we duck under the Bailey Bridge, there's the dramatic descent straight into the ultra-quick right-hand curve that leads into the start/finish straight. Fortunately, there's a cone at the apex for me to aim at, otherwise going off into the tyre wall is a gift. Alternatively, if I just put my left wheels in the gravel, it would probably hook the car at 100mph (160km/h) across the track and into the right-hand tyre wall. No such misadventure befalls us, and we're instantly hammering past the pits and the landmark Lime Rock control tower beside Front Straight, braking hard and lining up for Big Bend and another hectic lap. Huge fun!

Walter takes one of the new Exiges onto the skidpan, drifting and splashing, correcting slides and gyrating furiously, flicking huge rooster tails of water in the air.

Later, he fills us in on the scope of the driving school:

> We provide schooling across the country in four basic regions and we go to about thirty different tracks. Lime Rock is our base in the northeast, and we also have Sebring and Palm Beach International in the southeast with Atlanta in the mid-west, and Laguna Seca in California, where the other Exiges are. That's open all year round, while the others shut up shop for the winter by the end of November. The curriculum does not change, whether it's Laguna or Lime Rock. One of my favourite 'Skip Barberisms' is, 'Don't look where you are going, look to where you want to go.'

The Exiges are in good hands. Having owned several Lotuses previously, Walter is a flag-bearer for the marque.

> It took fifteen months, but Arnie [Johnson, Lotus USA CEO] gave us the six cars and it's been nothing but incredible. When people found out that we were getting Lotuses they literally wouldn't book a lesson until the Exiges arrived. Porsche, BMW and Lexus, they're wonderful cars but they look like rental cars when you put them next to an Exige.

Spoken like a true aficionado.

Lime Rock's West Bend is allegedly one of the most harrowing in North America, tightening up on itself while compressing the car's suspension as it sits down, hard up against the apex.

Set amongst forested rolling hills, Lime Rock's control building is the nucleus of the circuit and the Skip Barber Racing School.
LAURA DRYSDALE

Pupils at the Skip Barber Racing School learn the benefits and quirks of understeer and oversteer. Exiges are set up so they will oversteer very easily and the back end will step out, controlled on the throttle and by applying opposite lock.
JASON PARNELL

The Exige Cup 260 en route to the Skip Barber Racing School headquarters at Lakeville, home to Connecticut's deepest lake, for dinner at the aptly décor'd Boathouse Restaurant with Walter Irvine, Jim Altemus and Antonia Salm.
JASON PARNELL

Lotus Type 123 2-Eleven 2007–11

Layout and Chassis

Lotus-designed lightweight structure of epoxy-bonded and riveted aluminium alloy extrusions with integral steel seatbelt support structure and lightweight steel rear subframe. Ultra-lightweight (40kg/88lb) body panels bolted on for ease of removal. Launch edition exclusive three-way Lotus Sport colour scheme with decal pack. Six-point FIA compliant roll-over structure with integral harness bar

Engine

Type	Toyota-based WTL-I 16v 2ZZ-GE, transverse mid-engine
Block material	Metal matrix composite (MMC) and aluminium lightweight compact construction
Head material	Metal matrix composite (MMC) and aluminium lightweight compact construction
Cylinders	4 cylinders in line
Cooling	Water
Bore and stroke	82mm × 85mm
Capacity	1796cc
	Valves DOHC, chain-driven, 16 valves, VVTL-i (variable valve timing and lift with intelligent system), hydraulic tappets, 4 valves per cylinder
Fuelling	Multipoint sequential fuel injection, electronic ignition, electronic throttle control
Supercharger	Lotus Sport-developed Roots-type supercharger with unique rear-mounted air-to-air intercooler
Engine management	Lotus T4e engine control unit
Max. power	252bhp (188kW) at 8,000rpm
Max. torque	179lb ft (242Nm) at 7,000rpm
Emission control	Three-way catalytic converter (UK SVA pack only); full on-board diagnostics (OBD)

Transmission

Gearbox	Close-ratio C64 6-speed transaxle driving rear wheels. Switchable Traction Control System (LTCS)
Clutch	Hydraulic
Ratios	1st 3.116
	2nd 2.050
	3rd 1.481
	4th 1.166
	5th 0.916
	6th 0.815
	Reverse 3.250
Final drive	4.529

Suspension and Steering

Front and rear	Unequal-length double wishbones, Öhlins coil-over gas-pressured monotube dampers. Rear double-shear track control-arm brace, unique steering arms and front upper wishbones to suit ultra-low ride height
Steering	Rigidly mounted rack and pinion; 2.8 turns lock to lock
Wheels	Unique black forged alloy lightweight 5-spoke, 16in front, 17in rear
Tyres	Front: Yokohama A048 LTS (W rated) 195/50 R16
	Rear: Yokohama A048 LTS (W rated) 225/45 R17

Brakes

Type	Servo-assisted track-tuned 4-channel ABS with Lotus/AP Racing twin-piston fixed aluminium alloy front brake calipers, Brembo single-piston sliding rear calipers. Cast iron ventilated and cross-drilled discs
Size	288mm diameter, 26mm thick front and rear

Dimensions

Track	1,457mm (57.4in) front, 1,507mm (59.3in) rear
Wheelbase	2,298.7mm (90.5in)
Overall length	3,822.7mm (150.5in)
Overall width	1,714.5mm (67.5in)
Overall height	1,117.6mm (44in)
Dry weight	745kg (1,642lb)
Track pack format	725kg (1,598lb)
Track pack	High-downforce single-plane carbon-fibre rear wing, high-downforce front splitter, brake lights and rear indicators and FIA-approved driver's race seat with 6-point harness

Performance

Max. speed	155mph (294km/h)
0–100km/h (62mph)	3.8sec
0–100mph (160km/h)	9.1sec
Fuel consumption	Combined 30.4mpg (9.3ltr/100km)

ABBEVILLE ACTION

The Lotus Type 123 2-Eleven was delivered in three-way Lotus Sport colour scheme, seen here in the hands of two-time Le Mans winner and F1 driver Gijs van Lennep during a track-day session at Abbeville Circuit, France.
ANTONY FRASER

Twice a year, specially invited sports car fans from Belgium, Holland and Britain head for Abbeville race circuit in northern France, where enthusiast collector Johan Dirickx hosts a week-long track-day session. Invariably, this attracts an assortment of Lotuses, including Elises, Exiges and 2-Elevens, not to mention the occasional VX220. I attend regularly, and this is an account of a typical Abbeville programme.

Star of the show several years running is 1971 Le Mans winner, Gijs van Lennep, who laps consistently in a 2-Eleven and is having such a good time it is hard to prise him from the cockpit. A regular on the historic racing scene and a high-performance instructor at Zandvoort circuit, Gijs is enthusiastic. 'The Lotus is the ideal tool for the job. It sums up Colin Chapman's values perfectly – light weight and a good chassis set-up.'

Opposite-locking around the sinuous 1.5-mile (2.4km) circuit at the action-packed meeting, no one can outdo sideways king P-Jay for spectacular drifting in his VX220 Roadster. Also on hand is Gijs's Zandvoort instructor colleague, Yannick Dillen, fast lady extraordinaire. Yannick drives a dozen laps of Abbeville with me buckled up in the passenger's full harness. Such is the 2-Eleven's ferocious competence on a winding track that I still clutch the side tube of the roll-cage to keep out of her way as she shifts in and out of corners. Afterwards, as the tension drains away, she turns to me, totally composed, and remarks:

> Impressive isn't it? It's light on the steering, and it's on semi-slick Yokohamas that you can drive on the road, so it's really good fun! I'm using all the ratios and I do some left-foot braking to influence the nose of the car, force it down to make it steer a bit better, and that works, because you have a little bit more weight on the front, and then all of a sudden it turns in.

Out on the track, all this seems instantaneous as I watch her feet dancing on the pedals, her arms twirling from lock to lock, hand darting from steering wheel to gear lever and back again. Both the 2-Eleven and its driver have a voracious appetite for bends, and Abbeville has thirteen of them. For a couple of seconds on the main straight I can relax, before tensing up for the rest of the full-

Yannick Dillen is an instructor at Zandvoort and Assen circuits; here she treats JT to a few fast and furious laps of Abbeville in Johan Dirickx' 2-Eleven.
ANTONY FRASER

BELOW: **There is nothing that circuit driving instructor Yannick Dillen likes more than a session in a 2-Eleven, such as here at Abbeville Circuit in France.**
ANTONY FRASER

on lap, where I'm hurled forwards and backwards in my seat – or would be if it wasn't for the harness straps – legs braced against the footboard. All is a blur as we arc from one turn to another, braking late, tyres squealing, clipping apexes, riding the rumble strips, and dashing relentlessly on to the next challenge.

Yannick hasn't come to terms with the on-board traction control switch yet.

> You have a maximum and a zero, but if you switch it off completely then the inner wheel on the back is spinning so much that when you rev it up you don't get out of the corner – but if you put it too high then it takes the power of the engine away, so I am trying to find out what the ideal position of the button is. I'm an instructor, not a race driver, so I am not used to setting the car up to my liking: I just try to go fast with it however it handles. But the Lotus is really good fun, and not too expensive on tyres and brakes because of the weight.

She makes it sound simple, but it's always a salutary lesson to be driven round a circuit by a professional. Just leave it till you've digested your breakfast.

SPA-FRANCORCHAMPS

I handled an Exige under the guidance of Ron Simons for some circuit track-driving instruction at Spa-Francorchamps.

I first met ebullient Dutchman Ron Simons at the Nürburgring in 2005. I'd just bought a Porsche 964 from Roock Racing at Leverkusen and intended to give it a shakedown around the Nordschleife on one of its public access days. Trouble was, the 964 still bore its German export plates, which, along with trade plates, are a no-no on the Ring; if you crash and damage their Armco, they can't pursue you to reimburse them. So, although I'd paid the €15 to go on track (for one lap, if memory serves), the gatekeeper wagged his finger and turned me away. Ron Simons happened to be on the spot, carrying out his track driving tuition, and he saw my plight. 'Come out with me in my Alfa 75,' he suggested. So, my son Jules and I piled into the Italian tin-top, and Ron showed us how it's done. He even let us fetch another Alfa 75 V6 (like the one we'd had as a family hack) from his nearby depot and have a crack in that. So we ended up with ten hectic laps, unexpectedly, though not in the 964, and I've always felt grateful to Ron just for that.

Fast forward to 2012, and I'm at Spa-Francorchamps with my colleague Antony Fraser to do a story for *911 & Porsche World* magazine on Ron's flourishing RSRSpa operation. That included lapping Spa in a Porsche 997 GT3 and a Lotus Exige S. Perfect material for our Lotus book too! Here's my 2020 interview with Ron.

Having driven both Spa and the Nordschleife a few times, with Ron and his tutors in the passenger seat, I can wholeheartedly endorse his operation and recommend having a go yourself.

Johnny Tipler helms an Exige S belonging to Ron Simon's RSRSpa circuit driving school through the esses at Les Combes, Spa-Francorchamps, in July 2012.

ANTONY FRASER

A pair of RSRNürburg's Exige Ss in Nürburg village ahead of a day on the Nordschleife.
KOSTAS SIDIRAS

BELOW: **Partners in crime? Ron Simons and Johnny Tipler after enjoying a few laps at Spa-Francorchamps, May 2019.**
KOSTAS SIDIRAS

We can hear from someone who did. One of RSR's clients is Paulo Tavares de Melo, and I chatted with him over coffee in the Spa-Francorchamps paddock café, where he provided a eulogy on the Exige.

> I have been racing for most of my adult life, but always in small, front-wheel-drive cars, because back in Brazil, this was the most economical way to get your speed fix and bang fenders on the weekends. I never really had the chance of experiencing a rear-wheel-drive car on a race track until Ron Simons, from RSRSpa, introduced me to the Lotus Exige. The track? Of all places, Spa-Francorchamps!
>
> The Exige 240 initially caught my attention because of its size. It looks like a go-kart on steroids, and I wondered whether I would fit in it. Once you are in your seat, you immediately realize that you are in for a fun ride. Your butt is almost touching the ground and the steering wheel, pedals and gear shift lever are placed in just the right positions. I fired up the Toyota engine and took a couple of easy laps around the circuit to warm up the tyres, test the brakes and gearshifts.

JT: So how long have you been using Exiges?

RS: My racing/driving school and track car rental shop, RSRNürburg, has been using Lotus Exiges for a good ten years now.

JT: You began with a fleet of Alfa Romeo 75s, didn't you?

RS: We started with the Alfa Romeo 75 TS in the late 1990s. Rear-wheel drive, no ABS, light-alloy 2000cc engine, transaxle, and inboard rear brakes. It looked like a boxy sedan but underneath it was designed like a race car. This was, in a way, the same pure, honest momentum driving machine as our replacement car, the Lotus Exige.

JT: There have been other makes too.

RS: The Alfas were getting very old after hard use by 2005, and we had to find a replacement. For a while, the Renault Clio Cup was the one. Good car but it also gave us lots of trouble – gearbox and clutch – and also what was wrong was that it was front-wheel drive. We had to replace the Alfas with something serious to be able to satisfy our clients in the long run.

JT: And is that where the Exiges came in?

RS: From 2010, and we were very proud to land a works deal where Lotus was supplying us Exiges for the school. At the peak, we had almost twenty cars in the fleet. The cars were also used for our scenic and historic road tours in the Eifel and Ardennes, for guided convoy training and one-on-one coaching at the racetrack.

JT: Well, only last year you very kindly took us on an unforgettable tour up the Mosel, visiting riverside vineyards whilst driving from the Nürburgring to Spa in one of your Caymans. But how do you rate the Exiges?

RS: These cars are rock solid. Very low use of brakes, tyres and fuel. I don't think we ever did a clutch on any one of them. Only a few synchromesh replacements in the gearbox over all the years. The handling is very predictable and track-focused. With its 150mph (240km/h) on a little over 900kg (1,980lb), this was a serious piece of kit. The cars came without any warranty, which made us a bit nervous at first. However, this proved to be a non-issue, since the cars were perfect, and almost nothing went wrong in all those years.

JT: And could your pupils go out on track in all weathers?

RS: We supplied four sorts of tyres that pupils could choose from – wet weather road tyres, full racing wets, semi-slicks, and full slicks. Especially in the wet, the car's limits come right down at

Taking a tight line around La Source hairpin at Spa-Francorchamps in an RSRSpa Exige.
KOSTAS SIDIRAS

The 2-Eleven is the car of choice for Ron Simon's more experienced pupils, or for those wishing to step up from the Exige.
KOSTAS SIDIRAS

Putting car and driver to the ultimate test – achieving a quick lap of Spa-Francorchamps. As Ron Simons says, 'The Exige is a seriously fast car that *you* need to drive.'
ANTONY FRASER

the Nordschleife; but it's the same at Spa. With the full racing wets fitted, it's a very competitive car again, which is very predictable and with a sweet balance.

JT: Do you generally find that the punters can cope with the Exige?

RS: We often had to answer the question, 'Is it easy to drive?' Well it is, and it isn't. It all depends on the conditions, which tyres are mounted, and especially the skill set of the driver. It is very easy to drive, but don't get me wrong. The Exige is a seriously fast car that *you* need to drive – as opposed to, for example, a Nissan GTR, where the car is actually driving you. Without the right feel, skill, and confidence, it is a lethal package. We never put inexperienced drivers in these cars, since, more often than not, it proved to be too much for them to handle.

JT: So the driver is the weakest link, then?

RON SIMONS INTERVIEW *continued*

RS: Yes, the weak part in this case is the driver. Due to the burgeoning popularity of both tracks, Spa-Francorchamps and the mighty Nürburgring Nordschleife – and circuit driving in general, because where else can you have fun in a great car – we notice that skill levels don't match up to what is needed to keep the package safe – and by 'the package' I mean the car, the driver and instructor. Therefore, to keep these clients happy as well as safe, we needed cars that were easier to drive with the right nannies on board to keep the customers out of trouble.

JT: Have you had many cars damaged over the years?

RS: There was a time when we did need a lot of body parts due to crashes. People are simply not aware of their own limitations, I guess. Damage was mostly limited to just a front or rear clam. Expensive, yes, but fully and easily reparable. The core chassis of the car was mostly not touched, and therefore the car stayed in an 'as new' condition.

JT: At what point did you expand your fleet?

RS: We tried to upgrade our existing fleet with the new Exige SV6 when it came out. However, the car proved to be too much at first, and also was too expensive on consumables and initial investment, compared with the Porsche Caymans, for example.

First, we had the Alfa 75s, then these Lotus Exiges, and now we have BMW M2s and the Porsche Cayman GTS and GT4. But we still have returning customers asking for the Lotus Exige, and so we keep a few for that reason. We also still use our Lotus 2-Eleven, the Cup 260, and a very quick Komo-Tec Exige S (+75bhp) for the taxi hot laps at both tracks. The sensation of speed in the open-cockpit 2-Eleven is mind-blowing at Spa-Francorchamps where, on a good day, Blanchimont and Eau Rouge–Raidillon can be taken flat out.

The archetypal Nordschleife blast: a couple of RSRNürburg Exiges blitz the hallowed 14-mile (20km) circuit.

KOSTAS SIDIRAS

Ron Simons upgraded his fleet of track-driving instruction cars to include the Exige S V6 Cup, seen here at Spa-Francorchamps.
KOSTAS SIDIRAS

I quickly felt comfortable, and soon picked up the pace. That's when you really come to appreciate this awesome car. The engine is a perfect match for the car. I was impressed how well it performs, allowing you to understand how the car behaves at speed, and Spa was the perfect place for it. Because of the track's high-speed nature, you are constantly pushing the limits of the car, and that's where it really shines. The braking and, especially, the cornering ability of this car are absolutely incredible. I was able to keep up with much faster cars during the middle part of the track (from Les Combes to Fagnes). It really likes to be driven hard and to be thrown around, but, at the same time, it is very forgiving if you go past its limits. Like a go-kart, you end up sweaty and with a huge smile on your face after a track session. Since my first experience with the 240, I have gone back to Spa every year and, between the Exige 240, the 260 Cup and the 2-Eleven (oh my God, what a car!), I have now turned more than 1,000 laps in a Lotus at Spa. It would be an understatement to say that it is one of my favourite cars.

The 2-Eleven is so consistently popular with RSRSpa customers because of its racing credentials that Ron Simons retained the school's cars rather than replace them, not only to keep his clients happy but because there are no economically priced substitutes.
KOSTAS SIDIRAS

BORDER PATROL

Storming the wet and windswept Scottish Borders in a lemon-yellow Exige S, I discover the landmarks on the Jim Clark Trail.

If only I had GPS. It's not that I'm lost, it's just that Edinburgh's A720 southern bypass has so many speed cameras that I'm leery of taking the Exige S above 60mph (100km/h), dual carriageway or not. At least the TomTom would predict them. It's the supercharged car, which means rearward visibility is limited for the tail-gunner, so I bide my time till we turn off the A1 to head for the hills. It's here that the Lotus will come into its own.

I've collected our tasty slice of lemon meringue pie from one of the most prolific Lotus salesmen in the country, feisty Graeme Robertson of Murray Motors, whose dealership is just off the A720, a stone's throw from Ingliston and Edinburgh airport. There are several fine cars in his showroom, including a rare 340R and a gorgeous Elise in the blue and white Scottish racing colours of Écurie Ecosse.

The Jim Clark Trail

Strictly speaking, I should have started this pilgrimage on the north side of the Firth of Forth at Kilmany in Fife, where Jim Clark was born on 6 March, 1936. Although there's a statue of him there, Clark left Kilmany when he was only six, and so I go south to the Borders, his true turf. Following A1 signs for Galashiels, Hawick and Carlisle, I'm heading for Berwickshire and the Jim Clark Trail, an unofficial pilgrimage route linking places connected with our racing hero. Soon enough, I'm done with the main road, and hook off right at Haddington towards Gifford on the B6369. This is a land of long, straight B-roads with taxing right-angle corners at field boundaries where, thanks to hedge-free topography that provides a commanding view of the turns, I take a deep breath and use the whole road. The Exige stays firmly planted on course, hardly lifting off from the straightline velocity.

I make a right in Gifford, a pretty four-square village, onto the B6355, climbing up drove roads with their broad grass verges. The route thrusts up onto dry-stone-walled rough pasture, smooth asphalt bucking up and down with the contours. It's looking more and more remote, and at Danskine the 'drrrrr' of a cattle grid warns me I'm onto unfenced moorland, where the road width is scarcely more than single track. Round the next bend there's a sheep sitting on the side of the road – it doesn't bat an eyelid as I brake and jink by. Livestock notwithstanding, this is Lotus country: fast, uphill sweeps, off-camber turns, and blind crests. It's also lambing time, so I'm on my guard for strays; I can only put my foot down where the way's clear, and mud from tractor tyres is another local hazard.

The Exige controls have a refreshing immediacy: a flick of the wrist to change direction, tiny steering inputs weave the car through the bends, with similarly flexible wrist action

The Exige S stayed firmly planted, retaining the straightline velocity attained on Berwickshire's long, straight B-roads, anchoring hard to negotiate taxing right-angle field boundary corners.

JASON PARNELL

The Exige S rushes along the Borders back roads, familiar to Jim Clark, no doubt, and where he must have cut his motoring teeth.
JASON PARNELL

shifting the lever between third, fourth and fifth. Nimble footwork brings instant advance and retard. The surface is particularly uneven, and the steering kicks back as I ride the bumps. A few miles on, I'm at the summit of the Lammermuir Hills, 163m (535ft) above sea level, and high enough to see across Firth of Forth to the Fife coastline perhaps 20 miles (32km) to the north.

The beautiful Borders road quickly plunges downhill into an avenue of beech trees flanking a farm, and the cattle grid heralds fenced roads and rough pasture, thronged with ewes and lambs. Whiteadder Water morphs from stream to lake, shaded by silver birch and conifers, and there's yet another brief summit and a couple of bear-right turns down into Duns. I go left to Chirnside, 8 miles (13km) on the fast A6105, passing rally driver Louise Aitken-Walker's family garage on the way out of town. (She won the FIA Ladies' World Rally title in 1990 in an Opel Kadett with Swedish co-driver Tina Thörner, and was awarded the Jim Clark Trophy for the best performance in motor sport by a Scot.) On this curving A-road, the Exige delivers ferocious performance, and in fourth and fifth you feel like you can move mountains. It's incredibly quick and peerless in its responsiveness to steering, accelerating and braking.

Beside a chapel on the high road through Chirnside is the monumental town clock, dedicated to Jim Clark, and designed by his mentor and friend, local architect Ian Scott-Watson. The Border Reivers' mounted rider symbol is incorporated in the granite column, and a two-dimensional Lotus 25 is mounted at the summit alongside the clock. Close to the town's low road is the parish church where he is buried. I walk to the wall running along the top of the cemetery, and here's his headstone, no grander than any others, but obvious just now because of wreaths and bouquets placed by fans marking the fiftieth anniversary of his death. To its right is his parents' plainer stone, their dates showing that they outlived their son by little more than a decade.

Heading out of Chirnside, I pass the garage of Jim's cousin, Doug Niven, Scottish saloon-car champion in the late 1970s in a variety of V8-engined Fords and a 5.0-litre VW Beetle silhouette racer. Three miles (5km) east on the A6105 is a right turn into a lane leading to Edington Mill, a conversion of new apartments on the Whiteadder Water. Before you get there, you pass Edington Mains, where a large farmyard and barns dwarf the unassuming sandstone house where Jim lived and farmed, until tax exile took him to Paris and Bermuda in 1967.

I've an appointment at 44 Newton Street in Duns, home of the Jim Clark Museum, to meet Ian Scott-Watson, who's promised me a post-lunch guided tour of nearby Charterhall circuit, where young Jim cut his racing teeth. The compact museum displays a chronological arrangement of trophies, models and related photographs of the local hero, given to Duns town council by his parents after his death. Originally called the Jim Clark Trophy Room, it first opened in 1969. A refurbishment in 1993, funded variously by Hazel Chapman, Tom Walkinshaw, Peter Collins, Peter Windsor

The Jim Clark Motorsport Museum at Duns, Berwickshire was enlarged and refreshed before being opened by Sir Jackie Stewart on 31 August 2019.
LAURA DRYSDALE

BELOW: **The Jim Clark Motorsport Museum in Duns is a shrine to the late Formula 1 World Champion, a treasure chest containing many of the trophies and memorabilia garnered during his racing life.**
JASON PARNELL

and the Scottish Motor Racing Club brought an elevation of status from trophy room to museum. Duke Video provided footage of Clark in action, one film with commentary by Ian Scott-Watson, and nowadays it attracts over 10,000 visitors each year. Among the souvenirs that catch my eye is a booklet of original photos taken by Jim's farmer friend Eric Bryce.

I visited the JC shrine again in 2019 with Laura Tipler and Glenys Watt during another refurbishment launch, which was attended by a host of racing celebs including Sir Jackie Stewart and Jim's erstwhile girlfriend Sally Stokes and her racer husband, Ed Swart. Whilst trophies and documentary movies remain the museum's bedrock, now there's one of Jim's Type 25s and a works Lotus Cortina installed, giving a more tangible element to the experience.

Charterhall Airfield

A short hop south of Duns, just off the B6460, is Charterhall airfield. Exposed on a windswept arable plateau, it's like Snetterton would be if nothing had happened there for fifty years. Racing began here in spring 1952, with Mike Hawthorn winning a Formule Libre race in a Cooper-Bristol. Famous names who competed included Stirling Moss, Giuseppe Farina and Roy Salvadori, and it's where Jim Clark took his first win, on 5 October 1957. The Borders and District Motor Club, of

Jim Clark's F1 World Championship winning Coventry-Climax 1.5-litre V6-powered Type 25 R6 also features large in the Duns Motor Museum, currently on loan from the Tinguely Museum in Basel. During 1963, 1964 and 1965 he drove it in ten Grands Prix, winning the Dutch, Belgian, British and French GPs. The R6 was also driven in period by Clark's team mate Trevor Taylor as well as other F1 stars, including Mike Spence, Pedro Rodriguez and Peter Arundell, eventually starring in the Metro Goldwyn Mayer movie *Grand Prix*, shot in 1966, in the hands of Phil Hill.

which Ian Scott-Watson was a prime mover, relocated from Charterhall to Ingliston, close to more populous Edinburgh, in 1964, hastening Charterhall's decline into closure in the late 1960s.

In plan, the circuit is anvil-shaped, not so different from Silverstone's Club circuit layout, and related to other airfield tracks like Snetterton, but not the curvaceous perimeter runway types like Goodwood, Croft or Thruxton. The main runway formed the mile-long top straight, where the white markings defining the grid and start/finish line are just about visible, even today. A footbridge provided spectator access to the paddock, which is still fenced off from the former raceway. At the end of the straight came a sharp right-hander, leading onto another straight, perhaps 300m (320yd), and a fast left-hander followed by a tight right and a squirt up to the final bend before the main straight. The corners were delineated by 5-gallon oil drums, half-filled with sand.

There's been no revival or makeover, so the surface is in truly bad shape: bumpy, tinged green with moss, covered in stones, cratered with potholes and swathes of abraded tarmac. Today it serves as a stage on the Jim Clark Rally, originally run in 1970 as the first closed public road rally on mainland Britain. The rally's now based in Kelso, south of Charterhall, and includes 100 miles (160km) of special stages in and around the Lammermuir Hills.

Ian Scott-Watson, whose architectural practice is based in Greenlaw, 6 miles (10km) west of Duns, is the perfect guide to the circuit, because he was there right from the start of Jim Clark's career. Jim started off in 1954 by racing and rallying the family Sunbeam Talbot saloon, and two years later Ian let Jim drive his DKW saloon, his Porsche 356 and, crucially,

The Jim Clark Motorsport Museum was enlarged in 2019 to accommodate a couple of his racing cars, one of which is this Lotus Cortina, in which he won his class in eight out of nine rounds (John Whitmore won the other) to take the 1964 British Saloon Car Championship. The car is currently owned by four-time IndyCar champion and fellow Scot, Dario Franchitti.

Before Jim Clark joined Colin Chapman at Team Lotus, his mentor was Ian Scott-Watson, who provided the young Scot with a range of his cars to race, from a Sunbeam Talbot and DKW to Porsche 356 and Lotus Elite.
JASON PARNELL

his Lotus Elite. It was clear from the outset that Jim was something special, so Ian stood back and gave Jim his head.

> He really was a super bloke. To me, he was just a good mate. He did change a bit over the years, but basically he was still the same Jim at the end. He was due to come home the week after Hockenheim. I had been looking forward to seeing him. I hadn't seen him for about nine months, because he was based in Paris for tax reasons. The tax regime in those days was ridiculous: I think he was only allowed to spend fourteen days a year in the UK. Before he got his own plane, I used to pick him up and take him to the airport, and he would lend me his car until he was back again. So, at one point I had a Lotus Cortina with wishbone rear suspension: there were just two of them made – Colin [Chapman] had one, and Jim had the other. It was great fun to drive. Once I came down from Edinburgh on the A1, doing as usual 100mph [160km/h] wherever I could. I turned off onto the track to his house, and the rear suspension collapsed; I was down to about 5mph [8km/h]. If that had happened half an hour earlier, I wouldn't be here today.

So, did Ian have any influence on Jim Clark's driving skills?

> I gave him the chance to race, but I didn't actually teach him. I didn't need to: the very first time we went to a meeting, he was 3 seconds a lap quicker than me, within five laps of going out for practice. It was entirely natural. It embarrassed me at the time, because I thought I mustn't be much good, but when he got into Grand Prix racing he was often 3 seconds a lap quicker than everyone else, so I think maybe I wasn't bad as all that.

Ian is a fund of stories. I spot the billowing windsock – incredibly, planes still occasionally use Charterhall – and that spurs him on. 'Colin Chapman was a keen flyer,' says Ian, 'and Jim caught the aviator's bug very quickly.' But his technique in the air owed a certain amount to his skills on the track, as Ian explains:

> Jim bought a twin-engined Piper Comanche, though he wasn't as good a pilot as Colin; I would have flown anywhere with Colin, but Jimmy was inclined to bank far too steeply, and you were almost falling out of the door. I designed a villa for Colin in Ibiza, and sometimes he flew me out, just him, me and [his wife] Hazel.

An element of mystery surrounds Ian's Elite, the one that Jim Clark used to make an indelible impression on Chapman at 1958's Boxing Day Brands meeting, and to such good effect during the 1959 season.

> It was ESH700, the first one off the line. According to the information I had before the race, it was to be chassis 1036, but it was 1038 that we got. I can never prove it, and no one would ever admit it, but I think Colin had just taken 1036 out for a run and he crashed it. He wrote off quite a few over the years.

The Elite was entered for Le Mans under the Border Reivers' banner, but with no time to prepare it adequately, Chapman provided another car, with the proviso that Clark share it with Sir John Whitmore. That was far from ready, too:

> We had to do thirty-two modifications to it before we could race it. New gearbox, new suspension, just about anything you could think of had to be replaced. We got thirty-two huge crates into the transporter at Cheshunt, and they said, 'Right, you will have to put all those on before you can race. We almost missed practice it took so long.

In the event, the Clark/Whitmore Elite was delayed by starter-motor problems during pit stops, and did well to finish tenth overall, and second in class behind the trouble-free Elite of Lumsden and Riley.

Time to move on. Charterhall's surface is so bad that a lap of the circuit is unedifying; you just spend all your time avoiding potholes. It's brightened up though, with glorious views south to the Cheviots, where phenomenal driving roads through beautiful scenery beckon. But beware the speed cameras: between Greenlaw and Dalkeith I count at least four, even out here in the sticks. Happily, there are none on the moors, and I can squeeze the lemon once more. The Exige S is all about the elegance of the supercharger's power delivery rather than brute force; it's sharp, yet seamless as it takes exactly your chosen line through the bends. Gentleman Jim would have loved it.

ABOVE: **Synonymous with Lotus racing successes in every sphere of the sport, Jim Clark made his mark driving mentor Ian Scott-Watson's Elite, probably the first to be sold privately, here at Charterhall, Berwickshire, possibly in 1958.**
ERIC BRYCE

Pretty much any backdrop suits the Exige, this one being Dalhousie Castle, 12 miles (19km) south of Edinburgh, and an ideal stopover or starting point for the Jim Clark Trail.
JASON PARNELL

THE GUY MUNDAY INTERVIEW

In a life inextricably bound up with Lotus and Caterham, Guy Munday has been the voice of Lotus open days for the past three decades. He gave me chapter and verse over coffee at Salthouse on the Norfolk coast.

You'll probably be familiar with Guy's personable voiceovers crooning over the tannoy as he broadcasts the commentary at Lotus Club gatherings and Lotus Cars' Hethel open days. His expertise in the marque goes back over thirty years, and one string to his bow is coordinating at the Lotus Driving Academy. Early in 2020, he messaged me to say he was about to run in a couple of brand-new Elises for the Driving Academy – they now switch cars on an annual schedule – and why don't we meet up? That was a no-brainer, so on a beautiful spring day (prior to lockdown) we met up on the north Norfolk coast, along with photographer Stephanie Ewen of Red Fin Photography.

JT: We first met when you were selling Caterhams in Salisbury in 1993.

GM: Yes, we were an independent Lotus and Caterham dealer, and then Lotus awarded us the dealership for Hampshire and Wiltshire. I was in touch with Lotus Cars at the time, and they asked me if I fancied taking on the sales side at SGT in Maidenhead. SGT was a long-standing Lotus dealership, but they weren't performing. It was a fabulous place, near Maidenhead, and you've got Slough and Silicon Valley on your doorstep, so there was no reason why it shouldn't have worked. They were one of the best Alfa Romeo dealers in the UK and Mitsubishi dealers as well, but the Lotus showroom was literally round the back with the lights switched off.

JT: What was your role at SGT, then?

ABOVE: **Lotus and Caterham specialist Guy Munday not only buys and sells the cars, he provides commentary at Lotus Cars open days, and administers the Lotus Driving Academy, which includes guided tours of Classic Team Lotus too.**
STEPHANIE EWEN

Photographed on a north Norfolk coastal road trip, the entry-level Elise 1.6 Sport 220 was a crucial model in the company's Driving Academy fleet.
STEPHANIE EWEN

GM: My first task was to sell an old Lotus Esprit S4 which they'd had as a demonstrator for about eighteen months. They expected the customer to come to the showroom, but I preferred to be more flexible than that. So, I drove the car 5 miles [8km] to the customer and sold it to him. I took SGT to the top of the pole: we became the most successful Lotus dealership, and when the Elise came out we sold 145 cars in one year – 1998 – and in 1999 I sold seventeen Esprits, and that was at a time when the Esprit was flatlining.

JT: How long were you at SGT?

GM: From 1995 to late 1999. My reward for putting them at the top of the table was two pay cuts caused by lopping percentages off my commission. I was bemoaning this to Chris Mennem, who'd been UK sales manager at Lotus Cars, and had since become general manager at Stratton Motor Company in Norfolk. He invited me to join Stratton in October 1999, and I was there for fifteen years until October 2014. SGT has completely disappeared now, unfortunately.

JT: What was the best-selling car while you were at Long Stratton?

GM: Always the Elise. I was there from 1999, so from the end of Series 1 production, and then obviously the Series 2 Elise. We were very supportive of the Autobytel Race Championship, and we raced a couple of cars in that, which gave us a bit of a profile. The Series 2 Sport 190, which had the Rover K-series engine, was a Lotus Motorsport product, and we had a good relationship with the motor sport department. We sold a good number of the total forty-eight built, and in my early days we were probably the most successful Esprit V8 sellers, because I loved that car, and if you actually believe in what you're selling it's reasonably easy to sell. I also sold the last six UK-spec Esprits. That all kicked off on Lotus's stand at the British Motor Show in 2002, when the general sales manager said, 'We're going to stop making the Esprit; it's not public knowledge yet, and it's going to upset a few people.' I said, 'I'll tell you what, put me down for the last six cars.' He said, 'Are you sure?' I said, 'No, I mean it.' And I went back through my old customer database and managed to sell all six.

JT: How was the new Evora received at the time?

GM: On 1 September 2009 I sold the first retail Evora! That's because I stood on the Motor Show stand on every single day in 2008 when they launched the car, and I got a huge number of orders in the bag. They told us the internet system was going live at 10am on a certain day, so one of the girls back at Stratton Motor Company sat patiently by the computers, and the moment it went live we banged in our orders! In the event, Lotus said, 'Look, you can't have all of the first seventeen cars; that's not fair to the other dealers. We'll give you the first three or four.' Anyway, there was a film crew there, and the first one I sold appeared in a video that Lotus made at the time. It was a good day, and it's always nice to get one over your dealer colleagues!

JT: While you were at Stratton, how was the business affected by the uncertain climate at Lotus, going from the Dany Bahar regime to Jean-Marc Gales?

For fifteen years, Guy Munday was sales manager at the Lotus dealership Stratton Motor Company, during which time the Elise in S1 and S2 guise was always the best-selling model.

Launched in 2009, Guy Munday sold several of the first Evoras off the production line. This one was at a press reception at the Mas de Pierre hotel, St Paul de Vence, near Nice.

GM: Well, I think everybody lost a little sweat during Dany Bahar's tenancy. I wasn't alone in thinking there was absolutely no way his strategy was going to happen, and I was always very sceptical he would ever see it through. He even stated publicly that he didn't much care for the whole small car platform, and totally dismissed the Evora. He wanted Lotus to be a British-based Ferrari, and that didn't make the job any easier selling the Elise between 2009 and 2012. The biggest problem with selling the Elise was probably when, a couple of years earlier than that, they stopped making the basic 140bhp version, which was still reasonably good value; when that got taken away and the starting point was £32,000–£33,000, all of a sudden, the job got a lot harder. We were still coming out of recession, and I recall that being a very difficult time because we didn't sell many cars.

JT: When Mr Gales was in charge there weren't many cars made, were there?

GM: No, everything was a bit up and down at that time, for sure. I know Jean-Marc wasn't the most popular of people, but actually he was there to pick up the pieces after Dany Bahar had vacated with all his very expensive employees and friends, who'd left no money, so Gales was basically there to steady a very rocky ship. Suppliers were going unpaid and were left in the cold, and the factory was on short-time working, which would have had an effect on waiting times because cars simply weren't being built.

JT: Since you left Stratton you've been working for yourself?

GM: Yes, my day job is buying and selling cars like any other car dealer, really. I retain relationships with a good number of the main Lotus dealers, and if they've got something a bit older or higher mileage that they don't want, they might put it onto me, either for me to contact the customer direct, or for me to underwrite for them when the deal is done.

JT: How old do the cars you sell tend to be?

GM: I don't go very new, because there's not a lot of point in trying to compete with the established dealers. If I've got a £60,000 Lotus Exige and a dealer has got five or six of them, then somebody is going to look at five or six cars, rather than the one I've got. My ideal stock is somewhere between five and twenty years old, and ideally between £16,000 and £30,000, so I'm not treading on anybody's toes.

JT: With the Elise, would a low-mileage Series 1 car be worth more than a high-mileage Series 2 car?

GM: Absolutely! A low-mileage Series 1 is probably one of the most desirable Elises you can find; they're taking on collector status already. But an early Series 2 Elise isn't really a collector's car at the moment; it's just an old Elise. So, a good specification, very low-mileage Series 1 with all the right attributes, service history and spec will make £20,000, but you can buy a Series 2 Elise for £12,000 or £13,000.

JT: What's the turnover of Evoras like? Do you see many?

GM: Yes, I do, and I like them. But I'm not really dealing in many of the later, more performance-oriented versions; again, that's the domain of the main dealers. But you can buy an Evora for the same price as a decent Elise – an early Evora with a few miles on it is probably about £30,000, and they're a really good grand touring car. We tend to forget that the early cars are ten years old now, and they're very good value, though to my mind it's still a relatively new car.

JT: Do you see any other related models, like VX220s or the Type 121 Europa?

GM: Yes, I sold a couple of Europas during the course of 2019, though finding them is very difficult. When they were new we had a bit of trouble selling them, which is why there were only a few hundred made. But now they're sought by collectors, and finding them at a reasonable price is very difficult. I tend to stick with Lotus if I can, but in the five years I've been solo I've sold just two Vauxhall VX220s, and on the Caterham side of the fence I've also sold a few.

JT: How is Lotus going to perform with Geely backing?

GM: From a personal point of view, I think the sky's the limit. They've proven with Volvo the wonderful things they can accomplish. So, we're just hoping that a little bit of that magic dust falls on Lotus. We're both of the view that it's their ambition to turn Lotus into a McLaren or British Ferrari equivalent, but whatever they come up with, I'm looking forward to selling Geely products in a few years' time when they come my way. From an owner and enthusiast point of view, I want to see my favourite brand succeed under Geely's tenure.

ABOVE: **Chatting with Guy Munday over coffee in Salthouse, north Norfolk. Being pragmatic, he tends to specialize in selling Lotuses that are between five and twenty years old and between £16,000 and £30,000 in price, so he isn't treading on main dealers' toes.**
STEPHANIE EWEN

With a portfolio of cars across the spectrum of Lotuses, Guy Munday sells a few Evoras, though earlier ones, rather than the more recent performance-oriented ones. This is a 2009 press car I borrowed, pictured in Norwich Cathedral Close.

THE GUY MUNDAY INTERVIEW *continued*

JT: Do you have your own Lotus, or are you constantly turning them over?

GM: I've got a collection of Lotuses. My first connection with Lotus was watching Grand Prix racing back in the 1970s, and I worked for Caterham before I worked for Lotus, so I've always kept an affinity with Lotus and Caterham Sevens. At the moment I own five Lotus Sevens: a Series 2, a Series 3 and Series 4 that work, and I've got a couple of Series 2s that need restoring. I've also got a Lotus Eleven, a Lotus Cortina, and a couple of Elise S1s that I don't really want to sell but if the offer was right I would. I've also part-owned an ex-Andretti/Peterson/Nilsson Type 78 F1 car. I'd love to get into single-seaters again, but they're quite an expensive hobby…

JT: What about speaking at Lotus Club meetings and doing the commentary at Factory open days?

GM: It's an honour to be invited to do that; they entrust me with taking the microphone and speaking to people and talking about cars, confident in my knowledge and having the trust in me not to ask the wrong questions – for example, not embarrassing one of the engineering team who can't talk freely about what they're doing – so it's discretion assured. Since 1998 I've done all of the big anniversaries – the fortieth, the two fiftieths, sixtieth and the seventieth, and some other events in between. I thoroughly enjoy doing it, and it does enable me to ask questions of people I wouldn't generally get an opportunity to ask questions of.

JT: What is your favourite Lotus?

GM: Of the ones I've not owned and I wish to own, it's actually quite an obscure one: it's a Lotus Type 73, which, as I'm sure you know, is the black and gold JPS-sponsored Formula 3 car from 1972. I know where they both are – and they will never be for sale. It's not my favourite Lotus, but it is the one I most covet. If I could only have one car, it would be one of my Lotus Sevens.

JT: So, with your own business plus your role at the Driving Academy, you're certainly able to fill your days.

GM: Definitely! I've got a customer base which goes back twenty-five years or more. For example, I'm in the process of acquiring a Caterham that I sold when I worked for that company, and I left them twenty-seven years ago! They do pop up every now and again. If I'm not buying or selling Lotuses, or working at the academy, my personal Lotus collection certainly keeps me out of trouble. And I do ensure that I leave enough time to actually enjoy them on the beautiful Norfolk roads, like we've experienced today with the Elise Sport 220.

Guy Munday regularly commentates on proceedings at Lotus gatherings, such as the two-day Lotus Festival at Snetterton in June 2009.

Suitably liveried, the Lotus Driving Academy Elise Sport 220 gets a shakedown run, helmed by Guy Munday.
STEPHANIE EWEN

THE LOTUS DRIVING ACADEMY

Guy Munday knows so much about the Lotus marque that it's not surprising that he's in demand at the Lotus Driving Academy. He describes the Elises that are used.

> This yellow one is a Sport 220. It's got the 1.8 Toyota engine, 218bhp, and this particular car is actually standard spec, because of course the Driving Academy doesn't have a requirement for things like stereos, carpets and creature comforts. It's brand new for this season. The last cars had done two seasons, and they were starting to show their age, so this is brand new for this year. It is our intention, going forward, to change them every year. We have four cars, of which three are right-hand drive and one left-hand drive, which is approximately the right ratio; we always try to accommodate the drivers with the right car in terms of it being left-hand or right-hand drive if we can, so running one left-hand-drive car works out about right, given the number of clients coming from countries where they drive on the right.

Guy's role at the Driving Academy includes hosting, co-ordinating and, on certain days, undertaking the factory tours. The Driving Academy is a franchise, so it's not actually directly administered by Lotus Cars themselves. Occasionally, they also offer tours of Classic Team Lotus (which is just across the road from the main factory). As Guy says:

> On the days when there are no factory tours I tend to drive a clipboard, just making sure the right person is in the right car at the right time, that the instructors are kept fully occupied, that the customer has their helmet on and is ready to go, so that on changeover there are no massive delays, because we tend to be up against it, time-wise. We adhere to a full-on day's schedule, so I'm always having to make sure everybody is in the right place at the right time, ready for a quick turnaround, making sure the coffee pot's on, keeping everybody happy.
>
> There are four levels to the Driving Academy: Bronze, Silver, Gold and Platinum. Bronze is a good introduction to safe road driving as well as track driving.
>
> We use the North Circuit for some of the morning sessions, and the South Circuit for some of the morning sessions, and then in the afternoon we open the whole track up for the complete 2.2-mile [3.5km] experience. They're 20-minute sessions, so customers get three 20-minute sessions in the morning and two 20-minute sessions in the afternoon. We divide the group in two, so half are driving while the other half come with me on the factory tour and Classic Team Lotus tour. Then, half-way through the morning we turn the group around and go again! The number of laps they get depends a little bit on the ability of the driver, on how quick the drivers are. They're timed sessions rather than distance covered, so when time's up, all the cars come in regardless of the number of laps they've completed. It's non-competitive, so we try to

The Lotus Driving Academy employs four Elises and an Exige 410, with Guy Munday here at the factory.
JASON PARNELL

continued overleaf

THE LOTUS DRIVING ACADEMY *continued*

space the drivers out around the circuit so they shouldn't really encounter other traffic. It's pretty much teaching you to be a safe road driver rather than an out-and-out race driver.

The Silver day raises the game a bit.

There's no track driving in the morning, but we still have three separate disciplines that are set up on the track. We've got a slalom, which teaches you how to thread curves together by looking, not at the next gate on the slalom, but two or three gates further on. So, your entry speed and your exit speed need to be judged so you don't compromise the next one, because if you go too fast into the first one then you're out of position for the second. It's all about maintaining speed and momentum through all of the gates.

For the second discipline, we set up cones across the track and we invite the clients to imagine it's not a set of cones but a family of people: there's a pram and pushchair and a dog, and if you're going too fast then you're just going to pass straight through them. It's all about judging your braking, to demonstrate how good the braking is on an Elise, and how ABS works as well, to get you out of trouble and enable you to still have some steering input to drive around the problem rather than ploughing straight through. People are usually quite surprised at how late you can leave the braking, and during the course of the session you're encouraged to get closer and closer to the obstacles without actually mowing them down.

The academy instructs on how to make use of oversteer and understeer.

The third discipline utilizes the low-grip circle, and on a Silver day we encourage understeer and oversteer, to show you how to get out of it once it's happening. The Elise has a little bit of understeer built in – most manufacturers will build in a little bit of understeer – because the easiest way out of it is generally to lift off and hit the brakes, which is what Mr Average naturally tends to do in a panic situation. If you've got a big oversteer moment, the last thing you want to do is lift and hit the brakes, but we encourage the car to understeer to see how far you can push it. We then encourage you to provoke oversteer to see how far you can go with that, how much lock you can keep on, and how to get out of it again. It's really about encouraging safe road driving, and we treat it as one big roundabout, really. If you go into a roundabout too hard, and you get yourself into an understeer or an oversteer situation, you need to know how to get out of it again.

Skies and dunes: great panning shot of the Elise Sport 220 travelling swiftly through the curves on north Norfolk's coast road.
STEPHANIE EWEN

Of the driving Academy's Elises, three are right-hand drive and one is left-hand drive, seen here, to accommodate clients coming from countries where they drive on the right.
STEPHANIE EWEN

BELOW: **Safe pair of hands: Lotus specialist and aficionado Guy Munday at the wheel of a 2020 Elise Sport 220, navigating the Norfolk coast road.**
STEPHANIE EWEN

Those three disciplines become relevant in the afternoon, because we open up the full 2.2-mile track, and you put into practice what you've learnt in the morning. For instance, at the end of the straights you will be braking – and braking as late as possible and as straight as possible, which you've learned on the brake and steering discipline in the morning. The complex of curves shows you how to look through the first curve into the second and third ones to get your positioning and speed right so you don't lose momentum. There's a hairpin at each end where you can put your understeer and oversteer into practice, so it's all relevant to safe road driving, but also track driving to a degree.

The Gold level takes things up to the next level.

We set up a grand slalom, spread everything out over the entire back straight, with unequal spacing between the gates, allowing a reasonable distance to accelerate, change gear, brake, change down again ready for the next sequence of gates. Also, what we teach there is heel and toe; everybody has heard about the technique, but very few people really understand what it is and what benefits it brings, so we teach them how to do throttle-assisted gear changes, how to execute later braking into the corner whilst taking the downchange in a nice smooth manner. The afternoon track time brings slightly more advanced techniques into play.

The Platinum level is more race-based.

We go into things like data logging as well. We only employ people with some race experience on the Platinum day, and we've got Rob Barff, who's raced at Le Mans; Adam Wilcox, who was Autobytel Champion back in 2000, and David Brise (Tony Brise's nephew). The data logging looks at acceleration and braking points, revealing where you can make up lap time on certain points on the circuit, using the recently learned race techniques.

continued overleaf

THE LOTUS DRIVING ACADEMY *continued*

The culmination of the Driving Academy is the 'Licence Weekend': if you successfully complete the Bronze, Silver and Gold, then you're awarded your Driving Academy licence.

> If you do all those days, plus the Platinum, then we call that 'the Carbon Weekend', which is the ultimate experience currently on offer. There are also some stand-alone days, for example, the Exige Experience. A lot of people use the Exige days prior to making a purchasing decision if they're considering buying one. We use our car on the Lotus test track so they can see whether it's exactly what they want, and from Lotus's point of view it's a good incentivizing conversion tool as well. We've got the four Elises, but there's also an Exige 410 that we use on the Gold and Platinum days, but with the Exige Experience you get three sessions, one of which will be in the Exige. Finally, we also offer the 'Scare Yourself Sensible Day'. That's the starter session – the Christmas present, birthday present, Father's or Mother's Day present. It's an affordable way in, a half-day session consisting of a twenty-minute drive and a factory tour, a taster to encourage people to do further days as well.

There are approximately a dozen instructors.

> Most of them have other commitments, as a lot of them are active racing drivers, and if they've got a race weekend then they can't work for us. We use Lotus's own staff as well, and you get a slightly different experience from them. There's a difference between what a racing driver can teach you and what somebody like Dave Minter, who's been Lotus's ride and handling guru for forty years, will teach you. You get a different experience from them than you do with the race drivers: they tend to be more sympathetic on the cars and encourage a smoother drive. Dave and his revered ride and handling colleague Alistair McQueen set up the Driving Academy back in 1998, and it's run pretty well. Alastair was very much responsible for the basic format to which we still adhere to this day. The emphasis is very much on safe road driving, and it's worth pointing out that the Driving Academy is responsible for selling a good number of cars to punters.

The Lotus Driving Academy was set up in 1998 by Alistair Stewart and Dave Minter, and todays offers four levels of complexity, taught by a combination of racing drivers and Lotus ride-and-handling experts.
GUY MUNDAY

The Driving Academy uses the Exige 410 on the Gold and Platinum days, as well as the Exige Experience.
GUY MUNDAY

Lotus Elise Cup 250 2016–20

Layout and Chassis

Lotus-designed lightweight structure of epoxy-bonded and riveted aluminium alloy extrusions with integral steel seatbelt support structure and lightweight steel rear subframe. T45 Motorsport hoop

Engine

Type	Supercharged Toyota-based VVT-I 2ZZ-GE; transverse mid-engine
Block material	Metal matrix composite (MMC) and aluminium lightweight compact construction
Head material	Metal matrix composite (MMC) and aluminium lightweight compact construction
Cylinders	4 cylinders in line
Cooling	Water
Bore and stroke	82mm × 85mm
Capacity	1796cc
Valves	DOHC, 16 valves, variable valve timing and lift with Valvematic system, hydraulic tappets, 4 valves per cylinder
Fuelling	Multipoint sequential fuel injection, direct electronic ignition
Supercharger	Charge-cooled Magnuson R900 supercharger utilizing Eaton TVS technology
Engine management	Lotus electronic T4 engine control unit
Max. power	243bhp (181kW) at 6,800rpm
Max. torque	184lb ft (250Nm) at 4,600rpm
Emission control	Three-way catalytic converter Euro IV emissions compliant with full on-board diagnostics (OBD) CO_2 emissions 208g/km

Transmission

Gearbox	Close ratio 6-speed manual transaxle driving rear wheels
Clutch	Hydraulic
Ratios	1st 3.116 2nd 2.050 3rd 1.481 4th 1.166 5th 0.916 6th 0.815 Reverse 3.250
Final drive	4.529

Suspension and Steering

Front and rear	Unequal-length double wishbones, Eibach coil springs over Bilstein gas pressured monotube dampers. Adjustable ride height and adjustable front anti-roll bar. Lotus dynamic performance management. Aerodynamically optimized rear diffuser. Driver selectable ESP modes
Steering	Rigidly mounted rack and pinion; 2.8 turns lock to lock
Wheels	Ultra-lightweight silver forged 10-spoke alloy wheels, 16in front, 17in rear
Tyres	Front: Yokohama A048 LTS (W rated) 195/50 R16 Rear: Yokohama A048 LTS (W rated) 225/45 R17

Brakes

Type	Servo-assisted track-tuned 4-channel ABS with Lotus/AP Racing twin-piston fixed aluminium alloy front brake calipers, Brembo single-piston sliding rear calipers. Cast iron ventilated and cross-drilled discs
Size	288mm diameter, 26mm thick front and rear

Dimensions

Track	1,457mm (57.4in) front, 1,507mm (59.3in) rear
Wheelbase	2,298.7mm (90.5in)
Overall length	3,822.7mm (150.5in)
Overall width	1,714.5mm (67.5in) excluding door mirrors
Overall height	1,117.6mm (44in)
Dry weight	899kg (1,982lb)

Performance

Max. speed	154mph (248km/h)
0–60mph (96km/h)	3.9sec
0–100mph (160km/h)	12.2sec
Fuel consumption	Urban 28.0mpg (10.1ltr/100km) Extra urban 47.1mpg (6.0ltr/100km) Combined 37.7mpg (7.5ltr/100km)

LOCAL HERO: THE ELISE CUP 250

Just as I thought the book was done, press officer Alastair Florance told me that a couple of cars had literally just rolled off the assembly line straight into the press fleet, and would I like to review them for the book? No question, obviously, and a day or two later I was helming a Burnt Orange Elise Cup 250. First journo to get a go! In a box-ticking exercise that the local tourist office would be proud of, I motored with alacrity from one Norfolk beauty spot to another, evaluating the car's prowess along the way.

The fabulous Elise Cup 250 was drawn to one of north Norfolk's honeypots, Cley Windmill.
LAURA HAMPTON

The Elise Cup 250 is created on the usual lightweight aluminium chassis, and powered by the supercharged 1.8-litre Toyota straight-four that just loves to rev, producing 243bhp at 7,300rpm. True to form, lightness is key, and it weighs 931kg (2,048lb), having been stripped of niceties: there's no power steering or air-conditioning, and the stereo is not standard issue. It uses a lighter lithium-ion battery, as well as carbon-fibre seats and lighter forged alloy wheels. Suspension consists of coil-over Bilstein dampers and anti-roll bars, and it runs on Yokohama A048 tyres, 195/50 × 16 front, 225/45 × 17 rear, allied to ABS, traction and stability control.

Aerodynamics have a role to play, not just in presenting a dynamic and purposeful image; the front splitter, side sills (no step!), rear diffuser and wing conspire to produce 66kg (145lb) of downforce at 100mph (160km/h) and 155kg (341lb) at top speed. Specifying the aero kit in carbon-fibre saves another 10kg (22lb).

Accessing the cockpit is most easily done with the roof off, which it was all the time during my tenure. Removing the canvas top is easily done by one person; with doors open, bring the two little levers inwards with your thumbs, releasing the hood's side rails, then roll it up inwards, while springing the two parallel supporting rods out of their housings on header rail and roll-over hoop. Stash the roof and rods, rolled up into a bundle, behind the seats – or in the minimal boot

The Elise Cup 250 is powered by the supercharged 1.8-litre Toyota straight-four, producing 243bhp at 7,300rpm.
LAURA HAMPTON

RIGHT: **The purposeful, no-frills cockpit of the Elise Cup 250, a fine amalgam of bare aluminium chassis and touches of Alcantara.**

FAR RIGHT: **One of the niceties of the Elise Cup 250 is its naked gearshift linkage, which would doubtless be fascinating to watch in action were the driver not otherwise occupied.**
LAURA HAMPTON

if you've no baggage. Then put one leg over the side sill, and brace your torso by holding onto the sides of the seat and lift your other leg in, and slide down into the womb-like seat.

All controls fall neatly to hand: pedals nicely spaced, plus left footrest; shift lever with naked linkage; wheel and switchgear. On the dashboard, to the left of the amply proportioned steering wheel rim, are the light switches and Sport and Traction buttons. Playing around with these modulates throttle response and traction control; the Sport setting allows the tyres to spin up enough to induce a little oversteer, which is more applicable on track but amusing to have on the play list. Speedo and rev-counter are right behind the wheel, with a difficult-to-read digital display of speed – this being a left-hooker the speedo was in km/h – and fuel gauge. My confidante on this adventure, Laura Hampton – World Explaura – and I decide that we could bear to travel long distances in these Alcantara-clad seats, which seem to me to be amply supportive when cornering rapidly. The view in the mirror is dominated by the large transom of the rear wing – though one only really notices that when stationary, and it doesn't impede rearward vision.

The unlock button on the key needs pressing to disable the alarm – leave the car un-started for a couple of minutes and it needs pressing again. Activate the ignition with a turn of the key. Foot on clutch, press starter button, and it fires up enthusiastically. There's the guttural tickover, and it certainly makes its presence known. Despite the absence of EPAS, the non-assisted rack of the Elise imparts unimpeachable steering feel when out doing the business on the open road. The shift is notchy and slots exactly into place as you'd expect. There's no other car with which you're totally at one when you address the controls, and the Elise imparts a feeling of security that it would look after you if things got out of hand.

Our route from Hethel takes us first to Heydon, a rural idyll in north Norfolk and a village where I have lived a few times over the years; Laura still lives nearby.

Refreshed at the inimitable Earle Arms, we head coastwards next day, to Blakeney and Morston, taking a circuitous route over rural byways via Holt and Langham, many of them former drove roads with broad verges, which helps sight the car through bends. We arrive quayside at Wells-next-the-Sea, haven for the Dutch barge-restaurant The Albatross, where fish and chips are eaten, legs dangling over the harbour water. Heading west, Holkham Park is closed due to Covid, though the dunes car park is thronged. From here to Burnham Overy there's a titillating blast on decent A-road, with a few demanding third-gear zigzags thrown in.

Fairground Ride

Speed-wise, the supercharger spins up so fast that the car really does take off extraordinarily smartly. There's instantaneous power on tap, and equally instantaneous engine braking too – when I lift off, the speed drops instantly too, with no overrun, and this can be used to advantage in fast cornering. And here, it's so sure-footed I can make it do anything I want; it is too accomplished and precise to be classified a hooligan; it's a finely honed athlete, all taut musculature, nimble as a lightweight boxer.

Pausing for refreshments at the incomparable Earle Arms, Heydon, before getting on with the drive story.

The Elise ride is supple, yet the way it dispatches its power and deploys it on the road is truly a visceral experience.
LAURA HAMPTON

Talking of which, the Elise is the swishing rapier to the Boxster's slashing cutlass – if apt comparison is required. Some of these corners, which I know quite well, one might lift for in the Boxster, but take flat with no lift in the Elise. While the Porsche is serene, the Elise is visceral. Yet the ride is supple, and it's light on its feet, while the AP Racing brakes have a firmness and confidence-inspiring consistency that's more than adequate in any situation when the anchors need applying. It carries its speed through corners, and its poise and balance never disappoint, while there's so much mechan-

The Elise Cup 250 can do leisurely as well, top off and side windows down, motoring through north Norfolk.
LAURA HAMPTON

ical grip that understeer and oversteer don't even enter the vocabulary. It flows through our coastal corners sublimely, whilst delivering constant feedback on all its responses as I power through the turns. It obliges you to be accurate with the controls, only deploy as much throttle or steering lock as you need, and be in the right gear for any circumstance; fail to do that and it sulks. On the other hand, you can just potter, if traffic, distracting scenery or conversation requires it.

Even at a low 2,000rpm, the sound of the tuned four-pot engine resounds noisily – and agreeably (as far as I'm concerned) – off north Norfolk's red-brick walls and hedges. The acoustic crescendo is proportional to revs, and that's what the Toyota unit excels at – revving. In truth, there's not much call for anything much beyond 5,000rpm, but it's useful to know it's available. On a twisty back road, slotting from one gear to another – third, fourth, maybe second for tighter corners – I accelerate as hard as I like through the bends, and carry the speed without braking all the way through a complex, straightlining the esses where sight allows. My snapping sidekick Ms Hampton observes gleefully that 'It's a fairground ride for grown-ups!'

Travelling swiftly with the top off, I'm consciously crouched down slightly behind the screen as I can feel the slipstream playing with my hat – and side windows are only down in a practical sense when going fairly leisurely, otherwise it is drafty. Heading back east, the back roads beckon once again, and we pass through Warham with its front-room pub, to Binham with its ruined Romanesque abbey, fetching up at Cley with its medieval mini-cathedral and smoke house – and its Landmark Trust windmill for the money shot. We've enjoyed a marvellous mix of roads of all different widths, cambers and surfaces, in proper full-summer countryside, and under the circumstances, I can think of fewer better places to give the Cup 250 its head.

THE EXIGE CUP 430

'I think you'll find this is the fastest car you've ever driven!' So said Lotus Cars' press officer Alastair Florance as I prepared to leave the Lotus factory enclave with this Vivid Green sports GT. Oh, yes, I thought; perhaps a tad overconfident? But was he right? My god, I think he was!

I'm no stranger to very high-performance cars, including the 1,000bhp 997 GTronic from 9ff and various Ruf Porsches of around 800–900bhp; and I once hit 200mph (320km/h) at Bruntingthorpe proving ground in a Ruf CTR3. Indeed, I've driven an F1 car – a Prost-Peugeot 3.0-litre V10 (ex-Alesi/Heidfeld) – around the 'Mickey-Mouse' Circuit du Var. And a Porsche 917 (ex-Elford/Attwood Le Mans car) around Donington Park circuit. All are extraordinarily quick. And, no doubt, the road-going, production line Porsche Cayman GT4 is also fantastically competent – I did a feature on one of those (John Statham's car at Autostore) last year. But, and here comes the kicker, having spent a week playing with the Lotus Exige Cup 430, I think that, point-to-point, there actually is nothing quicker. Alastair was right after all!

Designed for Power

So, this, then, is the ultimate Exige experience. Here's why: the Cup 430 designation refers to its extraordinary brake

Looking like a refugee from a nineteenth-century John Constable painting of idyllic rural Suffolk, the Exige Cup 430 is, paradoxically, probably the fastest car available, point to point.

LAURA HAMPTON

Surmounted by its charge-cooler and supercharger, the Exige Cup 430's 3.5-litre Toyota V6 powertrain delivers a consistent 430bhp.

RAVEN COZENS-HARDY

horsepower rating, developed by its 3.5-litre Toyota V6 powerplant, charge-cooled and supercharged to pump out a consistent 430bhp.

The colossal 430bhp and 440Nm is transferred to the gearbox by a 240mm-diameter clutch. Traction out of corners is maximized by motorsport-derived variable traction control, linked directly to the ECU and managing the surge of torque. The six-position rotary switch manipulating it is located on the steering column. It's only active with ESP switched to off, and five pre-set traction levels (1, 3, 6, 9 and 12 per cent slip) as well as 'off' are displayed on the instrument cluster.

The Exige's exterior aero extensions are obvious for all to see, and during my week's tenure, I notice a lot of observers studying them and contemplating what they might be there for: the front splitter with its rubber bib, the side-steps – *not* running boards! – and that lofty plank of a rear wing high on its cantilever pylons: all in carbon-fibre and conspiring to generate 171kg (377lb) of downforce. It doesn't take long behind the wheel to discover that it's a road and track weapon to be taken seriously, and not a poser's piece. The radical aero package is not for show, and when Laura, my lenswoman, was quizzical about the aero add-ons, I assure her that nothing is fitted without a purpose. The Cup 430 generates as much downforce at 100mph (160km/h) as its more modest sibling, the Exige Sport 350, does at 170mph (274km/h). The Cup 430 has an ultra-lightweight front clam with unique carbon-fibre ducts, and wider radiator apertures for the benefit of cooling, while the front splitter and air-curtain design help reduce drag, and generate 76kg (168lb) of front-end downforce. The straight-profile motor sport wing (as opposed to cranked) and the aluminium diffuser at the lower back end conspire to generate a further 95kg (209lb) of downforce at the rear.

The external carbon-fibre panels include the front splitter, front access panel, the roof, the diffuser surround, the enlarged air intake side pods, the one-piece tailgate and engine lid and the race-derived rear wing, all of which are motor sport-grade quality. This level of construction and technical specification largely accounts for the Cup 430's £100k price tag, and the fact that it is double the price of an Elise is down to its staggering speed and capabilities: that's

Fisherman's wharf: the wonderful Vivid Green Exige Cup 430 posed beside Southwold's estuarine shacks.
LAURA HAMPTON

The rear of the Exige Cup 430 is surmounted by its straight-profile motor sport wing, with an aluminium diffuser under the back end, generating 95kg (209lb) of downforce.
LAURA HAMPTON

what ultimate performance costs. I dare say you'd be struggling to match this, even in a McLaren 570S costing £150k, and the Lotus is a darned sight nimbler than a £155k 911 Turbo. Horses for courses, though.

As is to be expected, the weight factor – or lack of it – plays a part too. Weighing just over 1,110kg with a full tank of high-octane fuel, the power-to-weight ratio hits a staggering 387bhp per tonne, and with a beefy 325lb ft (440Nm) of torque punching from 4,000rpm, the 0–60mph dash takes a blink-of-an-eye 3.2 seconds. Top speed is an eye-watering 174mph (280km/h) and, having experienced how blindingly fast it spears away when subjected to determined pressure on the accelerator pedal, I dare say 170mph is easily achievable on a long straight such as Silverstone's Hangar Straight. On an autobahn max-out, that's rather academic, because this is not a motorway car; its abilities and proclivities are wasted on anything other than rural and provincial blacktop – and the more remote the better.

That's all down to the ride and handling set-up, which is optimized for track work, and that extends to curving country roads, too. The Cup 430's race-derived suspension spec includes revised steering-arm geometry that increases bump steer, and its handling characteristics can be altered by tweaking its Nitron three-way adjustable dampers (high- and low-speed compression plus rebound adjustment) and Eibach adjustable front and rear anti-roll bars, both as standard. Keen punters can thereby run a firm, aggressive set-up on track and dial it back for the journey home – though

Dynamism of a green machine: the Exige Cup 430 is a phenomenal performer on smooth countryside blacktop.
LAURA HAMPTON

that's outside our current remit. Tyres are Michelin Pilot Sport Cup 2 (215/45 ZR17 front and 285/30 ZR18 rear), applied to ultra-lightweight forged alloy wheels that can be painted red, black or silver at no extra cost. Braking is by forged four-piston AP Racing calipers and higher thermal-capacity two-piece J-hook brake discs front and rear. Should you wish it, the Cup 430 is also race-ready, as it has a T45 steel roll-over hoop installed – although it doesn't impinge. It also comes with a lithium-ion battery, baffled sump, and front and rear towing eyes. A motoring agnostic asked whether the word 'tow' was actually a Norfolk misspelling of 'two'…

OK, as I've said, apart from 911 GT3s and Turbos and limited editions from German specialists, the nearest car I've driven to the Exige Cup 430 is the Porsche Cayman GT4, so I'll say a few words about that as it's valid in context. It's a benchmark Porsche for a rather peculiar reason, and that is that it's the first one that's been permitted to be more powerful than a 911. Till now, Caymans and Boxsters have been subordinate to 911s. The GT4 borrows its 3.8-litre flat-six from the 991 Carrera S, revolving it through 180 degrees so the engine is amidships with the gearbox to the rear. The GT3 motor, which would have perhaps been the desired powerplant, would not fit in the Cayman engine bay due to its induction system. However, the Carrera S unit's power and torque remain the same at 380bhp and 310lb ft. The suspension is also largely sourced from the 991 GT3 parts bin, and it's also 30mm (1.2in) lower than the standard Cayman, and the front track is 13mm (0.5in) wider. Its brakes are also carried over from the GT3, and the extra spec includes a half cage, carbon bucket seats from the 918 Spyder and plumbing for a fire extinguisher. No question, it's a phenomenal car, performance-wise, and capable of colossal velocity. As I dived around the bendy bits where I did the test drive it was perfectly poised, soaking up the curves regally, in an almost dismissively haughty fashion. It has a different character to the Exige, though. Visceral, sure, but less hugging, not so encapsulating and enrapturing as the Lotus. I'm getting ahead of myself, but when the time came to hand back our Green Goddess at the Hethel factory, it was with heavy hearts. Back in my Boxster, I felt I was hauling granny's barge!

Interior Beauty

Anyway, back to the matter in hand – the Exige Cup 430. Within the cabin, the dimensions appear different to the Elise; looking in the rear-view mirror, the first thing I see behind me in the engine compartment is the throttle linkage, which fascinates as I press and release the accelerator pedal and it responds accordingly, nodding like a miniature well-head oil pump. Behind that, atop the V6 Toyota motor, is the intercooler, a major piece of kit that's not installed on the Elise. Then there are the carbon slats of the engine lid, and the transom of the rear wing. Following traffic is still adequately observable between these slats and, in practice, I find myself relying more on this mirror than the pair either side on the doors, despite the bisected view. It's a hard-top, so the band of vision is through the windscreen and door windows, not aided and abetted by upward vision were the top removed. My forward view is framed by the front wings (fenders) with their aggressive razor-tops and twin cooling slats.

The no-nonsense cabin of the Exige Cup 430, with carbon-fibre wrapping the side sills and seats, and door panels upholstered in Alcantara, while the exposed shift linkage provides a technical contrast.
RAVEN COZENS-HARDY

Though there's carbon-fibre a-plenty cladding the exterior, the black 'Chapman Tartan' is only used to cover the side sills in the cabin. More or less everything else is upholstered in Alcantara – door panels, dashboard facia and roof, handbrake gaiter, tactilely sculpted Momo wheel rim – and, contrastingly, the naked shift-linkage is also a nod to weight-saving tech. The binnacle containing the two main gauges – speedo and rev-counter – is directly ahead of the wheel, while a digital read-out strip showing fuel, time and speed in km/h is barely discernible. The Alcantara-clad race seats are comfortable enough, and the relationship of seat to pedals is straightforwardly achieved, fore and aft, but without power-assisted steering it can be an arm wrestle in a tight parking situation. As for the driving position, though it might at first seem too close to the wheel – relationship of legs to pedals is perfect – in actual fact, the bent elbows posture allows much more intimacy and physical power over the wheel, important when negotiating a high-speed corner or twisty zig-zags where control is paramount.

Flying around East Anglia

Let's get motoring! Laura Hampton and I are all set to head down to the Suffolk coast for me to evaluate the Green Machine's performance and handling, and for her to take some photos. It starts on the button, and getting off the line requires a little bit of concentration to balance clutch and throttle. Accelerating is a dramatic business, and it kicks off vigorously, almost violently. Driver and passenger are at one with the car as it zooms into orbit like a space capsule. In fact, 'zoom' is the acoustic soundtrack too – the whistle of the supercharger spooling up between shifts, the banshee howl from the titanium tailpipe as revs soar past 5,000rpm when it comes on the cam, then stuttering on the overrun as I back off the throttle; the exhaust note makes its presence felt within the car in a different, more sonorous way to the more raucous 4-cylinder Elise.

Our route takes us south from our north Norfolk base, and we give Norwich a wide berth, heading for Beccles and the southern Broads. Once beyond Beccles, the A145 towards Southwold presents some really fine twists and turns, sharp and shallow, allowing me to really explore the Exige's abilities, and the closer we get to Henham – site of the Latitude Festival – the more it reveals its true personality. This is an extraordinarily fast car with abilities far in excess of normal roadgoing expectations, providing a genuine ongoing thrust (rather than a kick) in the back as we hurtle down the road. The steering is totally accurate and judiciously weighted at speed, and turn-in is as sharp and as accurate as one could wish for. In the bends, its chassis provides indisputably peerless traction and unwavering power delivery. The tyres grip assiduously, and it catapults the occupants inexorably in the desired trajectory, arcing right and left. The G-forces we're feeling here raise the question of whether full harnesses might be more appropriate than the regular lap-and-diagonal belts.

Whatever, the Cup 430's capabilities in these settings are fantastic, and the uncompromising ride and the way it steers implacably around corners is confidence-inspiring. I know this route well, having driven it on the 35-mile (56km) daily school run, Norwich to Leiston, back in the 911 days, so I'm familiar with all the apexes, nuances of camber and surface undulations. Now, though, in the Exige I can go quicker still, and sometimes, I take a deep breath and just go for it, knowing that I can trust it to grip right the way round, no matter how tight the turn, provided I keep the lock on and the power down. Its progress is unshakable – especially awesome when I can straightline a section of two or three curves. It is astonishingly fast when I really try with it, and the steering wheel jinks as it bump-steers its way along these country roads, its nose hunting the driving line like a scent

The Exige Cup 430's steering is totally accurate and judiciously weighted at speed, with turn-in as sharp and as accurate in the corners as you could wish for.
LAURA HAMPTON

hound. I can feel the rock-hard suspension pitter-pattering over the bumps and, unsurprisingly, the ride is track day-hard and uncompromising. I'm seeing 4,000–5,000rpm through the gears, powering it through the esses, and of course it will go happily to 7,000rpm. But frankly, the V6 is so torquey that most of the time it's happy to throb along at 2,500–3,500rpm.

Where appropriate, I employ engine braking to slow down – the throttle is so sensitive that, just as revs soar very quickly, so they drop with similar rapidity. It's plenty torquey enough to cope with driving any corner in a ratio higher than might be considered normal, but there's nothing to beat a downshift ahead of the turn to give extra grunt, in terms of both traction and sound. Short-shifting is also fun, especially in less rustic environs. My feet are dancing on the pedals, my left hand slotting from one notch to another, the steering wheel bucking slightly in my palms as it scuttles over the undulations in the tarmac. It's the closest thing to flying on the ground!

True confessions: I'm a hopeless case – whatever book I'm working on, I always find myself hooked on the car – or bike – I'm writing about. (There are exceptions – I have done books about trucks and heavy equipment, but those are another story, literally.) So, here it is, here's the verdict; next to a Lotus – and an Elise or an Exige in particular – even a Boxster, the most agile of Porsche's modern cars, is bland. And now I crave the rawness, the tactile qualities, the direct seat-of-the-pants intimacy between machine and road surface that an Elise and its siblings provide. I haven't owned a Lotus since the days of the JPS Motorsport press office – which was an Elan S4 SE that spent much of its time *hors de combat* for one reason or another. But now, as recent outings in the current crop of Elise and Exige concentrate the mind, it's time for another one.

The Exige Cup 430's steering wheel jinks as it bump-steers along country roads, while the ride is track-day hard and uncompromising.
LAURA HAMPTON

APPENDIX

CHRONOLOGY

1996–2000	Elise S1
1997	GT1 road car
1998	Elise Sport 135
1998–9	Elise Sport 190
1999–2001	Elise 111S
1999	Elise Type 49 Gold Leaf Heritage
2000	340R
2000	Elise Sport 160
2000–2	Exige S1
2000–6	Elise S2
2002–5	Elise
2003	Sport Elise 135 and 135R
2004–8	Elise 111R and Federal car
2004–7	Exige S2
2005	Sport Exige 240R
2005	Sport Exige 400
2005	Exige Espionage (Harrods display)
2005–8	Europa S
2006–7	Exige Cup 190 and 240
2006	Exige GT3
2006–10	Elise S
2006–11	Exige S
2006	Exige S British GT Special Edition
2007–11	2-Eleven
2007	Exige GT3
2008–9	Europa SE
2008	2-Eleven GT4 Supersport
2008–11	Elise SC

Introduced in 2000 as a race car for the road, the Exige evolved from the Sport Elise, with 602 examples built over two years.

Released in 1999, this Series 1 Elise pictured at Goodwood House was the first of the 'heritage editions', with 134 units marketed as the Type 49, resplendent in the Gold Leaf colours that clad Team Lotus racing cars from 1968 to 1971.

ANTONY FRASER

2008–9	Exige Cup 260
2008	Exige Sprint
2008	Eco Elise
2008	Exige 265E and 270E Tri-fuel
2008	Europa Diamond Anniversary
2009–11	Exige S and Cup 260
2009	Exige S Type 72
2009	Exige Scura (matt black stealth finish)
2009–11	Elise Club Racer
2011–20	Exige S
2012	Exige R-GT
2012–20	Exige S Roadster
2013	Exige V6 Cup, Exige V6 Cup R, Elise S Club Racer, Elise S Cup R
2014	Elise S Cup
2016	Elise 250 Special Edition, Elise Race 250, Exige 350 Special Edition, Elise 3-Eleven
2017	Elise Sprint, Elise Cup 260, Exige Race 380, Exige Cup 380, Exige Cup 430
2018	Exige Cup 430 Type 25, Exige Sport 410, Exige Type 49 and Type 79
2020	Elise Cup 250, Elise Classic Heritage editions, Exige 20th Anniversary

SPECIAL MODELS

Sport 190
Sport 135R
Type 23
Type 25
Type 49
Type 72
Type 99T
Eco Elise
Sports Racer
Club Racer
Tri-fuel 270E
California Edition

CARS SHARING THE ELISE PLATFORM

Lotus Europa S
Lotus 2-Eleven
Lotus Exige
Lotus Elise GT1
Lotus GT3
Lotus 340R
Rinspeed sQuba
Tesla Roadster
GM VX220
Pininfarina Enjoy
Dodge Circuit

Posed at the entry to Druid's Bend at Brands Hatch, the Elise 340R took the model into the realms of its open-wheel Lotus Seven ancestor, and its designation reflected its power-to-weight ratio of 340bhp per tonne.
WILLIAM TAYLOR

Showboating: a little out of its natural environment, the Exige Cup 430 visits the fishermen's shacks beside Southwold's River Blyth estuary.

INDEX